P9-DDB-811

"In suitably fast-paced prose, Goldstone tells the enthralling story of the fraught early days of the 'Horseless Age.' The cast in the high-stakes battle includes brilliant engineers, Gilded Age tycoons, and reckless daredevils both on the track and in the boardroom—a heady mix of motors, money, and testosterone. Silicon Valley's billionaires have nothing on these guys for either ingenuity or ruthlessness."

—Ross King, author of *Brunelleschi's Dome*

"*Drive!* is an exquisite treasure. Titanic court battles; personal feuds among robber barons; hair-raising, death-defying early automobile races; and a slice of history, beautifully researched and written, that shaped the country in the early twentieth century—there is something in this book for all lovers of epic, transformative struggles."

—Dale Oesterle, Reese Chair, Moritz College of Law, Ohio State University

"A wonderful, story-filled saga of the early days of the auto age . . . While aspects of Goldstone's book will be familiar to auto buffs, the story is so compelling and well-crafted that most readers will be swept up in his vivid re-creation of a bygone era. The book abounds with detailed accounts of races, auto shows, and heroic cross-country journeys and explains in plain English the advances in automotive engineering that transformed early vehicles from playthings of the wealthy to functional, low-cost cars for the masses. 'Horse Is Doomed,' read one headline in 1895. This highly readable popular history tells why."

—*Kirkus Reviews* (starred)

BOOKS BY LAWRENCE GOLDSTONE

Drive!: Henry Ford, George Selden, and the Race to Invent the Auto Age

Birdmen: The Wright Brothers, Glenn Curtiss, and the Battle to Control the Skies

Inherently Unequal:
 The Betrayal of Equal Rights by the Supreme Court, 1865–1903

Dark Bargain: Slavery, Profits, and the Struggle for the Constitution

The Activist: John Marshall, Marbury v. Madison, and the Myth of Judicial Review

The Astronomer

The Anatomy of Deception

Off-Line

Rights

WITH NANCY GOLDSTONE

Out of the Flames: The Remarkable Story of a Fearless Scholar,
 a Fatal Heresy, and One of the Rarest Books in the World

The Friar and the Cipher: Roger Bacon and the Unsolved Mystery of the Most
 Unusual Manuscript in the World

Deconstructing Penguins: Parents, Kids, and the Bond of Reading

Used and Rare: Travels in the Book World

Slightly Chipped: Footnotes in Booklore

Warmly Inscribed: The New England Forger and Other Book Tales

WITH VERNONA GOMEZ

Lefty: An American Odyssey

DRIVE!

DRIVE!

HENRY FORD, GEORGE SELDEN, AND THE RACE TO INVENT THE AUTO AGE

BALLANTINE BOOKS

NEW YORK

Copyright © 2016 by Lawrence Goldstone

Published in the United States by Ballantine Books, an imprint
of Random House, a division of Penguin Random House LLC, New York.

BALLANTINE and the HOUSE colophon are registered
trademarks of Penguin Random House LLC.

All photos courtesy of the Library of Congress unless otherwise indicated.

LIBRARY OF CONGRESS CATALOGING-IN-PUBLICATION DATA
Names: Goldstone, Lawrence, author.
Title: Drive! : Henry Ford, George Selden, and the race to invent the auto age /
Lawrence Goldstone.
Description: First edition. | New York : Ballantine Books, 2016. | Includes
bibliographical references and index.
Identifiers: LCCN 2016002581 (print) | LCCN 2016010457 (ebook) |
ISBN 9780553394184 (hardback) | ISBN 9780553394191 (ebook)
Subjects: LCSH: Automobiles—History. | Automobile industry and trade—History. |
Automobiles—Design and construction—History. | Automobile driving—History. |
Transportation, Automotive—History. | BISAC: HISTORY / United States /
20th Century. | TRANSPORTATION / Automotive / History. | BIOGRAPHY &
AUTOBIOGRAPHY / Science & Technology.
Classification: LCC TL15 .G645 2016 (print) | LCC TL15 (ebook) |
DDC 338.4/762922209041—dc23
LC record available at http://lccn.loc.gov/2016002581

Printed in the United States of America on acid-free paper

randomhousebooks.com

9 8 7 6 5 4 3 2 1

First Edition

Book design by Christopher M. Zucker

To Nancy and Lee

CONTENTS

DRIVE!

A DAY IN COURT

On November 30, 1900, a ruling was handed down in United States district court in Buffalo, New York, that seemed certain to alter the landscape of America, both literally and figuratively. It would propel a few to wealth rivaling that of the Vanderbilts, Astors, and Belmonts and perhaps even approaching the Croesian heights of Pierpont Morgan himself. But for the majority of Americans, the decision foretold higher prices for a potentially inferior version of an item soon to become a necessity.

On that day, Judge John R. Hazel affirmed that, according to a patent granted in 1895, the gasoline-powered automobile had been invented by one and only one man, George Baldwin Selden of Rochester, New York. As a result, each and every gasoline vehicle produced in the United States could be sold only with the permission of the inventor and must include tribute in the form of licensing fees, the amount to be determined by the patent's owners.

Any edict of this magnitude was bound to generate controversy, as Hazel's did, but this decision featured a particular oddity that made the ruling positively bizarre: George Selden had never and would never attempt to build any form of the device he had claimed as his exclusive property.

The lack of an actual product, however, promised to have as little impact on George Selden's bank balance as it had on his lawsuit. In an era when monopoly interests were defended by the courts and venerated by large segments of the ruling elite, the granting of sweeping licenses on minimal evidence of utility was not considered outlandish. The beleaguered patent office, drowning in applications both serious and frivolous, had become little more than a way station on the road to riches. For the next eleven years, George Selden and the savvy financiers who had hitched their wagons to his paper star collected fees from virtually every major manufacturer of motorcars in the United States. Many of the companies who had been on the wrong side of Judge Hazel's decision soon banded together to form a sort of sub-monopoly, funneling fees to the Selden cabal while they extracted even larger fees from their customers. And so might it have continued, except for the energy, conviction, and out-and-out stubbornness of one man, a prototypical revolutionary, seething with contempt for an established order that had rejected him and willing to take any risk to wrench away its power.

In an irony that only two decades hence would elicit wonder—or guffaws—that man was Henry Ford.

Ford, who would come to epitomize the very interests that he fought with ferocity in the Selden case, was, as his decade-long war of attrition began, a maverick with a dream—to bring the motorcar, then largely a plaything of the wealthy, to the villages and farms of America.

Many Americans believe that Henry Ford invented the modern automobile, or at least the assembly line and mass production. He did neither. In fact, there is no significant invention in automotive technology for which Ford could personally take credit. Nor was he the first man to consider the egalitarian possibilities of automobile marketing. Ford's genius—like that of Steve Jobs a century later—was in his ability to improve and to adapt to the demands of the marketplace virtually any process or component with which he came in contact. To produce an automobile within the financial reach of the common man meant it had to be cheaper, lighter, and more reliable, so that was what Ford set his mind and his prodigious energies to create. Then, since the common man needs to be informed of the newest miracles of which he can avail himself, Ford, again like Jobs, also had both the ear and the flair for controlled overstatement that characterize the consummate salesman. That he projected cold sobriety in his public pronouncements made Ford's self-promoting homilies that much more credible. Henry Ford might not have been the brilliant inventor of legend, but he was a man whose skills were the perfect match for his ambition.

But inconsistencies and exaggerations should not eclipse achievement. Henry Ford succeeded where others failed. He envisioned and then created a product that fundamentally and profoundly transformed American society—and this from a man who left school at seventeen and, like many of the other great engineers of the period, was completely self-taught. He acquired some technical knowledge through books or pamphlets, but he developed his ideas almost exclusively through trial-and-error tinkering. From the day he began, he envisioned crisp, elegant solutions to problems of structure, function, and style. And unlike some of his contemporaries—Wilbur Wright, for example—Ford knew when to bring in associates and how to delegate tasks he either could not or should not undertake himself. He also knew when to abandon financial backers who were not up to his vision and to begin afresh. Ford's business acumen was every bit as formidable as his skill as an engineer, quite possibly more so.

When, toward the end of his life, Ford proclaimed, "I invented the modern age," the statement did not prompt a great deal of skepticism and has not since. To understand how accurate the assertion is, however, one must place Ford's work in the context of the development of the vehicle that he sold in such staggering numbers, yet such a portrait has remained elusive. Ford was obsessed with his public image. Biographies written by employees or sycophants, and one faux "autobiography" written with a publicity man, were ceaselessly promoted, while any article or book that delved into the darker corners of the Ford legend was mercilessly suppressed. His sense of public sentiment was acute—he knew never to whitewash. He was therefore painted not warts and all but rather with just enough strategically placed warts to render him both believable and touchingly human. In the end, Henry Ford marketed himself even more effectively than he did his Model T, and rendered himself a figure of such fascination and incongruity that, like a brilliant light shining in the dark, anyone looking into it would be blinded to the surrounding landscape.

Of course, a man of Henry Ford's stature cannot totally control what seeps into public view. The contradictions are renowned—the anti-Semite who freely employed Jews; the pacifist who hired thugs to repress his workers; the family man who hounded Edsel, his only son, to an early grave. But a key element of Ford's great talent was in neutralizing the negative and even turning it to his advantage. (His apology to Jews in 1927—totally insincere, as it turned out—seemed so heartfelt that even Jewish leaders applauded his contrition.) Then there was pure mythology—the philosopher who was illiterate (Ford merely couldn't spell); the engineering genius who could not read a blueprint (he could, and quite well).

But of greater significance are the contradictions in the Ford factories, and these receive surprisingly scant discussion. Ford is almost universally credited with "democratizing" the workplace—employing whites, blacks, women, immigrants, the disabled, even criminals, and paying each of them the famous five dollars a day for eight hours of toil. As Charles Sorenson, forty years a Ford executive, put it, while comparing Ford to Abraham Lincoln, "One preserved the Union and emancipated the slaves. The other evolved an industrial system which revolutionized American life and work and emancipated workers from backbreaking toil."[1] But Ford's workers were hardly emancipated, and their toil was as deadening as was a slave's in the cotton fields. In fact, in democratizing the workplace, Henry Ford dehumanized work.

Hannah Arendt, in *The Human Condition,* differentiated between "labor," which she defined as mindless repetition to produce the bare necessities of life, and "work," in which human beings produce something durable and lasting, using tools to create from the natural world objects that advance the species through pleasure and beauty. Work is prideful and creative and contributes to human progress; labor is, in essence, servitude. While members of Ford's assembly line may have been part of a process that resulted in a "creation," none produced anything as an individual, and thus his workers became, in fact, regressions in the human experience. Even worse, any employee who performed his or her task slower—or faster—than the regular, mindnumbing pace of the assembly line was dismissed. That the survivors were paid, even paid well, did not give them dignity or otherwise alter the bankruptcy of their working lives.

Preoccupation with the man has, then, overwhelmed a study of the process—not only the process that created the Ford Motor Company but also the process that created the automobile age as a whole. Henry Ford, despite another common perception, came onstage not in Act I, Scene 1 of the automobile saga but when the drama was already well under way. Nor, when he did appear, was he alone onstage. Although Henry Ford capitalized on the immense demand for automobiles that allowed millions to be sold, he did not create it. That was done for him, mostly by an amazing array of race car drivers and adventurers who kept the dizzying advances in automotive technology on the front pages of newspapers around the world. Misstating his place in the evolution of the automobile distorts not only Ford's contribution to its development but the nature of the innovative process itself, and of those who ultimately exact from it the greatest profit.

George Selden presents a different problem—how does history assess the contribution of an idea, especially one that neither was translated into practical reality nor became the direct inspiration for the innovations that followed? Selden is portrayed in most accounts as no more than an opportunist, a fraud, an unscrupulous lawyer who used his father's wealth and political connections to subvert the patent system. Through chicanery, it is said, Selden was able to maintain rights to a device that he never intended to build but which secured him licensing fees from those who did the work he declined to undertake.

But George Selden was not a fraud, at least when he originally filed his patent application in 1879. He was, at that point, a visionary, the first American to apply a nascent technology—internal combustion—to a vital and original purpose: a self-propelled "road carriage." And gaining a patent for an unrealized theory was the last thing on Selden's mind. With the assistant he had hired with funds from his own pocket, Selden fabricated a prototype three-cylinder motor and had every intention of building a vehicle to house it. Had he been able to access the wealth and political connections he is accused of relying on, George Selden almost certainly would have succeeded.

But Selden's father, rather than being an ally, refused to either contribute a dime to help his son achieve his dream or provide even a cursory introduction to any of the many wealthy and powerful men who were his intimates. Quite the reverse: Selden's father contributed only ridicule and derision to his son's efforts, so Selden was left to use his lawyer's skills to at least profit from an idea he had before anyone else. If George Selden had secured sufficient funds to experiment and then build his machine, formative and with an inferior technology though it may have been, he might now be remembered with the same veneration as the Wright brothers. Instead, he is little more than one of history's footnotes.

Even as he was finally granted his patent in 1895, both Selden and his idea seemed doomed to oblivion. Then, in a stunning turnabout, the Selden patent was rescued and used as a lever to create what might well have been the largest and most profitable monopoly the world had ever known. That edifice Henry Ford brought down and, in doing so, not only claimed much of those riches for himself but also created the culture that has been both America's boon and its curse.

George Selden is not the only player in the automobile saga obscured by the blaze of Ford's light. Almost a certainty, for example, is that not one American in ten thousand knows the name of the man who built the first modern automobile—and that he was neither American nor German.

In fact, the odyssey of Selden and his patent, from obscurity to fame and back again, is a unique and enthralling drama played out on a stage populated by a cast of outsized and compelling personalities. In addition to Ford and Selden, there are Selden's partners, William Collins Whitney and Thomas Fortune Ryan, voracious Wall Street speculators who could have been plucked from today's headlines; myriad visionaries, including Isaac Rice, the chess master who is considered the father of the electric car and who founded the company that today makes America's nuclear submarines; hustlers and swindlers; political bosses and political hacks, sometimes on the federal bench; impresarios such as William Kissam Vanderbilt II, heir to a great fortune, who began promoting car races in his teens, built Motor Parkway—the nation's first road designed specifically for automobile traffic—and founded the Vanderbilt Cup, America's first great annual road race; daredevils and race car drivers, including Barney Oldfield, who went from being a kitchen helper in an insane asylum to becoming the most famous driver of that or perhaps any era, who drove before crowds that sometimes exceeded a quarter million and would race against not only other cars but horses, locomotives, airplanes, and, in one case, heavyweight champion Jack Johnson; and master manipulators such as William Crapo "Billy" Durant, whose idea for a consortium of carmakers—which he called General Motors—became the model for automobile manufacturing and marketing for almost a century, and who, but for the shortsightedness of his bankers, would have persuaded Henry Ford to sell his company at what would have later proved to be a fire sale price.

The early automobile also figured in a series of remarkable events, from early rallies in Europe, including the "Race to Death," to the competitions at Grosse Pointe that first brought Henry Ford to the attention of the public, to the first cross-country journey in 1903, which featured two men and America's most celebrated dog, to a remarkable New York–to–Paris race in 1908, in which the participants traveled *west*. And, of course, there was courtroom drama, Selden against Ford, the resolution of which likely shaped American business and culture more than any other in our history.

But for all the glorious backdrop, this is at its core the story of a man unwilling to abandon a vision he was convinced was correct, who possessed just the right combination of brains, insight, bitterness, and anger to allow him to become one of the world's great innovators—and the richest man in America. But with all that has been written about Henry Ford and the rise of the auto culture, there is no narrative account of Ford's ascension against the backdrop of the Selden patent, nor one that includes accounts of racing, especially in Europe, which are crucial to any work that seeks to place Ford and his stunning innovation in the context of the extraordinary time in which he lived.

For a machine as common and essential to modern existence as the automobile, its story is surprisingly rife with misconceptions. For one thing, the internal combustion engine was not developed to power automobiles. In fact, the use of such a device on something as small as a motorcar was considered laughable until *after* George Selden filed for his patent. Like many modern devices, the internal combustion engine was inspired by a weapon of war and was originally conceived during one of the great scientific crossroads of human history as a theory looking for an application.

CHAPTER 1

POWER IN A TUBE

The latter half of the seventeenth century was a remarkable time, when science was called "natural philosophy" and one so engaged roamed freely over the intellectual landscape. Men such as Newton, Leibniz, Robert Hooke, Descartes, and Robert Boyle were all renowned for discoveries or innovations in a variety of disciplines. Christiaan Huygens was another of that century's masters. An advisor to France's Louis XIV for fifteen years, Huygens is best known for his work in astronomy, optics, and timekeeping—he discovered Saturn's moon Titan, and invented what came to be called the grandfather clock. But like most of his contemporaries, he was drawn to the more conceptual problems of the day, working in the mind as much as in practical spheres, theorizing on such diverse topics as the force of gravity and probability in games of chance.

One possibility that fascinated him was the use of controlled explosions as a power source. Since the only substance available to generate such a reaction was gunpowder, that became his default fuel, and cannons, some of which were huge and could propel a projectile weighing more than a quarter ton, provided the shape of the housing.

And, since the objective was to generate energy and not to kill one's neighbor, the canister would need to be closed at both ends. Finally, for maximum efficiency, whatever was employed inside the canister to be driven by the explosion would need to conform to its shape, a tool we now call a piston.

Huygens built such a device in 1673, but he made an odd discovery. After ignition, rather than being driven outward by the force of the explosion, his primitive piston was drawn back. Oxygen had yet to be identified as an element, so Huygens was unaware that the explosion had burned off the gas, creating a partial vacuum and therefore an atmospheric imbalance that the piston was sucked in to equalize. Motors that ran on this principle would be known as "atmospheric engines." Only later would experimenters discover that in order to fully harness the force of the explosion, it would be necessary to compress the fuel in the cylinder before ignition.

While Huygens had produced a theoretical prototype, his construction had obvious flaws, the most significant of which was that there was no means to keep the contraption running, since the cylinder had to be reloaded after each discharge.* Gunpowder, a solid, was not at all suited to any device that was meant to run continuously. So primitive was Huygens's apparatus that no one thought to improve in-cylinder explosive devices for almost two centuries. The encased piston, however, was almost immediately utilized to provide power generated from other sources. In 1690, Denis Papin, a French mathematician who had once been Huygens's assistant, created a partial vacuum in a cylinder by condensing steam, a spur that eventually inspired one of history's most significant technological advances.†

As iron came increasingly to replace wood, the great engineering challenge of the period was the development of an effective means to pump water out of mines and thus allow miners to access ore much deeper underground. In 1712, the year Papin died, Thomas Newcomen, an English iron merchant and lay preacher, built on both Papin's work and the experiments of another Englishman, Thomas Savery,

---

* This would be termed a "single non-repeatable cycle."
† Papin worked a good deal with steam. He also invented the pressure cooker.

and fabricated the first practical steam engine.* He placed a boiler beneath a cylinder, forcing steam into the chamber, and then used water from a tank above to cool the cylinder and condense the steam. The resulting partial vacuum allowed atmospheric pressure to draw the piston downward. A valve between the boiler and the cylinder would open to allow the steam to enter, and then close when the cylinder was full; another valve from the water tank would open when the cylinder was full, and then close after the piston had been sucked downward. A rocking beam—a sort of seesaw—attached at a pivot point above the cylinder and had a chain fastened on one side that ran a pump, which would suck water from a mine as the piston descended on the opposite side.

Newcomen's engine could run continuously and reliably and was thus a boon to mine owners. But it was also highly inefficient. The cylinder had to be hot when the steam entered, then cold to create the vacuum, then hot again to continue the cycle. Such rapid and extreme changes of temperature engendered substantial heat energy loss and also put a strain on the iron cylinder wall. For all its shortcomings, however, Newcomen's engine remained the state of the art for three-quarters of a century, until James Watt developed a vastly improved design, one that has remained more or less unchanged ever since.

Watt's engine was direct drive, that is, the piston was driven by the steam entering the cylinder and not sucked into a partial vacuum, as with atmospheric engines. He avoided energy loss by allowing his cylinder to remain hot. Waste steam was driven into a separate vessel by the downstroke of the piston, where it was condensed and then returned to the water tank to begin the water-steam-water cycle once more. A far more sophisticated system of valves controlled the movement of water and steam among the various components. Watt's ingenuity did not end with the engine's internals; he perfected methods for converting the piston's reciprocal (up-and-down) motion to rotary

---

* Savery built an actual steam pump, though it lacked sufficient power to draw water from anywhere but the shallowest depths and thus was never employed for its stated purpose.

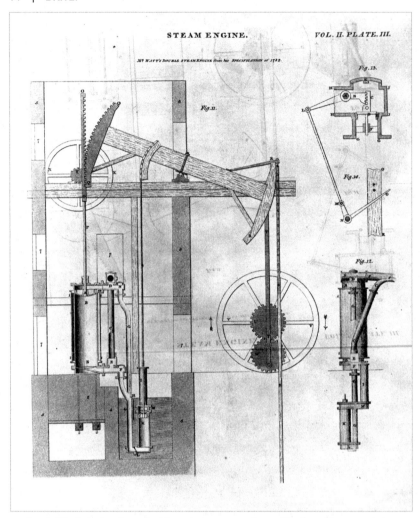

James Watt's design for a double-action steam engine, with planetary transmission and linkage rods

motion using gears, and also a linkage system to gain power from piston strokes in both directions, not just one, as with the chain.*

* Watt would have preferred a crank, but that device was under patent and he balked at paying licensing fees. The gear system he employed was called "planetary," because the gear attached to the connecting rod revolved around a fixed gear attached to the driveshaft. As the driveshaft moves up and down, the movable gear will move around the fixed one—like a planet orbiting the sun—which turns the horizontal shaft to which it is attached. That device was actually invented by a Watt employee, William Murdoch, but Watt submitted the patent application under his own name in 1781. The linkage system, however, a brilliant and simple mechanism of three rods that moved in a figure-eight motion, was Watt's own brainchild.

Watt's engine and transfer system were far more powerful and efficient than Newcomen's, using only half as much coal to produce twice the output. Since no ignition was necessary—steam was created externally in a boiler and then piped into the cylinder—steam engines avoided the problem that had doomed Huygens's explosive prototype. With the supply of the two fuels for steam engines, water and coal, essentially inexhaustible, there seemed little incentive to experiment with gunpowder or any other combustible alternative.

With his partner and fellow Lunar Society member Matthew Boulton, Watt marketed his device in 1776, thus beginning an industrial revolution on one side of the Atlantic at the dawn of a political revolution on the other.* The steam engine was soon employed in virtually every commercial process that demanded a consistent and reliable power source. Perhaps no other mechanical device in history caused such a rapid and profound change in the human experience. In many ways, the modern urban industrialized world could be thought to have sprung from the mind of James Watt.

Although Watt's engine, like Newcomen's, had been designed for stationary use, it was inevitable that the notion of applying steam power to locomotion would soon follow. Within decades, both steam locomotives and steamships would transport millions of tons of goods and millions of travelers greater distances and in less time than had previously been thought possible.

Applying steam power to personalized conveyances was another obvious extension of the technology, but it would require any such device to be engineered a good deal smaller and substantially lighter than had by then been achieved. The first man to successfully build a steam-powered carriage was a French engineer, Nicolas Cugnot, who in 1769, predating Watt, fashioned a heavy three-wheeled cart with a

---

* Boulton was one of a series of brilliant scientists and patrons of science who lived in Birmingham during the last quarter of the eighteenth century. Some of them, including Joseph Priestley, Erasmus Darwin, Josiah Wedgwood, William Small (Thomas Jefferson's tutor), and Samuel Galton, met once a month at the time of the full moon to discuss issues of the day, and thus dubbed themselves the Lunar Society. Also in 1776, Adam Smith published his groundbreaking economics treatise, *An Inquiry into the Nature and Causes of the Wealth of Nations,* so it well might be argued that three revolutions were initiated in that remarkable year.

large boiler hanging over the front, driving the single front wheel, leaving the entire platform free to haul munitions or artillery. Cugnot's cart was quite cleverly constructed, with two cylinders operating alternately, utilizing a ratchet that created rotary power and also allowed the vehicle to be driven in reverse. In a demonstration in Paris, Cugnot's *fardier à vapeur* ran for fifteen minutes and attained the heady speed of 2 miles per hour.

But in a subsequent demonstration, due to "the violence of its motions," as *Automobile* magazine later described it, Cugnot's machine seemed to have literally "broken down a brick wall which stood in its way."[1] Soon afterward, his sponsor, French foreign minister Étienne-François Choiseul-Ambroise, fell out of favor at court. With the coming of the revolution, Cugnot's invention was abandoned entirely. And so the first practical, mechanically driven conveyance ever to grace a public road was cast aside, never to be resurrected, not even when ex-artilleryman Napoléon Bonaparte was hauling cannon across Europe.[*]

In the first decades of the nineteenth century, a series of Englishmen, first Richard Trevithick and then Sir Goldsworthy Gurney, built steam carriages that carried passengers.[†] Gurney's traveled the 9 miles between Gloucester and Cheltenham three times a day at 12 miles per hour. In 1831, Walter Hancock began a shuttle between London and Stratford in an omnibus that could carry fourteen passengers.

Revolutionary though this transport might have been, the British public did not clamor for steam conveyance. The boilers threw off copious amounts of smoke and soot, which was not endearing either to those who had paid premium prices to ride in the thing or to anyone passing nearby. In addition, the boilers often exploded, the crankshafts regularly broke, and the vehicles had a disquieting habit of

---

[*] Cugnot's preserved wagon does, however, occupy a prominent place in the Musée des Arts et Métiers in Paris.
[†] Trevithick is best known for producing the first steam locomotive, but his invention of the high-pressure steam engine, which was far more efficient and therefore could produce more power at a smaller size, would prefigure the later development of the steam-powered automobile.

colliding with pedestrians or livestock, or crashing at what was then considered high speed. It is not difficult, therefore, to see why most of the populace preferred to travel cheaply and reliably in a carriage pulled by the more familiar and always agreeable horse. So irritating were steam tractors that, in 1865, Parliament passed the Red Flag Act, limiting the top speed of steam vehicles to 4 miles per hour and requiring that a man waving a red flag, presumably on foot, precede any such conveyance on a public highway.

Although steam tractors—heavy, bulky, and slow-moving—continued to find application, particularly as farm vehicles, little progress was made in advancing the basic technology. At the close of the eighteenth century, however, coal, which powered the steam engine, yielded a promising alternative fuel source. In 1796, William Murdoch, the same Boulton & Watt engineer who had invented the planetary gear system to convert up-and-down motion to rotary power, lit his house with a new fuel, coal gas, a mixture of hydrogen, methane, and carbon monoxide obtained by heating coal in the absence of air. The resulting product could then combust if mixed with oxygen. Coal gas, foul-smelling and sooty as it might have been—and explosive if not properly vented—quickly enjoyed widespread use to heat homes and businesses, and for street lighting. By the second half of the nineteenth century, most major cities in Europe and the United States had run gas lines, which were widely accessed by both municipal and commercial customers.

Of course, if coal gas could burn, it might also be used to drive a piston. It took sixty years, but in 1860, a Belgian, Jean Joseph Étienne Lenoir, adapted the Newcomen engine to coal gas and created a horizontal, double-acting piston with a shaft attached to a flywheel.* To ignite the gas-air mixture, Lenoir employed a constantly burning flame outside the cylinder that was sucked inside by the vacuum created

* "Double-acting" means the piston moves back and forth, with gas entering on either side as the piston passes, a sort of mechanical tug-of-war. A flywheel is a large wheel attached to a rotating shaft that "stores rotational energy"—in other words, allows the shaft to rotate at constant speed even if the energy powering the shaft is intermittent.

when the piston passed by. Lenoir's motor could run continuously and produce up to 20 horsepower.[*]

Lenoir patented the design in 1861, and it was soon licensed by a number of French manufacturers. Between three hundred and four hundred were eventually sold for use in light industry. But practical application only emphasized the Lenoir's flaws. With ignition occurring before the piston reached the end of its stroke, the engine dissipated a good deal of the piston's potential power. Also, as an atmospheric apparatus with no compression of the fuel in the cylinder, it burned excessive amounts of both gas and the oil that is needed in any engine in which every other piston stroke transmits power.[†] One hundred cubic feet of gas were required to produce a single horsepower. The Lenoir was thus suited only for smaller tasks, where the more complex, economically scaled steam engine was too costly. It would also work only as a stationary device, with gas piped from an outside source. When Lenoir mounted his motor on a three-wheeled carriage-like vehicle, its range was minuscule because the gas in the tank he carried was depleted within moments.

But once the technology had been introduced, major improvements were soon made. The same year Lenoir received his patents, two Germans, Nikolaus Otto and Eugen Langen, theorized that compressing the fuel would add power and efficiency, and that the mixture should be ignited as the piston became tightest against the top of the cylinder, when compression was greatest. In 1864, they founded the Deutz Company to conduct their research. There they would eventually employ two young engineers named Wilhelm Maybach and Gottlieb Daimler.

---

[*] "Horsepower," a measure introduced by James Watt, is a rate of doing work, expressed as the fraction work/time. One horsepower is equal to 33,000 foot-pounds per minute.

[†] Engines that are powered at every upstroke of the piston are called "two-stroke" and require a mixture of gas and oil in the cylinder. Both substances are burned off at ignition. Two-stroke motors are quite powerful in smaller machines but less efficient and more brittle than engines that are powered at every other upstroke, called "four-stroke." Modern examples of devices that use two-stroke motors are leaf blowers, chain saws, snowblowers, and motor scooters.

But Otto did not succeed in building a working compression engine—the explosions in the cylinder were too powerful. Rather than continue to experiment with compression, he and Langen settled for building an improved atmospheric engine. They exhibited their design at the Paris World's Fair of 1867, the Exposition Universelle d'Art et d'Industrie, and orders came rolling in. Although the Otto, as it came to be called, was almost unbearably loud, described as "clanging like a rapid-fire pile driver," the market for stationary power plants that could be installed on the factory floor had grown exponentially; Otto and Langen would eventually sell about five thousand of these new machines, the world's first mass-produced mechanical engine.[2]

The motor utilized a single inverted piston and, like the Lenoir, could run continuously off a city gas line. But Otto's engine needed only 45 cubic feet of fuel to achieve 1 horsepower, a vast improvement. Otto was also the first to convert the up-and-down reciprocal stroke to rotary motion by using a rack-and-pinion arrangement—a linear gear meshing with a circular one—and a one-way clutch, which disengaged the gears during the piston's return stroke.

Although the Otto was still technically an atmospheric two-stroke engine, it exhibited some crude characteristics of the more modern compression engine that Otto had first sought to build. Revenues from its sales funded a return to the research that Otto was convinced would yield a greatly improved product.

In 1876, he built one: the first modern internal combustion engine. Both atmospheric power and the two-stroke design were scrapped. Instead, he used four strokes to complete a full cycle. During the first stroke, downward, a mixture of gas and air was sucked into the cylinder; an upstroke, generated by the flywheel, compressed it; a flame was introduced into the cylinder to detonate the fuel, and a downstroke, the power stroke, occurred; the piston was then sent back upward, again by the spinning flywheel, which forced the burnt gases out an exhaust valve. This four-stroke operation, fuel efficient with great endurance, has remained the state of the art ever since. And although Otto's invention utilized only one cylinder, it would not be long before fabricators built a multiple-cylinder engine, with the tim-

4 THE 'OTTO' CYCLE GAS ENGINE

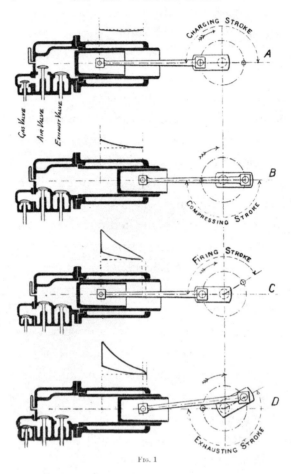

Fig. 1

Otto four-stroke engine

ing of the power strokes offset, thereby providing a continuous flow of enormous power while eliminating reliance on the flywheel. As an additional selling point, although it was still sufficiently loud to make conversation difficult in its proximity, the new creation was such an improvement over its predecessor that it was dubbed, without irony, "the silent Otto."

Otto received a patent for his design, but in 1886 he made an unpleasant discovery. In 1862, a French engineer named Alphonse-Eugène Beau de Rochas had received a patent for a similar four-stroke design, in which he also postulated that compression of the fuel in the cylinder was necessary to create a power stroke that could efficiently drive a piston.* In what would be a harbinger of the Selden-Ford duel, Beau de Rochas had never actually built an engine but had simply applied for his patent based on an idea and some crude drawings. Nonetheless, Otto's patent was revoked. But Otto proved to be as astute in the boardroom as in the workshop. By 1886, he had filed for and received so many other patents for minuscule improvements to his initial design that it remained difficult to develop a practical four-stroke engine without licensing an Otto patent.

But it turned out that Otto's was not the only design for a gas-powered internal combustion engine.

---

* Beau de Rochas was a man of brilliant ideas and no follow-through. Among his notions were a railroad tunnel under the English Channel, the incorporation of steel in high-pressure boilers, and a telegraph for submarines—which, of course, now exist—as well as more fanciful projects, such as driving canal boats by a chain on the canal bottom that stretched the length of the waterway. But he was also evidently an extreme eccentric who rarely made any money and could not save what little he did. When his four-stroke patents lapsed, he could not afford to renew them, so they entered the public domain, costing him millions. When he died in 1893, his widow reportedly was forced to sell household objects to pay for her mourning dress.

CHAPTER 2

THE MAN WHO WOULD BE KING

E ven as gas power found increased industrial application, few of the hundreds of inventors who sought to create powered locomotion imagined the internal combustion engine as anything but a monstrosity—large, noisy, smoke-belching, bolted to the floor, and suitable only for the factory. If a road carriage was to be built, it would be steam powered. On that point, nearly everyone agreed.

Except George Selden. Even before the Otto engine pushed a piston, Selden was engaged in developing a gasoline-powered motor sufficiently small and light to be attached to a four-wheeled chassis. As noted, had the family connections with which he was later credited actually existed, Selden almost certainly would have built the world's first motorcar. But those connections, along with virtually everything about his invention, proved to be an illusion.

Selden was born in 1846, son of abolitionist Henry Rogers Selden, a distinguished judge and the future lieutenant governor of New York.

A founder of the Republican Party, the elder Selden turned down Abraham Lincoln's offer of the vice presidency in 1864, feeling himself unqualified. His record as a defender of equal rights was without blemish. He refused to enforce the Supreme Court's ruling in *Dred Scott*, corresponded with Frederick Douglass, and when Susan B. Anthony was arrested for illegally voting in the November 1872 presidential election, he asserted, "I could not see a lady I respected put in jail." Against her wishes, he posted Anthony's bond. Anthony forgave Selden, who then defended her pro bono, basing his argument on the Fourteenth Amendment guarantees of equal protection of the law. Such was his reputation that Anthony told friends, "I know I can win. I have Judge Selden as a lawyer." For his part, Selden stated, "In my opinion, the idea that you can be charged with a crime on account of voting, or offering to vote, when you honestly believed yourself entitled to vote, is simply preposterous, whether your belief were right or wrong. However, the learned gentlemen engaged in this movement seem to suppose they can make a crime out of your honest deposit of your ballot, and perhaps they can find a respectable court or jury that will be of their opinion. If they do so, I shall be greatly disappointed."[1] Both defendant and lawyer turned out to be mistaken. The judge, Associate Supreme Court Justice Ward Hunt, serving on circuit, took no chances on the sentiments of a jury by directing a verdict of guilty.*

In contrast to his progressive public persona, however, at home Henry Selden was a rigid, domineering father, subjecting his son to a steady stream of "hostility and ridicule."[2] In particular, he had little patience with his son's penchant for tinkering.

---

* He took no chances on Anthony either, refusing to admit her testimony and writing his opinion before the proceedings commenced. Hunt was an "associate" of powerful New York senator Roscoe Conkling, "the champion of partisanship," and was appointed to the high court by Ulysses Grant at Conkling's behest. Hunt served for six lackluster years before suffering a major stroke that left him unable to speak or attend court sessions. He refused to retire because in order to receive his pension, he was required to be a member of the court for ten years. To get him off the bench, Congress passed a provision granting Hunt his pension if he retired immediately, an opportunity Hunt did not pass up. Conkling himself was nominated to fill Hunt's seat and was quickly confirmed, but declined the post because he would not accept a diminution of influence.

Selden would later claim to have begun thinking about "road loco-motion" when, as "a boy of fourteen, he chanced to hear a conversa-tion between his father and a manufacturer of farm implements, about [a] self-propelled steam carriage for public roads."[3] Both ex-pressed the opinion that such vehicles were not feasible. The "steam carriages" that had been present on the landscape for decades were little more than portable power plants that could not be moved faster than 5 miles per hour. No one, the judge and his visitor agreed, would succeed in overcoming the standard inhibitions of size and weight. Even at fourteen, Selden insisted later, he was already convinced that steam had no future. "This conversation was to Mr. Selden what the spoon over the tea kettle was to James Watt—it started him thinking upon the subject that was to be the main theme of his life." Although this entire account may well be apocryphal—most of the available material describing Selden's early life is taken either from interviews he gave when he was a figure of extreme controversy or from his tes-timony in the patent suit—that George Selden's interests were in me-chanical devices and not legal statutes is without question.

But Henry Selden would brook no dissent in his determination that George should take up the law. When the younger Selden returned home after a brief stint in the Union Army hospital corps, his father insisted he begin a course of study at Yale that would prepare him for a law practice.[4] But a Yale education was not going to aid George Selden in developing a motor that could be mounted on a wheelbase and carry passengers, so George, exhibiting rare defiance, left Yale and instead enrolled in a "scientific school." There, in addition to his studies, he was free to experiment with a variety of mechanical de-vices.

In 1869, his father put an end to such frivolity and Selden returned home to enter the family profession. Not surprisingly for a man who wished to be an inventor, he chose to specialize in patent law. That had been Henry Selden's specialty as well—"one of our greatest pat-ent lawyers, one of our greatest judges, and the greatest scholar of the law I have ever known," as one admirer put it. George Selden appren-ticed for two years; then, while continuing to live in his father's home, he joined the bar in 1871. Whenever he found himself with free time, he padded off to a basement workshop. Selden developed one or two minor devices he wanted to patent, but during the precise period when Henry Selden was defending Susan B. Anthony's freedoms without pay, the father refused to offer his son either moral or monetary support.

As the 1870s drew on, Selden's basement experiments resulted in one or two minor patents, which he licensed to local firms, but his main focus remained the design for a workable motorcar. His epiphany occurred in 1876, when he traveled to Philadelphia to visit the International Exhibition of Arts, Manufactures, and Products of the Soil and Mine, the first official World's Fair ever hosted within the United States, mounted as a centennial exposition to trumpet America's growing industrial might. Among the mechanical, agricultural, scientific, and cultural marvels exhibited in Philadelphia were the bicycle, the typewriter, Heinz ketchup, and Hires root beer. Also on display were the giant Corliss steam engine, the steam locomotive *John Bull,* and a new sort of engine, called the Ready Motor by its creator, George Brayton, an English inventor living in Boston. As reported in *Scientific American,* "The distinguishing features of this engine are that it can be started in a very short time, that it is economical in its consumption of fuel, and that, owing to the constant maintenance of carburetion, it is claimed, the danger of explosion of the hydrocarbon vapor is as greatly reduced as to be practically obviated."[5]

The most important word in *Scientific American*'s description was "hydrocarbon"; Brayton's Ready Motor ran on petroleum. Although petroleum had been used as a crude lighting fuel for centuries, the vast industrial potential of oil and its distillates was only then coming to be understood. The first modern refinery had been built less than twenty years earlier, and America's first oil well had not been sunk until 1859 (with a drill powered by a steam engine). At first, petroleum was considered only as a source of kerosene, with other distillates either of limited utility or considered waste products. Brayton's engine was the first to be powered by petroleum and the first to use any form of liquid fuel.

The Ready Motor was an odd combination of the impractical and the prescient. The engine utilized compression, but not in the cylinder. Brayton pressurized the air in its own chamber and then passed it through vaporized fuel for carburetion.* The mixture was then passed into an "expansion chamber," where it was ignited by a steady flame—as opposed to the spark used as ignition in the Otto. In this second chamber, the "injected" fuel burned rather than exploded and drove a piston. The engine was two-stroke and reciprocal, meaning that the piston was driven back and forth by alternating expansions on either side. Each thrust allowed the spent fuel from the previous thrust to be expelled. The "constant-pressure" principle was later called the "Brayton cycle" and found application in gas turbines, which are now employed to power jet engines.[6]

Although the Brayton engine exhibited at the centennial exposition was immense—more than eight feet high—as soon as Selden saw it, he was convinced that he had found his model. The constant-pressure principle was perfect, he was certain, for "road locomotion"—and Selden, before anyone else in America, realized that a petroleum-powered motor could be made substantially smaller and lighter.

For the next three years, Selden experimented with various designs and configurations. Although he was still living at his father's house and was a practicing attorney, Selden never had a great deal of money—he was plowing virtually all of his earnings into materials for his experiments. As he put it, the pursuit was with "unremitting ardor interrupted by pecuniary embarrassments." Eventually he hired a mechanic—or "mechanician," as they were then called—to help him fabricate the compact, lightweight Brayton engine that his road carriage would require. His principal problem was fuel—he had settled on petroleum over the obviously impractical street gas, but, as many Brayton users had discovered, crude was smoky and fouled an engine as much as powered it. So Selden, again before anyone else, turned to petroleum distillates.

Other than kerosene, the distillates—including gasoline, whose

---

* "Carburetion" is simply the mixing of air and fuel to enable combustion.

main utility seemed to be as a stain remover—continued to be viewed essentially as waste. But Selden wasn't so certain, so he and his mechanic, William Gomm, devised a test. They put a match to kerosene spread on an iron plate; it wouldn't burn. Then to benzene, which burned slowly with a good deal of smoke. And finally to gasoline, which "went off like a flash" and left no residue.

With that flash, Selden had his power source. Gomm then built a three-cylinder engine—to generate sufficient momentum to allow the engine to be run without a flywheel. That plan turned out to be moot, however, since only one of the cylinders became operational. But while the engine coughed and sputtered, it started up and ran. Although Gomm could not keep it going for more than a few seconds, a problem Selden intended to solve in his next round of experiments, George Selden was the first American attempting to build a gasoline automobile, and the first to conceive of a multicylinder motor to power it.

But Selden's time and money problems would not go away. During this period of experimentation and even when the patent application was first filed, he had every intention of pursuing production. But with his father unyielding in his refusal to help with either capital or introductions, Selden was forced to solicit financing on his own—or, more accurately, to beg for it. Without his father's endorsement, he was rejected everywhere and often laughed at. All the while, he was barely meeting expenses.

So, unable to raise the funds to build a prototype, embittered by the jeers of the local gentry, and realizing that competitors would at some point come to the same conclusions as had he, in 1879 George Selden decided to ensure that he at least made some money. He filed for a patent for an "improved road-engine" based on a gasoline-powered modified Brayton engine. "The object of my invention," he wrote in the patent application, "is the production of a safe, simple, and cheap road-locomotive, light in weight and easy to control, and possessed of sufficient power to overcome any ordinary inclination." He had avoided the impediments to steam locomotion, "the great weight of the boiler, engine, water, and water tanks, the complicated apparatus necessary to adapt the machine to the roughness of the roads which it must traverse, the necessity of the attendance of a skilled engineer to prevent accidents, and the unsightly appearance of the locomotives built on this plan," he claimed, by the "construction of a road-locomotive propelled by a liquid-hydrocarbon engine of the compression type." The goal, remarkably farsighted for its day, was to "employ the most condensed type of fuel, to produce a power road-wagon which differs but little in appearance from and is not materially heavier than the carriages in common use, [and] is capable of being managed by persons of ordinary skill at a minimum of trouble and expense." Since he had yet to develop an engine that could run for any length of time, he avoided specifics by simply asserting that "a given quantity of liquid hydrocarbon [would be] injected by pump into the combustion chamber."

While this and other references to a machine that had already been built were false, the lack of an actual prototype had no bearing on whether or not Selden would receive his patent. But it had great bearing on whether or not George Selden *wanted* to receive his patent, at least at any time proximate to when the application was filed. Without an actual automobile to sell and no prospects for acquiring sufficient capital to build one, Selden could profit from his invention only by licensing it. But even that route was problematic. Perfecting a working model was a good deal more complex than rendering a set of drawings. With an idea so ahead of its time, few manufacturers were apt to take on the costs and risks of perfecting a product for which no previous industrial process had been developed. Even his motor was nowhere near the stage at which it could be mounted on a carriage. The last thing he would have wanted was to be issued a patent whose seventeen-year life might well expire before there was any chance to profit from it.

Selden may or may not have been one of history's great innovators, but he was definitely a talented patent lawyer. If he couldn't control when the technology was ready for his idea, he would control when his idea was ready for the technology. The patent system was a jerry-built labyrinth, ripe to be manipulated in any number of ways, and

George Selden knew them all. In this case, the most propitious strategy was revision and delay, to keep the application pending until opportunities to profit from the idea had manifested themselves.

So for the next sixteen years Selden made fully one hundred alterations to his original application, in some cases adding specifics, in others taking them out, and in still others performing ludicrous secretarial chores, such as flattening out wrinkles in the paper. In each of these, he took the maximum time allotted by the examiner, often two years, all to ensure that his application was not approved until motorcars had become a reality.

With the filing of the patent application, Selden's life as an inventor came to an end. He was from then on nothing more than a lawyer with himself as a client. His gamesmanship was brilliant, and by the time he ended his long march, automotive technology had leapt into the practical. By deft management, Selden's approved 1895 patent—which reverted to the 1879 filing date but had an expiration date of 1912—bore only passing resemblance to his original application and incorporated many of the features of the automobiles that were by then selling in increasing numbers. On that paper product alone, Selden expected to become one of the richest men in America.

But after he obtained his patent . . . nothing happened. Three years later, Selden's motor, which had never been completed, lay rusting in the basement of the family home. With the caliber of both engines and the carriages that held them by that time making Selden's construction look childlike, none of the scores of manufacturers of genuine automobiles offered him licensing fees, and Selden lacked the resources to demand any. So obscure had Selden's patent become that when researchers for automobile manufacturers went hunting through the registry to protect themselves against potential infringement suits, they never even noticed it. Selden remained in Rochester, eking out the same insubstantial living as he had since entering the law. Sixteen years of clever manipulation, it seemed, had yielded him nothing.

CHAPTER 3

▧ MADE IN GERMANY . . .

G eorge Selden may have been the first person in the United
States to conclude that petroleum distillates might hold the
key to horseless travel, but he was not the first altogether. In
Austria, a decade before Selden cobbled together his three-cylinder
motor, a prominent engineer named Siegfried Marcus had not only
hypothesized that gasoline might be precisely what was needed to
power an internal combustion-driven motorcar, but he had also actually built one.

When he began tinkering with motor transport, Marcus, a native
German, had already produced a string of inventions that made him
a wealthy man and left him uniquely prepared to take on the task at
hand. One of these was "a hand-powered magneto-electric device
useful for a military field telegraph without batteries. This led him to
an electric ignition device for explosive mines, which was adopted by
the Austrian, Prussian, and Russian armies. By the 1880s, he had a
reliable magneto-electric ignition system for gas engines that could be
driven by the engine itself."[1] Marcus also invented the T plunger for
explosives, which was soon standard for both military and civilian applications. He was sufficiently acclaimed that Empress Elisabeth, wife

of Franz Joseph I, engaged him to install a system of electric bells in the Hofburg Palace in Vienna. From a steady stream of royalties—Marcus would eventually hold more than 150 patents—he was thus able to finance a workshop equipped with all the tools and instruments that might be needed to produce a motorized vehicle.

Marcus was not seeking profits. Something of a throwback to Huygens's era, he was drawn to problems as intellectual challenges. He particularly enjoyed the complex and the seemingly insoluble. But luck plays a role in scientific inquiry, and Marcus more or less stumbled onto gasoline as a power source. Austria-Hungary possessed some of the richest petroleum reserves in Europe—it had established the world's first oil refinery in 1858—and so petroleum products were an important component of the national economy. As in the United States, kerosene was the prized distillate, with gasoline considered useful only as a solvent. After some experimentation, however, Marcus, like Selden, determined that gasoline held great potential as a fuel; unlike Selden, he realized that the liquid must be either atomized or rendered into a vapor for it to combust. For a conveyable, self-contained engine, as would be needed in a motorcar, a small, efficient device would be necessary to disperse the liquid and then mix it with air so that it might be ignited in the cylinder.

To create a workable mixture of fuel and air, which Marcus called "carburetion," he filled a vessel with gasoline over which a brush rotated, sending minute droplets into the air above the pool. Suction created by the piston's downstroke drew the mixture into the cylinder, where it was condensed during the upstroke—momentum provided by a flywheel—and detonated by a spark, thus beginning the cycle once more. The "rotating brush carburetor," as it was termed, was highly inefficient—it utilized droplets rather than vapor, and there was no way to control the amount or richness of the mixture fed into the cylinder—but for the first time, the internal combustion engine had been freed from the factory floor and adapted for potential use in a vehicle. Even if he had never chosen to build a vehicle himself, "with his carburetor and his electric ignition, Marcus had made liquid fuel practical so that his engines could be used anywhere."[2]

Sometime in the late 1860s or early 1870s, Marcus mounted a two-stroke engine on a handcart and took it out for a spin. The machine could neither steer nor brake, but since it also could not tackle even the mildest grade, there was little danger of a runaway. Nor, with a range estimated at one-tenth of a mile, could it threaten havoc much beyond the door to Marcus's shop. Still, the sight of a motor-powered carriage ambling along the streets of Vienna elicited gasps, and word of Marcus's achievement spread across Europe.

Marcus returned to his workshop, and by the time George Selden was preparing his patent application, Marcus was well on the way to a second prototype. He had improved on the first version immensely, moving up to the more efficient four-stroke engine, installing brakes and steering, and developing a magneto starter to replace the assistants who had been required to lift the back wheels of the first incarnation off the ground and spin them to get the motor started.*

But Marcus chose not to publicly exhibit his machine until 1888, by which time two younger men had claimed the lead in the race to develop the horseless carriage.

Karl Benz was thirteen years Marcus's junior, born out of wedlock in Karlsruhe in 1844. His father drove a locomotive—and married Karl's mother soon after the boy's birth—but was killed in a railroad accident when his son was only two. Although Benz's mother had almost no money, she was determined that Karl receive a quality education, a task made easier when the boy demonstrated almost preternatural scientific aptitude from the moment he began school. Young Benz was sent to a prestigious scientific academy at age nine, a polytechnical

---

* For forty years, Austrian schoolchildren were regularly taught that Siegfried Marcus had built the first automobile. But Marcus was a Jew, and when the Nazis came to power, they destroyed his records and obliterated every mention of him that they could find. Thus, most of the details of Marcus's work have been lost. The second prototype, however, had been consigned to Vienna's Technical Museum and some quick-thinking employees hid it in a storeroom before it could be noticed by the Germans. That motorcar, now the property of the Austrian Automobile Club, is virtually all that remains of the man who could legitimately lay claim to the invention of the automobile.

secondary school soon after, and then was admitted to the University of Karlsruhe at age fifteen to study mechanical engineering. He was granted a degree four years later and, not yet twenty, went out into the world to make his living.

Benz was one of the plethora of automobile and aviation pioneers who began with bicycles. Both a rider and a mechanic, Benz, while still a student, had begun considering the means to adapt the basic bicycle design to a motor-driven carriage. Soon afterward, he took to sketching ideas for a high-speed motor in his spare time.

Despite his obvious talents, Benz had difficulty holding a job, drifting from one firm to another as either he or those for whom he worked became impatient and frustrated with the other. By his mid-twenties, he had come to understand that he was one of those people who could not work for anyone else, yet he lacked the wherewithal to strike out on his own.

Benz thought he had the problem solved when he took what little money he had been able to save and partnered with August Ritter to design and build machines to fabricate sheet metal. But choosing a business partner is a skill in itself, and Benz didn't have it. Ritter proved lazy and unreliable, and the new firm foundered. At one point, its tools were impounded and bankruptcy seemed inevitable.

But if Karl Benz was inept in choosing one sort of partner, he was utterly ingenious in another. Henry Ford would later call his wife, Clara, "the believer," for her unflagging support of his ideas and ambition, but it is difficult to imagine a wife more invaluable to her husband's success than Berthe Benz. She was a combination of cheerleader, mother, strategic planner, investment banker, and CEO. Not yet having married Karl, Berthe used her dowry to buy Ritter out and then pay off the firm's debts sufficiently to get her fiancé's factory up and running.

Their business brought in sufficient revenue to keep them operating, but Berthe was adamant that their future success lay in Karl's experiments with engine design and ultimately a motor-driven vehicle. To provide the wherewithal to continue the research, Berthe encouraged her husband to fabricate components that could be patented, thus bringing in licensing fees as well as providing elements of the final product. Over the course of the next decade, Benz obtained patents on either new or improved versions of a battery-powered ignition system, water-filled radiator, carburetor, spark plug, gearshift, and clutch. Ironically, the least advanced of Benz's components was his two-stroke engine. In 1883, Benz set up a production facility in—not surprisingly—a bicycle shop and set to incorporating these disparate elements into what would be the world's first automobile designed to generate its own power using an internal combustion engine.

He fell back on the old standby, the high-wheeler, for the design. The machine, which Benz would christen the Benz Patent Motorwagen, featured three bicycle-type spoked wheels (the front one smaller in diameter), a tubular steel frame, and a chain drive. Steering was by a tiller, and bench seating was provided for two. Benz had improved the motor considerably, employing a horizontally mounted one-cylinder, four-stroke engine, which could be water-cooled using Benz's patented radiator. Although his Motorwagen could generate only 0.9 horsepower, it could be started, run continuously, and attain a speed of just under 10 miles per hour. On January 29, 1886, Benz was granted the world's first-ever patent for a motorcar. In June, he drove the vehicle publicly through the streets of Mannheim.

As had the operators of the steam-powered bus services, however, Benz found that the public, while fascinated with his device, were not inclined to use it themselves, and certainly not to purchase it. During one of its first test runs, the tiller steering mechanism proved inadequate to prevent the Motorwagen from crashing into a wall, which did not help Benz gain popular acceptance. Nor could Benz's transmission, with one forward gear and one for reverse, allow the machine to negotiate anything but flat road or a coast downhill. Benz himself was not convinced that the Motorwagen could stand up to the rigors of an extended journey on the open road, leaving it suitable only for short trips within cities. Why, then, should consumers consider replacing the tried-and-true horse-drawn carriage, except for pure novelty? Sales were minuscule and the entire enterprise was threatened with collapse.

Benz Patent Motorwagen

Once again, Berthe Benz stepped—or in this case rode—into the breach. Early one morning in August 1888, before Karl was awake, Berthe wrote him a note. Then she gathered up their two sons and absconded with the Benz car. She drove some 65 miles on narrow, unpaved, bumpy roads from Mannheim to her mother's home in Pforzheim. It was the world's first automobile road trip. She purchased fuel from a pharmacy along the way—gasoline was at that time sold as a cleaning agent—and, in addition to one stop at a blacksmith's shop to straighten a bent axle, made two on-the-fly repairs herself. In one, she used her hatpin to clear a blocked fuel line, and in the other, she gained lasting fame with lingerie makers by employing her garter to insulate a short-circuit in the ignition system. Berthe solved the gearing problem by climbing hills in reverse. When she arrived at Pforzheim later that day, word of her jaunt was already making its way across Germany. She immediately telegraphed Karl, who must have been relieved that both his family and his automobile were safe. When Berthe returned home three days later, by then renowned across Europe, she gave her husband a list of improvements that the Motorwagen would need, including brake linings and an additional low forward gear, all of which Karl installed.*

Berthe's combination test drive and publicity stunt lifted both Benz and his company from near-oblivion to celebrity. The following year, he and Berthe took twenty-five improved Model 3 Motorwagens to Paris to exhibit at the Exposition Universelle. Held to commemorate the hundredth anniversary of the storming of the Bastille, the exposition was set on 240 acres of what is now the Champ de Mars. To ensure that this event would be the most opulent—and the most *French*—world's fair ever held, the organizers commissioned a specially built entrance arch that was guaranteed to announce to visitors just how unique their experience on the grounds promised to be. Despite furious criticism by a committee of three hundred famed artists, including Guy de Maupassant, Charles Gounod, and Jules Massenet, who denounced the structure as ugly and an affront to taste, the Eiffel Tower was nonetheless built and would prove to be the fair's most popular and enduring attraction.

Paris was the world's cultural center, and the five-month exposition drew luminaries from as far away as Argentina and Australia. One of the centerpieces was the Galerie des Machines, one hundred yards long, whose ceiling was supported not with pillars but with a series of parallel hinged arches, giving the space the feel of an inverted ship's hull. With the themes of the fair being modernization and progress, mechanical and industrial advances drew a steady stream of visitors, and no exhibit garnered more interest than the automobile. Aspiring automakers from Europe and the United States would return home

* In 2008, the German government declared a stretch of road from Frankfurt to Baden-Baden the Berthe Benz Memorial Route. There is now a biennial antique car rally along the route to celebrate Berthe's journey.

determined to create such vehicles of their own, and others would decide that the motorized carriage was not such a quixotic notion after all. By the time Karl and Berthe Benz returned to Mannheim, their future was secured.

But Benz was not the only person exhibiting an automobile at the fair. Another man, from Germany as well, had also succeeded in creating a motorized carriage. Each machine was precisely engineered and equally groundbreaking; each would have elements that survived into the next phase of automaking and others that were supplanted by superior technology. There are no reports that the two men ever met, either in Paris or subsequently, but their fortunes, and even their names, remain intertwined to this day.

Gottlieb Daimler was a baker's son, ten years older than Benz and only three years younger than Siegfried Marcus. Like Benz, he exhibited prodigious mechanical ability while still a boy.* As a student in his late teens, Daimler had already become known for his obsessive approach to work. He did not receive an engineering degree but at nineteen was hired out of the Advanced Polytechnic Institute in Stuttgart by the Karlsruhe Machine Works. Three years later, he was offered a promotion to supervisor, overseeing the building of steam locomotives. Instead, he returned to the Polytechnic to learn more about steam power. The more he learned, the more he became convinced that steam was a fatally flawed technology, doomed to be superseded by a fuel that could provide power more efficiently. He spent two years in England, working at engineering companies, and then returned to Germany, where—again like Benz—he was hired and then dismissed by a series of employers.

Daimler's movement from firm to firm also had nothing to do with competence; he was considered a master technician. But he was noto-

---

* At fourteen years old, while apprenticed to a gunsmith, he is reported to have designed and built a double-barreled pistol. Other accounts have Daimler building the pistol at ten, others not until he was eighteen—more credible, certainly, but less appealing.

riously difficult to work with, a perfectionist who seemed to have no need for time off. Only those equally committed and oblivious to the lure of leisure could thrive in his company.* In 1863, while working as the superintendent in another factory that produced steam locomotives, he found a kindred spirit in nineteen-year-old Wilhelm Maybach. An orphan whose education had been funded by patrons who noticed his aptitude for mechanics, Maybach would transition from Daimler's protégé to his partner, and the two would work so closely that it is impossible to discern which man had more input in the innovations that today bear only Daimler's name.

Maybach shared Daimler's determination to create an engine that could power locomotion and also recognized that steam power, while at that point the most advanced option, would not provide the long-term solution. Nor, he believed, would electricity. When Nikolaus Otto hired Daimler as technical director at his and Langen's Gas Engine Works at Deutz in 1872, Daimler brought Maybach on board as well, making the twenty-six-year-old chief designer. Both men had by that time come to believe that the four-stroke internal combustion engine could provide the breakthrough they sought and that gasoline was the fuel that would give the motor the widest range of application. But Otto, after his abortive attempt to build a compression motor, had decided to return to atmospheric engines; with that, the fissures that would eventually create an irreparable breach between the two men were formed.

Under Daimler's direction, Otto's company expanded and thrived. In the ten years Daimler worked in Deutz, he would not take a single vacation. But even as they were helping Otto attain prosperity, Daimler and Maybach were working privately on designs for the motor they were certain would supplant his. The most significant problem was in reducing the massive dimensions of the Otto so that it could be mounted on a vehicle. Unlike Benz, they were not at this point thinking solely of a motorcar, but rather of any conveyance that could be

---

* He did, however, eventually make time to get married and sire two sons, the eldest of whom, Paul, he doted on and took everywhere, while his wife and other son, Adolf, generally remained at home.

motor powered. They "soon realized that if its relative size and weight were to be materially reduced, the running speed must be greatly increased, this being the most obvious method of increasing the power without increasing the weight."[3] When they began, motors could barely achieve 100 revolutions per minute, thereby limiting both their efficiency and the power they could generate. Daimler wanted a motor that could achieve at least ten times the revolutions while producing equal or greater horsepower.

The first component they attacked was the Otto's flame ignition, in which, as Paul Daimler described it, "the compressed charge in the cylinder was put into brief connection with a burning gas jet by means of a moving slide, the flame being blown out by the explosion and relighted from a fixed gas jet. This method of ignition limited the speed of the engine to a comparatively low number of revolutions."

To replace flame ignition, Daimler and Maybach created the "hot tube," which was made of porcelain, open at one end, and extended into the cylinder. The porcelain was heated from the outside so that its temperature would be sufficiently high to ignite the fuel-air mixture forced into it during the compression stroke. Eliminating the need to relight a gas flame after each explosion allowed for much faster revolutions—thus allowing a proportional decrease in engine size and weight—but hot-tube ignition had problems of its own. Most significant was that the porcelain needed to be a precise temperature. If the tube was not heated sufficiently, it would fail to ignite the mixture; too much and it would explode, taking the engine with it. Even under optimal circumstances, the porcelain experienced enormous fatigue from changes in temperature and would often crack, requiring frequent replacement.

Imperfect as it was, however, hot-tube ignition was a step forward and convinced Daimler and Maybach that their plan for a light, fast motor was sound. Daimler, according to his son, "therefore severed his connection with the Otto Engine Works at Deutz and, returning to Cannstadt, near Stuttgart, his early home, he devoted his entire time and attention to the design of a light petroleum motor and motor vehicle."[4] Paul Daimler failed to mention that his father's parting with the man who had been his employer for a decade was bitter and acrimonious. Otto saw Daimler as an ingrate who had piggybacked off his ideas, and Daimler thought Otto a man hopelessly committed to outmoded technology.

With the money Daimler had made on his stock holdings in Otto Engine Works, he converted a greenhouse at the rear of his home to a machine shop. There he and Maybach worked in such secrecy that at one point police raided the greenhouse because neighbors were convinced the metallic sounds they heard coming from the building were the result of a counterfeiting operation.

But Daimler and Maybach weren't copying anything. They were devoting their full, extraordinary energies to perfecting the components of their motor. One of the most significant would be Maybach's design for an improved carburetor, the principles of which would dominate the industry for a century.* Before Maybach's breakthrough, carburetion was achieved either with a brush—Marcus's method—or, later, with a series of wicks that became saturated with fuel, much as a kerosene wick will become saturated in a lantern, and then were exposed to air drawn in from a surrounding chamber. With either of these designs, it was not possible to precisely regulate the amount of the fuel-air mixture that would enter the cylinder, and engines regularly either flooded or missed, sometimes within minutes of each other. Maybach ingeniously solved that problem by utilizing a float that sat atop the fuel reservoir. When the float reached the proper height, it activated a valve that stopped the flow of fuel to a separate chamber in which the fuel was exposed to air. The resulting fuel-air mixture, now in precise proportions, could then be drawn upward into the cylinder, compressed, and ignited.

In 1883, the lightweight, high-speed engine on which Daimler and Maybach had toiled for a decade was far enough along that they filed for a patent—which, for reasons never explained, was in Daimler's name only. But if Maybach was aggrieved by an omission that could potentially cost him millions, he never expressed that sentiment pub-

---

* In his article, Paul Daimler referred to this device as the "Daimler Carburettor," although Maybach, still very much alive, was certain to read it.

licly. Also for reasons never explained—although perhaps it was want of the more functional carburetor—it took an additional two years before they tested their motor on a prototype. The first vehicle to support the Daimler engine was, almost predictably, a bicycle.

It was a deftly constructed device, but stunningly uncomfortable, with the Daimler motor mounted directly beneath the driver's seat, between his legs, fed by a fuel tank directly above it, fastened to the underside of the seat. Maybach had yet to fully perfect his float carburetor, so the fuel-air mixture was achieved with a brush that passed over the fuel reservoir. Power was transmitted from the engine to the rear wheel by an arrangement of belts and pulleys. Daimler and Maybach set the cylinder vertically, a construct that Daimler dubbed the "grandfather clock." The engine was started with a crank, as would be all gasoline motors until the invention of the electric starter in 1896.* Two side wheels—positioned like training wheels on modern children's bicycles—kept the device from falling over sideways. With neither suspension nor, with the exception of thin sections of the frame, any means of protecting the rider's legs from the hot metal of the engine block, Daimler's motor bicycle was hardly practical. Still, in November 1885, when Maybach successfully drove the machine two kilometers on the streets of Cannstadt, it was hailed as the first publicly demonstrated gasoline-powered vehicle in history. (German newspapermen seemed to have forgotten about Siegfried Marcus.)

Initially the pair had used benzene for fuel because it did not need to be vaporized for carburetion, but, as had Selden, they found the distillate slow-burning, smoky, and inefficient. They then tried gasoline, which they employed exclusively thereafter.

After the motor bicycle experiment, Daimler next tried mounting his motor on a boat, but he had difficulty persuading anyone to ride in the craft: they were certain the motor would explode. It did not, and soon afterward Daimler-powered boats appeared on lakes and rivers across Germany and into Switzerland. After that, while Karl Benz was perfecting his three-wheeler, they purchased a stagecoach, tried their

---

* Electric starters would not come into widespread use for another two decades.

engine on a trolley, and even used it to power a balloon. Finally, in 1889, Daimler and Maybach settled on the automobile as the most promising application for their invention.

But Daimler and Maybach's greatest contribution was the motor itself. In 1887, well before they decided to mount their motor on an automobile, licenses were sold to other builders who intended to do that very thing.

CHAPTER 4

... PERFECTED
IN FRANCE

The Germans provided the impetus for motorized travel, but it fell to the French to create the modern automobile. In the 1880s and 1890s, a series of innovators attacked the problem from a variety of angles and in the process became both the most advanced and the most successful carmakers in the world.

The most important of these men was Émile Levassor, who joined with René Panhard, a fellow graduate of the École Centrale Paris, France's premier college of engineering, initially to build machine tools for woodworking. In the early 1880s, they purchased a license from Otto and Langen to build motors that could be used for power saws. But both followed closely the news out of Germany and, after learning of Benz's machine, became interested in building an automobile that could be sold in France. It soon became clear, however, that the gas-powered Otto would be difficult, if not impossible, to adapt for that purpose. One afternoon in 1887, while sailing on a lake, Levassor noticed a boat powered by a Daimler motor. After some inquiries, he contacted Édouard Sazarin, Daimler's French agent, to discuss the purchase of a license to build the light, high-speed motors in France.* When Sazarin told Daimler of the potential deal, Daimler journeyed to France to meet Levassor and was impressed by both his abilities and his vision, and they quickly came to terms. But Levassor and Panhard did not immediately begin to design automobiles. Their first idea was to produce only the engines and engage another manufacturer to construct the remainder of the car. They chose Armand Peugeot, another École Centrale graduate, whose family had been metalworkers for four generations. Peugeot, who had been manufacturing—what else?—bicycles, had also seen the potential of automobiles. He had completed an experimental steam carriage just months before Levassor approached him. Peugeot enthusiastically embraced the opportunity to use a Daimler motor instead, and in 1890 and 1891 he built several automobiles for Panhard and Levassor, based, as had become the norm, on the "horseless carriage" schematic.

But Levassor thought merely throwing a motor on a horse-drawn carriage—or a glorified bicycle—was shortsighted, and he decided he could create a better machine. Within months, he had produced a radically new design. The 1891 Panhard et Levassor was a true automobile, the first that did not simply mirror a horse-drawn carriage's silhouette. Levassor placed "the engine in front, a sliding change-speed gear arranged for various speeds, a counter-shaft for carrying a differential gear, and sprockets for a chain drive on to the back wheels."[1]

Levassor's design allowed for larger, more powerful engines whose size was not limited by the space under the seat or between the rear wheels. With a clutch that linked the engine to a variable-speed transmission, power went through a differential to chains that drove the rear wheels. Levassor observed of his creation, *"C'est brutal, mais ça marche"* (It is raw, but it works). Peugeot soon adopted the design, as within a few years did every other French carmaker. Eventually each of those features was incorporated in automobiles around the world, and a front-mounted engine with clutch-driven gearbox and rear differential has remained the industry standard to this day.

* Levassor was clearly negotiating for more than an engine license, for when Sazarin died the following year, Levassor soon afterward married his widow, Louise.

1898 Panhard et Levassor

These improvements, while groundbreaking, in no way meant that a ride in a French automobile was a peaceful, pleasant experience. To give a sense of what early automobiling was like, Charles Jarrott described a friend starting the engine of Émile Levassor's #5 in late 1896:

> Wellington, who was an expert on ignition burners (so he informed me), then proceeded to light the ignition lamps for the motor. His methods were drastic, novel to me, and terrifying to the bystanders. There was rather a big blaze, but, as he explained to me afterwards, that was a detail, and it really was not dangerous. Anyhow, when I say that he turned on the petrol tap, flooded the whole of the engine with petrol, turned the tap off, lit a match, dropped it inside the bonnet of the motor and then ran away, one can imag-

ine that my criticism of his expertness was somewhat more forcible than the expression of the word "primitive." And having assured the bystanders that the aid of the fire brigade was not necessary, and the flames having subsided, we got the burners to work with the aid of some methylated spirit, and then proceeded to start the motor.[2]

Still, the virtues of Levassor's creation were manifest in speed, endurance, and handling, and Panhard et Levassor and Peugeot quickly dominated the market. Paris boulevardiers, industrialists, and country doctors, the core groups of French car buyers, submitted so many orders for the machines that the two firms could not fill them all. Many carmakers abandoned steam, and by July 1895, during an exhibition on the Champ de Mars—only six years after Karl Benz had introduced his Motorwagen—thirty-six carmakers exhibited automobiles.

The French also solved the problem of what an automobile should run on. Wheels were originally made of iron, but soon this was supplanted by solid rubber. While less prone to distortions from striking rocks, ruts, or holes, solid rubber's ability to absorb jolts was only a marginal improvement over metal. A car rattling about did not merely create discomfort for the passengers; it could literally destroy a chassis or disable an engine. In 1890, two brothers who ran a family rubber business, Édouard and André Michelin, noticed that a bicycle tire invented by Scottish veterinarian John Boyd Dunlop was "pneumatic"— filled with air—which gave it remarkable resiliency. In Dunlop's version, the rubber shell was glued to the wheel; this made it unwieldy and time-consuming to repair on a bicycle, almost impossible on a motorcar. The Michelins improved on Dunlop's invention by creating a locking lip on the rubber, which was set into a matching shape on the wheel. The tires were thus easy to detach and repair when the tire was deflated. Pneumatic tires were also a good deal lighter than solid rubber, and, by absorbing vibration, they allowed a machine's frame to be lighter as well. They first marketed their "pneus" for bicycles with great success, and in 1895 they mounted the first set for automobiles on a Peugeot. In extremely short order, pneumatic tires became standard for every automobile made in Europe or the United States.

The Michelins also became famous for benevolent treatment of their workers. They created a system of bonuses based on the company's profits and also a medical plan, in which physicians hired by the company treated Michelin workers and prescribed medications, all at a fraction of the normal cost. Eventually the company built a hospital and a senior citizens' facility, subsidized housing, and financed a cooperative at which Michelin workers could buy food, clothing, and other necessities.

Temperamentally opposite from the Michelins, certainly in how he viewed the working class, was Count Albert de Dion, a playboy aristocrat whose father had married an American. De Dion had become interested in automobiles between sessions at the gaming tables or engaging in duels. Like Peugeot, he began with steam.

In 1883, he engaged a mechanic, Georges Bouton, and began manufacturing steam carriages, uncharacteristically granting the commoner Bouton equal billing in the partnership. In the late 1880s, steam became a far more practical alternative when yet another Frenchman, Leon Serpollet, aided by his brother Henri, perfected the "flash tube boiler." Also called the "mono-tube boiler," Serpollet's invention used far less water and converted it into steam much more quickly, all while providing a continual supply to the engine. That, in turn, considerably shortened the time it took to get the motor to sufficient pressure to engage the pistons, making for faster starts and the ability to run at higher speeds. Serpollet eventually built a racing car with a four-cylinder motor, which, for a time, held the land speed record.

Serpollet's design was adopted by almost everyone who wished to remain with steam power. De Dion therefore continued to build steam-powered cars—and would for a decade—but after the success of the Daimler motor, he and Bouton agreed that the future was with gasoline. Levassor had the exclusive French license, so Bouton designed an extremely light, 3-horsepower motor of his own that was capable of running at high speed and had electric ignition rather than flame. He initially mounted the motor on a tricycle, as had Karl Benz.

Bouton proved himself a first-rate engineer, and De Dion–Bouton motors gained a well-deserved reputation for performance, reliability, and durability, all at a reasonable price. Although they were unable to match the popularity of Panhard et Levassor, sales of the De Dions remained brisk throughout the first half of the 1890s.

Eventually, word of De Dion–Bouton motors made its way across the Atlantic and would-be automakers in the United States began to purchase them as well.* All this interest stoked de Dion's elitist sensibilities, and in 1896, before he had built a single four-wheeled gasoline automobile of his own, Count de Dion and a group of wealthy industrialists and car enthusiasts founded the Automobile Club de France (ACF) to promote both racing and French automobiles. Its headquarters were in an opulent four-story mansion on Place de la Concorde, purchased for 1.5 million francs, complete with balconies and roof garden.[3]

With the founding of the auto club, "automobilism," as it was called, took on an extra dimension. Count de Dion's palatial clubhouse became a meeting place of young right-wing aristocrats, and soon the automobile began to be seen by large segments of the public not as an agent of progress but rather as one of reaction. In response, municipalities with left-wing constituencies often enacted anti-automobile laws, such as speed limits of 6 miles per hour. De Dion himself was a member of the Chamber of Deputies, where he spoke out vociferously against Alfred Dreyfus. After a protest demonstration at the Auteuil racecourse in 1899 at which either President Émile Loubet or a police inspector was struck over the head with a cane—accounts differ—De Dion, an admitted ringleader, was accused of the act, forcibly restrained by the police, and subsequently jailed for two weeks.[†]

* James Ward Packard of Warren, Ohio, brought one home from Paris and soon was inspired to form the establishment that became the Packard Motor Car Company.

† De Dion denied striking anyone during the fracas. "He asserted that he had taken lessons in fencing, boxing, and kicking and that if he had hit anyone, the person struck would not have been capable of coming to court." *New York Times,* June 16, 1899.

1901 De Dion motor carriage

In 1899, de Dion and Bouton moved beyond motors and finally began making gasoline cars on their own, and these soon acquired a reputation as some of the finest machines produced anywhere. But one year before they did, a twenty-one-year-old engineering whiz named Louis Renault took an old De Dion–Bouton motor and mounted it on a car with a three-speed gearbox, with reverse and what at the time was called "propeller drive," a system for transmitting power directly to the rear axle without chains. Renault's system also featured a more efficient method of shifting gears from one speed to another.*

Renault, from a wealthy family of haberdashers, had built the car

---

* Chains, which tended to stretch and sometimes break, were also less efficient in preventing energy loss from the engine and crankshaft to the axles and wheels. Most of the improvements to motors and transmissions in the early days of automobile development were aimed toward losing the least amount of the energy created during the explosion within the cylinder as it was transferred along the various components, until it actually turned the wheels. The other area of development was attempting to create the most powerful explosion possible within the cylinder.

on a whim, for personal use and not to sell. But to celebrate Christmas in 1898, he drove his new machine, which he called a voiturette, from his family's country estate to Montmartre, in Paris, to join his brother Marcel and some friends. At Christmas dinner, someone bet that his machine could not negotiate the 13 percent grade up the hill to the restaurant. Renault drove up and back a number of times with a passenger seated next to him. Before he had finished dinner, Renault had orders for twelve voiturettes. He, Marcel, and a third brother, Fernand, founded Renault Frères a few weeks afterward. By March, they had rented factory space near their family home and begun to manufacture the Voiturette Type A. With motorcars that were light, sturdy, reliable, and easy to maintain—traits that would later be attributed to Ford's Model T—Renault Frères, although never quite outstripping Panhard, quickly became one of the leading automobile manufacturers in France.

CHAPTER 5

AN UNEASY ROMANCE WITH THE HORSE

A s the nineteenth century moved into its final decade, the impact of industrialization on demographics in the United States and Western Europe—much of it engendered by the use of piston-driven machinery, steam or gas, either in factories or in railroad locomotives—was unmistakable. Across America, immigrants and erstwhile farm families streamed into cities. The population of Manhattan, for example, grew from 515,547 in 1850 to 1,515,301 in 1890; Brooklyn, then a separate city, from 96,838 to 806,343; Chicago from a puny 29,963 to a muscular 1,099,850; Detroit from 21,019 to 205,876. While in many cases city boundaries increased as well, territorial expansion was generally outpaced by the influx of new residents. Sometimes territory remained precisely the same, as in Manhattan, an island that was stuck with its 23 square miles.

Logarithmic growth in population density caused any number of well-documented challenges. Strains on housing, educational facilities, sanitation, water, and even food supplies were inevitable. Often overlooked, however, is that with people cramming into living and working spaces, they were also forced to live in closer and closer proximity to the horse.

Unlike on the farm or even in a town, where unpleasant equine by-products were an inconvenience that could generally be sidestepped, in the cities there was no escape. Horses moved everything—they carried individuals and pulled private carriages, hansom cabs, and liveries. The milkman had a horse, as did the vegetable man, the knife sharpener, the chimney sweep, the mason, the carpenter, and the local doctor. Policemen were on horseback and a team of horses pulled the fire truck. In New York, "each day these same horses deposited 60,000 gallons of urine and 2,500 tons of manure on its 250-plus miles of paved streets. It took a strong stomach and the skills of an acrobat to cross a street. On damp days, pedestrians contended with syrupy puddles of foul-smelling manure alive with flies. In dry weather, the germ-laden droppings were pulverized by the animals' hooves into a fine powder carried everywhere by the wind, even into homes."[1] Revolting as these images are, the pollution did not stop there. "For a two-horse team to pull a fully loaded omnibus or streetcar designed for 40 passengers was strenuous work, especially since these were often overcrowded. Cruelty to animals was regarded as a necessary evil. Many horses died in the streets and their carcasses had to be hauled away."

Still, in the early days of automotive experimentation, the animal was considered "civilized" compared to noisy, smoky, bone-rattling motorcars, particularly among the wealthy—who were rarely forced to endure the worst of horses' various pollutions at close range. Few, certainly, saw those primitive machines as one day supplanting horse-drawn vehicles. A small number of visionary entrepreneurs, however, grasped that the potential market in horseless transportation was enormous. As soon as such vehicles began to make inroads, the advantages became manifest. So, where the city-to-city steam omnibuses might not have borne up in comparison to the reliable old horse, the reaction within city borders was far different.

Ironically, as industrialization had created a broader and deeper moneyed class, the very people who retained the most romantic image of the horse resided in the most obvious market for early horseless vehicles. Since early generation motorcars, like every new product, were certain to be more expensive than later models of the machine, persuading well-heeled buyers to abandon outmoded notions seemed to present an immense challenge. As it turned out, however, manufacturers needed little concern. The novelty of motorcars, coupled with the fact that no one else could afford them, made the wealthy and near-wealthy eager and ready outlets for the new products. A viable commercial entity seemed to be all that was required to transmute the horse-drawn carriage into a modern automobile.

While the Brayton Ready Motor might have piqued the interest of George Selden, another device exhibited at the 1876 Philadelphia fair, neither mechanized nor industrial but rather an instrument of leisure and diversion, was to have a far more profound impact on American technology. The bicycle would spur a craze; tens of millions would be sold in the United States in the coming decade and prompt a revolution in the manner in which Americans viewed their own mobility. It would not only provide impetus to the search for a horseless carriage—as it had in Europe—but eventually provide inspiration for a different sort of transportation miracle: powered, controlled flight.

The bicycle exhibited in Philadelphia was not even the kind we recognize today—the "safety bicycle," with both wheels of equal size—but rather the high-wheeled "ordinary" that contemporary Americans associate mainly with circus performers. At the time, not only were there virtually no bicycles in the United States but there were also virtually no roads on which to ride them. But to the successful entrepreneur, dearth represents opportunity, and that was precisely what another visitor to the fair, Colonel Albert Augustus Pope, recognized in that awkward high-wheeler.

Pope, born in Massachusetts in 1843, had been forced to become something of an opportunist after his father lost all the family's money in land speculation when Albert was ten years old. He began by hiring himself out plowing fields, graduated to selling fruits and vegetables, and then at age fifteen started his own produce business at Boston's Quincy Market. At the onset of the Civil War, Pope, still a teenager, had become sufficiently successful to be appointed a second lieutenant. He fought with Grant at Vicksburg and Petersburg, with Sherman at Jackson, and with Burnside at Fredericksburg, always receiving high commendations. By the war's end, Pope was a twenty-two-year-old colonel with command of his own regiment. He mustered out and began a shoe-supply business in Boston with $900 he had saved from his army pay. With a deft hand for finance and some clever marketing, he grew his business rapidly, and in three years it was the largest of its kind in the nation. Pope, who would go by "Colonel" for the rest of his life, had made himself a rich man.

After his visit to the fair, Pope, then in his early thirties, sailed for Europe to learn about bicycle manufacture and there solicited British fabricators to license imports into the United States. But relying on imports would eventually leave him vulnerable to competition. So, only months after he had acquired the American rights to some English patents, Pope approached the Weed Sewing Machine Company in Hartford, Connecticut, with an offer to lease the excess floor space in its factory to produce high-wheelers. His first runs sold out instantly, and Pope increased production, eventually buying the Weed Company and converting the factory solely to bicycle manufacture. He then initiated a program of horizontal expansion, unusual for its day, buying a rubber company, a steel company, and the largest nickel-plating factory in the world. Finally, he instituted a program of "integrated manufacturing operations," a rudimentary assembly line approach, which "prefigured the concentration of resources in the modern automobile plant."[2]

But for all his business acumen, Pope's greatest skill remained marketing. Clearly, sales of bicycles would be limited unless there were places to ride them, and American roads at that time, especially outside the centers of the largest cities, were dirt and gravel nightmares. In 1880, Pope hosted a conclave of manufacturers, bicycle enthusiasts, and shippers in Newport, Rhode Island, and there founded the League of American Wheelmen. The league's first act was to officially launch the Good Roads Movement, specifically to prod state, local, and even national officials to build improved roads.

In what would have been a surprise only to those unfamiliar with Pope's persuasive powers, the movement became an unprecedented success, and within five years, Good Roads had become a national obsession. The league eventually published pamphlets, such as *The Gospel of Good Roads,* and even *Good Roads Magazine,* whose circulation topped one million. Local groups demonstrated, held conventions, and lobbied legislators. As one wag put it, "In politics, machinery and economics the Colonel's tenets were simple. He believed in the Republican party, the bicycle, and good roads."[3]

With clever misdirection, Pope ensured that good roads were promoted not as a surface for bicycles but as the soul of a nation and the infrastructure that any modern industrial and agrarian country required. As he wrote in a widely disseminated pamphlet:

> The people everywhere throughout the country are awakening to the vast importance of better highways. They more fully realize not only the great commercial advantages of good roads but they see more clearly that the material highways of the country are highways in a spiritual sense as well; that the growth of society, education, and Christianity depend largely upon good means of communication between home, school, and church, and that no nation can advance in civilization which does not make a corresponding advance in the betterment of its highways.[4]

Although not at all constructed for this purpose, thousands of miles of improved roads would therefore be in place, waiting, when automobiles began to become fixtures on the landscape.*

The high-wheeler's design was obviously of limited utility to all but the nimble, so, to create the widest possible market base, Pope almost totally redesigned the product he had seen in Philadelphia, replacing the ordinary with the safety bicycle. In addition to lowering the profile and making both wheels the same diameter to provide greater stability, he used hollow tubing in the frame, and employed pneumatic

---

* As will be seen, Pope's roads would barely scratch the surface of what would be required to convert a horse-borne society to a motorized one, but they would nonetheless be sufficient to give automobilism a solid start.

rather than solid rubber tires. The result, the Columbia Chainless, "unexcelled by any domestic manufacturer," was lighter and easier to mount, dismount, and maneuver, and bore less friction on the wheels.[5] It opened marketing possibilities to older men, children, and especially women. Not only did bicycling become an appealing new way for gentlemen and ladies to spend time together, but women seized on the freedom of movement that cycling implied as a symbol of political freedom. One prominent ad for the Columbia Chainless featured a beautiful young woman in a flowing dress holding a wreath while standing next to two bicycles set on a platform. By the mid-1880s, a woman on a bicycle became a badge of liberation. Henry Selden's client Susan B. Anthony gushed, "The bicycle has done more for the emancipation of women than anything in the world."[*]

But bicycles, like any fad, eventually ran their course. With a saturated market and a growing fascination with motorized transportation, bicycle sales had dropped precipitously by the mid-1890s. But Colonel Pope was prepared. As many of his competitors began to close up shop, Pope was retooling his factory to house a new division of his company that would produce automobiles.

The colonel's dilemma was that with no experience in the field, he could not be certain what kind of automobile to produce. Steam carriages at that point remained the most popular, but gasoline power seemed to be fast overtaking steam as a preferable technology. Then there were electric vehicles, which had recently been developed by a pair of Philadelphia engineers; they were lacking in range but were fast and quiet. Even compressed air had been toyed with as a power source and showed some promise, although it would still require a good deal of work before it could be adapted to a commercial vehicle.

The problem seemed solved when Pope got word of a young graduate from the Massachusetts Institute of Technology who had built a gasoline-powered prototype that had been successful in test runs. The

---

[*] And, of course, bicycles were to inspire an entire generation of innovators, both on the ground and in the air. Wilbur Wright, Glenn Curtiss, Alexander Winton, Hiram Percy Maxim, and many others took the bicycle as the starting point for their experiments.

engineer had an excellent pedigree. His father, Hiram Stevens Maxim, had developed the first portable, fully automatic machine gun; built machines that some claimed had successfully attained powered flight; and invented the inhaler, the curling iron for hair, and a mousetrap that reset itself.

Pope summoned Hiram Percy Maxim to Hartford, watched a test run of what Maxim later called his "explosive tricycle," and hired him on the spot. Maxim, who would later pen *Horseless Carriage Days,* the most insightful and witty memoir ever written about the early automobile, was given a free hand in a refreshingly ad hoc effort to come up with something that Pope could sell.

Without informing either the boss or the local citizenry, Maxim, accompanied only by one or two close associates, often took his creations out on the streets of Hartford for tests late at night. More than a few times, the engine stalled and the machine had to be pushed to a downhill slope, coasted home, and secreted in a shed so Colonel Pope would be none the wiser.

Eventually Maxim's designs progressed sufficiently that he wanted to try for a "record run," north to Springfield, Massachusetts, and back, a distance of slightly more than 50 miles. The Good Roads movement had yet to visit this stretch, and soon after they'd left Hartford, Maxim and his companion were shining their lanterns on a narrow, rock-strewn path, barely wide enough for the car. Maxim provided perhaps the best description of what it meant to ride in an early version of "this throbbing, noisy, complicated, greasy accumulation of mechanical odds and ends."[6] Describing his own prototype, he wrote, "It was a real horseless carriage, even to the whip socket on the dash. It shook and trembled and rattled and clattered, spat oil, fire, smoke, and smell, and to a person who disliked machinery naturally, and who had been brought up to the shiny elegance and perfection of fine horse carriages, it was revolting."

The war between horse and machine cannot be appreciated by a population for whom the automobile is as common as the front door of a house. Maxim, however, described an encounter when his motorized vehicle came upon an equine-powered one, while traveling at

Hiram Percy Maxim

night on a country road north of Hartford, that resembled a scene from *Close Encounters of the Third Kind:*

> This junk dealer, bringing a load of junk to Windsor Locks in the silent night, was blissfully ignorant of the existence of such a thing as a motor-vehicle. As he wended his way along the lonely country road, up from the distance came a strange and unearthly noise, the like of which he had never heard in his entire life. This weird noise became a din. The din grew louder and signified that whatever was making the awful sound was approaching. A little flickering light appeared ahead, but before he could judge its distance in the dark, the monstrous thing was upon him and about to run him and his horse down. And the poor horse . . . just as he was about to be attacked and devoured by the terrible thing, he reared up and wheeled.[7]

Despite terrifying passersby both animal and human, Maxim persevered. On his third try, he finally succeeded in his Springfield run, and soon afterward made an even more arduous journey to Long Island Sound. By 1897, Maxim had progressed sufficiently that Colonel Pope saw commercial application within reach. It would turn out, however, to be a very different application from the one Maxim had struggled over all those bone-jarring miles to perfect.

CHAPTER 6

EARLY AMERICANS

W hile Albert Pope may have been the most sophisticated of the late nineteenth-century American entrepreneurs seeking to transform the bicycle into the automobile, he was not the only one, nor even the first. That honor went to two farm boys from Illinois, Charles and Frank Duryea, who in 1895 built and sold thirteen identical motor carriages, "the first automobiles to be regularly manufactured for sale in the United States."[1]

The Duryea brothers, eight years apart in age, got started when Charles, the elder of the two—born in 1861, only two years before Henry Ford—was a teenager. Charles had been fascinated with both motor vehicles and human flight since he was a boy, and for years had been visiting the local library and reading everything he could find on the subject, particularly in *Scientific American*. After the family visited the Philadelphia fair and he saw the high-wheeler exhibit, he set to building a bicycle from scrap and spare parts that lay about on his father's farm. Frank, still a boy, turned out to have a flair for mechanics and was an able assistant.

The experiment was successful, so the brothers stayed at it. Like thousands of other Americans, the Duryeas graduated from building bicycles for themselves and their friends to running a makeshift manufacturing operation, learning by trial and error how to build a workable machine, and then selling their product locally. In the mid-1880s, the two were making a decent living, but both thought they could go further. They visited Washington, D.C., and "agreed that an engine driven vehicle would be equally practical on the road."[2] The brothers left Illinois and moved to Chicopee, Massachusetts, where Charles continued in the bicycle trade and Frank found work as a toolmaker.

For two years Charles pored over the volumes of material detailing the developments in automaking in Germany and France. He drew up preliminary plans, got a local backer to put up $1,000, and "bought an old phaeton buggy into which his proposed structure was to be built."[3] In April 1892, he hired Frank away from the Ames Manufacturing Company and put him in charge of construction of a gasoline-powered automobile. Their first efforts were disasters. Frank later attributed the failures to Charles's primitive engine design, which included hot-tube ignition, by then already nearing obsolescence, and required that the motor be started by the manual rotation of a flywheel. Charles's engine also lacked a water jacket—because he "believed that since it was to operate in the open air, it would not overheat"—and had inadequate carburetion and no muffling system, which upset the engine timing.

After those first failed attempts, Charles returned to Peoria to continue in the bicycle business, but Frank remained in Massachusetts, working to improve the design. In September 1893, Frank successfully tested a one-cylinder automobile, attaining a top speed of 5 miles per hour. Four months later, Frank had completed a vastly improved model, and Charles returned from Illinois. The following year, Frank, again working alone, produced what might well be considered the first modern automobile built in the United States. Although Frank's machine steered with a tiller and its braking system was uncertain, Charles later wrote that "it was a real auto because it combined for the first time the auto essentials like spray-carburetor, electric ignition, throttle control, hand brake, anti-friction bearings, artillery wheels, air tires,

Duryea's 1892 gas buggy

live rear axle and engine shaft lengthways of the car."[4] He also took credit for the design.

The brothers incorporated the Duryea Motor Wagon Company in 1895, with Frank the designer and chief engineer and Charles handling the business side. To increase exposure, they entered their motorcars in races—which they generally won—and loaned one to the Barnum and Bailey circus, where it was exhibited daily and driven in street parades.

The Duryeas, however, found that success could be as thorny to navigate as country roads. As might be deduced by Frank's need to later pen an account of the events, the brothers had a falling out. Charles sold his majority interest in the company and again moved to Peoria, which he liked for "its resourcefulness and its industry and the friendliness of its people," and began an automobile company of his own, the Duryea Manufacturing Company of Peoria, Illinois.[5] When Charles's venture was incorporated on February 19, 1898, the Duryea brothers had founded the first two automobile manufacturing companies in the United States.

Charles's automobiles contained some novel improvements—they were the first to employ a planetary transmission—but he nonetheless found it impossible to attract capital. He later wrote, "Few believed autos were anything but a passing fad, a plaything the rich would quickly tire of and discard. Carriage makers in particular thus kidded themselves. Generally they fought us till they failed and went down with the flag flying—a very poor substitute for vision."[6]

In addition, reaction to automobiles by the local citizenry in friendly Peoria was no better than it had been in the English countryside. Charles Duryea's wife, Rachel, described their reception to the *Peoria Journal*: "We had tomatoes thrown at us, and we had things worse than tomatoes thrown at us. People said our automobile scared the horses and should be kept off the roads. Many times we had unpleasant experiences." In one Illinois town, if a horse refused to pass an automobile, the driver was required to "take the machine apart as rapidly as possible and conceal the parts in the grass."[7]

Whether or not the Duryea brothers would have succeeded had they stayed together is uncertain. Certainly Frank was an outstanding engineer and Charles had a well-honed promoter's flair. Separately, however, they soon faded into irrelevance. Charles, in particular, became an object of pathos. "He drifted down and out of the automobile world until he was reduced to running a question-and-answer column on a trade paper and writing pamphlets protesting that it was not Haynes or Winton or Ford or Olds who deserved credit for fathering the American automobile, but he, Charles Duryea."[8]

The Duryeas, however, were soon replaced by more aggressive and forward-thinking competitors. The most significant of these was a Scottish-born engineer, another bicycle manufacturer, who, like Colonel Pope, was heavily investing both time and money in motorized transportation.

Alexander Winton had immigrated to the United States at age nineteen. After a number of years working on steamships, he moved to Cleveland, Ohio, where, in 1891, he began the Winton Bicycle Company, one of the hundreds of small independents springing up across the nation to compete with the likes of Albert Pope. (The Wright

Cycle Company of Dayton, Ohio, was another.) Winton had a keen eye for detail and was precise in construction, and so he fared well in an industry where demand seemed always to overwhelm supply.

Also like Pope, Winton sensed the imminent saturation of the bicycle market and became convinced that the future was in motorized transportation. Although the number of automobiles sold in the United States by then barely numbered one hundred—and virtually all of these were imported from France and Germany—Winton saw it as a market ripe for exploitation.

He quickly rejected steam as a power source. The Europeans had by that time demonstrated that a gasoline engine could be powerful and compact, and have great range, in some cases more than 200 miles, so Winton began tinkering with gasoline motors. By 1894, around the time the Duryeas were bringing their automobile to market, Winton began building his first prototype.

In March 1897, Alexander Winton founded his automobile company in Cleveland. After only three months he had produced a 10-horsepower model that achieved the astounding speed of 34 miles per hour on a horse track. Soon afterward, Winton drove his automobile 800 miles, from Cleveland to New York City and back. One year and nine days after the company's inception, he sold his first automobile, one of two dozen that year. Winton built his automobiles by hand, and each had brightly painted sides, padded seats, a leather roof, and gas lamps.

Later in 1898, a Michigan man who had recently built an experimental gasoline vehicle was invited to Cleveland, but Winton thought him too old—he was thirty-five—and not especially impressive. When Winton declined to hire him, Henry Ford returned to Detroit to continue work on his own.

In October 1895, American motoring passed a milestone—it got its very own trade magazine when *The Horseless Age: A Monthly Journal Devoted to the Motor Vehicle Industry* was published in New York. *Horseless Age*—subscriptions two dollars a year, single issues twenty-five

cents—became the dominant entrant in what was soon to be a burgeoning field, and remains in publication to this day.[9]

The magazine itself opened with a "Salutatory," in which editor
and proprietor E. P. Ingersoll wrote:

> The appearance of a journal devoted to a branch of indus-
> try yet in its embryonic state may strike some as premature.
> But those who have taken the pains to search below the
> surface for the great tendencies of the age know when a
> giant industry is struggling into being. All signs point to the
> motor vehicle as the necessary sequence of methods of
> locomotion already established and approved. The grow-
> ing needs of our civilization demand it; the public believe
> in it, and await with lively interest its practical application to
> the daily business of the world.[10]

While Ingersoll was of course attempting to induce sales of his magazine, his statement turned out to be prescient.

In one of the main features of that first issue, Alexander Winton
described his new "motor-carriage," a four seat dos-a-dos with "an
eight-hp improved gasolene [*sic*] motor." The key features, Winton
noted, were:

> the hydro-carbon feeder, the electric igniter, and the regula-
> tor. The feeder converts oil to a fixed gas before entering
> the cylinders, without any of the objectionable feature of
> the carburetor now in general use. The igniter is absolutely
> positive in its workings, requires no adjustment, and will
> run for years without any attention whatever. The gover-
> nor is pneumatic and by pressing a button, the speed of the
> motor can be varied from 200 revolutions . . . to 700 or 800
> if necessary. The engine is entirely self-oiling [and] a con-
> denser or cooler is used to reduce the temperature of water
> for cylinders. Five gallons are all that is necessary and it
> does not attain more than 200 degrees Fahr., so that evapo-

ration is very light. My vehicle for two persons will not
weigh to exceed 400 pounds, and will be capable of a speed
of 30 miles per hour.[11]

Other machines were profiled, including Hiram Percy Maxim's
motor tricycle and a Duryea motorcar, although the article had
Charles, identified as the sole inventor, discussing America's first practical automobile from Peoria, while the company that was producing
it was noted as operating out of Springfield, Massachusetts. Although
Frank was shown at the tiller of the machine in the accompanying
photograph, he had not been interviewed for the piece.[12]

In all, more than two dozen motors or vehicles were featured—
among them automobiles, buggies, carriages, motorized bicycles, even
a sleigh—the vast majority gasoline-powered, although steam, kerosene, electricity, compressed air, and carbonic acid were also represented. This was a stunning array for a machine that had yet to be
marketed beyond a meager audience. (*Horseless Age* would soon establish itself as an advocate for gasoline motors and an antagonist to all
other forms of propulsion.)

Finally, there was an extensive section devoted to what was to be
America's first auto race, to be held the following month in Chicago,
sponsored by *The Times-Herald,* which was putting up $5,000 in prize
money. Entrants included the Duryeas, a Benz that had just recently
been manufactured under license in the United States, and more than
fifty others. The rules of the contest ran to an entire page in small
print.

But the lifeblood of any magazine is advertising, and the first thing
a curious browser would have noticed in the premier issue was a full-
page advertisement for Daimler Motors, "operated by either gas, gasoline, or kerosene,"[13] to be manufactured in Long Island City, New
York, at a site used to fabricate a different sort of product. William
Steinway, the piano maker, had been so taken with the Daimler motor
on a trip to Europe in 1888 that he purchased from Daimler a license
to be the sole distributor in the United States, and he then set up a
factory at the site of his piano manufacturing plant. Curiously for an

automobile trade journal, the Daimler ad was not promoting the use of the motor in motorcars but rather "for launches, triple, twin, and single screws. Paddle and stern wheels of the lightest draft," and "for stationary purposes." As the journal also reported, "Daimler Motor Launches are familiar sights in the New York waters, as well as in regions more remote, their reputation for speed, economy and general serviceableness being unsurpassed."

On page three was a half-page ad for the Duryea Motor Wagon Company of Springfield, Massachusetts, "manufacturers of motor wagons, motors, and automobile vehicles of every kind." And among the other manufacturers who took out ads was Charles Brady King, a well-known figure in the burgeoning city of Detroit, and one of the most prominent advocates of motorized travel, promoting his "patent gas engines for vehicles, launches, etc." King had been sketching designs for automobiles since 1892 and has been described as "the most technically knowledgeable of the early automotive pioneers and one of a handful of men who could envision the automobile as a part of everyday life."[14]

Charles King had been born on an army base in San Francisco in February 1868. His father was a Union Army general who had fought with distinction in eight major battles and would remain on active service until his death in 1888. King entered Cornell University in 1887 to study engineering but left after two years. In the early 1890s, he amassed a small fortune by inventing a variety of devices, including the jackhammer and a brake beam for railroad cars. He had become interested in gasoline motors after seeing a two-stroke engine exhibited at the Columbian Exposition in Chicago in 1893—at which he was awarded a medal for his display of pneumatic tools.[15] In 1894, he began a company to manufacture gasoline motors, pneumatic tools, and, ultimately, an automobile.

As *Horseless Age* went to press for the first time, King had yet to actually build a motorcar of his own, but he soon would. Five months later, on March 6, 1896, at age twenty-eight, Charles B. King gained the distinction of being the first man to drive an automobile on the streets of Detroit. It was powered by a four-cylinder, four-stroke engine of his own design.

Following along on a bicycle was a man in his thirties, old for a tinkerer, who, with King's help, had been experimenting with motor-powered vehicles on his own. This man would later claim the honor that should have been King's. In this, as in many distinctions that rightly belonged to others, this man would be almost universally believed.

Because Henry Ford always understood that history belonged to the man who wrote it.

CHAPTER 7

■ THE SELF-CREATED MAN

For a man who has provoked as much scrutiny as anyone in American history, save perhaps George Washington and Abraham Lincoln, Ford has to a remarkable degree remained an enigma. As one writer noted, it is impossible to discern whether Ford "was a simple man erroneously assumed to be complex, or an enormously complex individual with a misleading aura of simplicity."[1] Much of this confusion is thanks to Ford himself. Another observer noted, "Any effort to quote Henry Ford is like trying to nail Jello to the wall. Since Henry never wrote anything of substance in his life, and avoided public speaking, virtually all of his pronouncements are translations by various spokesmen."[2] Most of all, we are unable to pin down Henry Ford because he went to great lengths to avoid leaving any trail except the one he intended biographers and commentators to follow. Ford was obsessed with his own legend, and his ultimate success often overwhelmed earlier distortion or hyperbole.

For example, in 1921, Ford issued an autobiography whose expansive title was *My Life and Work*. Ford made no secret that the book was a "collaboration" with Samuel Crowther, one of his publicity men.[3]

Within this volume lay many nuggets of the Ford legend—how, say, in 1876, the same year that George Selden saw the Brayton engine in Philadelphia, the thirteen-year-old Ford came upon a man driving a self-powered steam engine on the rutted roads of rural Michigan. It was a large and ungainly affair, transported from farm to farm to perform a variety of tasks, threshing and the like. Ford stopped the man and bombarded him with questions on the workings of the marvelous machine. In what has been considered the definitive Ford biography, Allan Nevins noted that forty-seven years later, Ford remembered the incident "as though he had seen it only yesterday," recalling specifically how the machine ran, at how many revolutions per minute it operated, and even the name of its owner—Fred Reden.* From that moment on, the story went, Henry Ford became fascinated with self-driven vehicles and became determined to build one of his own.

But another biographer recounted that after the twelve-year-old Henry saw his first locomotive during a trip to Detroit, he peppered the engineer with questions on the workings of *that* marvelous machine, and that "seven decades later" he still remembered the engineer's name—Tommy Garrett.[4] From that moment on, Henry Ford became fascinated with self-contained motors and became determined to build one of his own.

One or both of these meetings might well have taken place, of course, and might even have evoked the fascination of which Ford later spoke. These, like many incidents in Ford's early years, have no independent confirmation. And any discrepancy or exaggeration in these tales is moot: whatever motivated Henry Ford to dissect and remake machinery is far less important than that he did it, and anyone is entitled to fib. But uncertainty as to the Ford legend stretches to areas that are not at all meaningless. More important, *My Life and Work* as well as two subsequent biographies penned in the 1920s by Ford flaks (William A. Simonds's *Henry Ford: Motor Genius* and Allan L. Ben-

---

* Reden's name is not mentioned in *My Life and Work,* although the incident is recounted in detail. Ford provided additional details, including the operator's name, as part of his testimony in a lawsuit, which, like the autobiography, came decades later.

son's *The New Henry Ford*) were used as key sources for the "authoritative" biography by Allan Nevins—itself the product of a grant by the Ford Motor Company Fund to Columbia University—which, in turn, was a key source for every biography written since.*

The result is a boyhood that seems a combination of Horatio Alger and Booth Tarkington. No one in the Ford family yelled, no one fought, there were no resentments or bitterness, Dad was firm but fair, Mom was warm and nurturing. It seems a bit surprising that a man who as an adult could be as gratuitously vicious and vindictive as Henry Ford grew from such idyllic beginnings. Telling also is that the trait to which most biographers point to humanize Ford is his love of practical jokes—which, of course, are based on laughing at a dupe and always involve at least a benign level of cruelty. And Ford's were often crueler than most.

Still, a reasonably accurate picture can be fleshed out of the man who would become the wealthiest in America. He was born in Greenfield Township on July 30, 1863, roughly three weeks after the Battle of Gettysburg, the eldest of six, to a farmer who had emigrated from Ireland as a twenty-year-old. Henry's relationship with his father has been portrayed as one with disagreements—Henry despised farm work and refused to take over the family farm—but largely strife-free. He adored his mother, and when she died in 1876, he was devastated. "A watch without a mainspring" was how he described the family after she was gone.

When Henry was fifteen—or thirteen, or perhaps twelve—according to friends and relatives interviewed by biographers, he was given a pocket watch for his birthday, which he immediately took

---

* There are numerous eyewitness accounts cited as well, particularly in Nevins's work, all of which support Ford's own story of his upbringing. Most were originally obtained by Ford employees, notably Simonds, or were otherwise gained under Ford Motor Company auspices after Ford had established himself very definitely as a man on whose good side one would choose to remain. By the time the later biographies were being researched, most of the remaining witnesses to Ford's upbringing were in their eighties or even nineties and Henry Ford had become a mythical figure. Ford critics, who were vociferous and abundant, were not given nearly the same exposure.

apart and then put back together. From there, he is reported to have taken to repairing pocket watches for anyone in the area who was in need.[5]

Whenever he did this—or even if he did it—Ford's ability to visualize, dissect, and reimagine mechanical devices was prodigious. Any period of technological change will evoke the latent genius specific to its era, and in the late nineteenth and early twentieth centuries, mechanical brilliance could find expression in a variety of venues, none more so than transportation. In *My Life and Work,* Ford declared, "My toys were tools—they still are! Every fragment of machinery was a treasure."[6]

Ford left the farm to work in Detroit at either age sixteen or seventeen. He walked the 6 miles to the city, as he hated horses. He moved in with his aunt and worked at a variety of jobs, most in machine shops. In 1882, for reasons never made clear, Ford gave up a job at a toolmaker's—which he later claimed to have loved—to return to the farm. Ford later insisted it was "more because I wanted to experiment than because I wanted to farm, and, now being an all-around machinist, I had a first-class workshop to replace the toy shop of earlier days." His father also gave him 40 acres of land, hoping he would clear and till it, but Ford had other plans for the property.[7]

Living at home turned out to have unexpected benefits. At a dance in 1885, Ford met a young woman named Clara Bryant, a friend of his sister's. He claimed to know within thirty seconds that she was the girl for him, the sort of romantic embellishment that became attached to many of his reminiscences. Ford—serious and a lifelong teetotaler, although not for religious reasons—was appealing to Clara, and the two soon struck up a romance. They would be married in 1888, on Clara's twenty-second birthday, and she would prove such a perfect mate that Ford would dub her "the believer" for her steadfast conviction in his plans, ideas, and eventual success. Ford would have had this relationship too portrayed as strife-free, but while they remained married until Ford's death in 1947, there were some serious strains, especially in the final two decades of Ford's life, most concerning Ford's overbearing, even abusive treatment of Edsel, their only child.

After the wedding, Ford remained in Greenfield, earning money by setting up a sawmill for the timber on the tract of land given to him by his father. Clara handled the family finances and drew up the plans for the couple's first house. A turning point seemed to arrive when Henry heard that one of his father's neighbors owned a stationary steam engine that had broken down. He convinced both men to give him a shot at repairing it. After he did so, he was hired to both operate the machine and maintain it. From there, he got himself a job repairing Westinghouse steam engines owned by the area's farmers. He may also have set up a workshop on his father's farm and built a steam engine of his own. Although a recent biographer is skeptical, insisting the account is "clouded" and "vague," Ford himself was definite enough.[8]

> It had a kerosene-heated boiler and it developed plenty of power and a neat control—which is so easy with a steam throttle. But the boiler was dangerous. To get the requisite power without too big and heavy a power plant required that the engine work under high pressure; sitting on a high-pressure steam boiler is not altogether pleasant. To make it even reasonably safe required an excess of weight that nullified the economy of the high pressure. For two years I kept experimenting with various sorts of boilers—the engine and control problems were simple enough—and then I definitely abandoned the whole idea of running a road vehicle by steam.[9]

He also claimed to have built a number of other motors including, in 1887, a scale-model Otto, which he then "gave away later to a young man who wanted it for something or other and whose name I have forgotten." These accounts, specific as they are, may be fanciful: as loyal a Ford associate as Clara later claimed no recollection of anything of the sort.

At some point—Ford said in 1886, although both Clara and his sister insisted it was 1890—he was called to the Eagle Iron Works, where, because of his talent with machines, he was asked to examine an Otto gas engine that had broken down. Fortunately for Ford, who was never much of a reader, he had taken to poring through magazines that described the latest advances in engine technology, including a piece on the "Silent Otto." Tinkering with a machine he had encountered only in print, Ford nonetheless got the motor running smoothly and as a result was asked to repair similar devices (although one contemporary insists that Ford did not repair that first Otto, but merely "saw it").[10] Ford later said that he recognized instantly the need to move from coal gas to liquid fuel in order to apply the Otto to road travel. In any case, from there he was called on regularly to repair both Ottos and steam engines, traveling regularly to and from Detroit.

In late 1891, Ford, returning from repairing an Otto in Detroit, announced to Clara that he intended to build an automobile, and perhaps even drew her a crude sketch on the back of a piece of sheet music. He further informed her that they must move to the city. Clara, the Believer, was described as "aghast" but agreed to abandon home and family and go wherever her husband had decided he needed to be.[11] Whether to learn about the electricity that sparked the Otto, as he later claimed, or simply to place himself in the midst of the mechanical devices to which he was inexorably drawn, Ford got himself hired by the Edison Illuminating Company in Detroit, where he quickly distinguished himself with mechanical aptitude and a ferocious work ethic. Within two years, he had risen from a $45-per-month engineer at a substation to chief engineer, on call twenty-four hours a day, with a salary of $100 per month. He, Clara, and newborn Edsel moved in to a house at 58 Bagley Street, which had a brick storage structure in the backyard: perfect for a workshop.

Although it is unlikely that Ford had been experimenting with motors before he moved to Bagley Street, as he later claimed, once there he began in earnest. His position at Edison gave him access to tools and machinery, and he even taught an engineering class at the YMCA for $2.50 a session to gain the use of their machine shop. By this time, largely because of the Daimler motor, the virtues of gasoline had begun to assert themselves, so Ford concentrated his efforts there.

First Ford shop

At some point Ford met Charles King. Although they were said to have become friends, it must have been difficult for the hypercompetitive Ford to deal with a man five years his junior who had already achieved great acclaim as an inventor and who seemed to be far ahead in the development of the very instrument on which Ford had set his sights. More likely is that the affable King was taken with Ford's drive and obvious talent, while Ford saw King as someone whose efforts he could trail until they could be surpassed, much as Ford would trail along on a bicycle while King drove an automobile for the first time on the streets of Detroit.*

With King's support, Ford pressed on. He told of obtaining parts for his engines in odd ways, such as cylinders he fashioned from "an exhaust pipe of a steam engine that I had bought."[12] Others worked

---

* In addition to his mechanical achievements, King would become known as an artist, musician, poet, and mystic. He was generous, helping other would-be inventors, such as Ransom Olds, without asking anything in return, and was extraordinarily well liked. There are no reports of him ever conducting himself in business with the ruthlessness that characterized most industrialists.

with him, Ford admitted, but the ideas were his and he supervised the operation.

"The hardest problems to overcome," Ford wrote, "were in the making and breaking of the spark and in the avoidance of excess weight. For the transmission, the steering gear, and the general construction, I could draw on my experience with the steam tractors. In 1892, I completed my first motor car, but it was not until the spring of the following year that it ran to my satisfaction."

From there, Ford described in detail a machine that "would hold two people, the seat being suspended on posts and the body on elliptical springs. There were two speeds—one of 10 and the other of 20 miles per hour—obtained by shifting the belt, which was done by a clutch lever in front of the driving seat." Finally, Ford insisted that his "gasoline buggy" was the first and for a long time the only automobile in Detroit. "It was considered to be something of a nuisance, for it made a racket and it scared horses. Also it blocked traffic."

Although eventually Ford did build the machine he described, the rest is nonsense, and that Ford thought to foist such a tale on the public only thirty years after it supposedly happened—and almost everyone involved in the early automobile business in Detroit was still alive—is testament to the hubris that he had developed from his rise to prominence. (Ford loyalists, such as Edward "Spider" Huff, one of those who was assisting Ford in the project, later swore the story was true, despite overwhelming evidence to the contrary.) More surprising is that almost all the Ford biographies, even recent ones, have dismissed this outright lie as a lapse of memory or muddling of dates, while at the same time attributing to Ford a remarkable "magpie memory."[13]

This particular fable is made even more preposterous by being in direct conflict with another of Ford's favorite reminiscences. On Christmas Eve 1893, according to Ford and other family members, Clara was preparing dinner for the next day, when her family, the Bryants, would be coming, and seven-week-old Edsel was sleeping in the next room. Henry had been working on a "simple experimental engine," the one with the gas pipe cylinder that he later asserted had been mounted on his two-seater the previous spring. He had fashioned a flywheel from an old lathe.

"He brought the engine into the kitchen, mounted it on a board, and clamped it to the sink." The fuel had to be fed by hand, using a metal cup as a crude makeshift carburetor. The engine ran, to Henry's great satisfaction and Clara's delighted surprise. "I didn't stop to play with it," he told William Simonds. "I wanted to build a two-cylinder engine that could be used to propel a bicycle."[14]

According to King, his assistant Oliver Barthel—who later went to work for Ford—and a third man who worked for Ford at the Edison plant, "the kitchen sink/engine episode occurred at the end of 1895, not 1893," and was performed in front of King himself.[15] Furthermore, Ford's inspiration was not self-generated, as he insisted, but was sparked by an article in the November 7, 1895, edition of *American Machinist* in which Edward J. Pennington described cobbling together a workable internal combustion engine from bits of scrap and other spare parts, an assertion that, ironically, turned out to be untrue, as Pennington was later exposed as a fraud. Whatever else this story tells us, it firmly establishes Henry Ford as a man willing to take credit for the work and ideas of others—and as a man willing to abet or even encourage subordinates to lie for him, traits that would dominate his reminiscences for the remainder of his life.

When he published his autobiography, Ford included virtually nothing concerning his developmental work but encouraged the perception that he received no guidance directly or indirectly. He recounted, "I had to work from the ground up—that is, although I knew a number of people were working on horseless carriages, I could not know what they were doing."[16]

But he did, and in some detail. Not only had Daimler and Benz, among others, been marketing automobiles in Europe, with which Ford was familiar from his reading, but he quite clearly knew about the Duryea brothers' gasoline automobiles as well. King even gave him four valves to help construct his engine when Ford could not make his work. By the time Ford began to experiment in earnest, he had no shortage of sources on which to draw and no shortage of others willing to lend him expertise and support.

But from the first, Ford brought to his designs a vision that, if not unique, was at least rare. A report in 1898 on one of Ford's early vehicles by R. W. Hanington, an engineer who had worked for Duryea but found that operation "a total failure," was to the point: "The whole design strikes me as being very complete and worked out in every detail. . . . A first-class carriage, well thought out and well constructed, but employing no novel feature of great importance. Novelty, rather than good design, has been the idea of most of the carriage builders. Simplicity, strength, and common sense seem to be embodied in Mr. Ford's carriage, and I believe that these ideals are the essential ones for a successful vehicle."[17] Those qualities would distinguish almost every Ford car, none more than the Model T.

Two years before Hanington's report, in spring 1896, Henry Ford had completed his first vehicle, largely the same as the one he had described as being completed three years earlier, although the actual product was missing a number of the refinements he included after the fact.* He called it the "quadricycle," and it was essentially a motorized four-wheel bicycle, with chain drive, a tiller for steering, and no brakes or reverse gear.

But before Ford could test his invention on the street, King beat him to it. On the night of March 6, King took his motorized carriage out for a drive. "Motorized dray cart" would be a better description, since that is what King's contraption most resembled, down to its 1,300-pound weight and heavy metal-capped wood wheels that clattered over the cobblestone streets. But it ran, and it was first.

King's ride was widely reported in the press the following day, an account that was eerily similar to the one Ford attributed to his own vehicle in *My Life and Work*. As the *Detroit Free Press* described the event, "The first horseless carriage seen in this city was out on the streets last night. It is the invention of Charles B. King, a Detroiter, and its progress up Woodward Avenue about 11 o'clock caused a deal of comment, people crowding around it so that its progress was impeded. The apparatus seemed to work all right, and went at the rate of 5 or 6 miles an hour at an even rate of speed."[18] King himself observed, "Horseless carriages are extensively used in Paris as delivery

---

* It lacked, for example, a bench seat for two. Ford had installed a bicycle seat instead.

Ford quadricycle

wagons, carriages, and even ambulances. I understand the Prince of Wales has ordered one. They are much in vogue among the English aristocracy, and will undoubtedly soon be here. I am convinced they will in time supersede the horse."[19] Although one biographer observes that "if [Ford] felt at all crestfallen that King had beaten him to the street, he has left no record of it," it is difficult to believe that, pedaling along behind, a man with a temperament like Ford's did not experience some level of resentment.[20]

In any event, the machine that Ford took out on the streets three months later was superior to King's in almost every way. It was almost a half-ton lighter, more maneuverable—going forward, at any rate—and had a superior motor, although he did suffer a breakdown that was repaired with materials from the Edison plant. As would be true for the machine Hanington critiqued, nothing was particularly inventive on the quadricycle—Ford had seen similar transmissions as well as motors, and the overall design was a hybrid of many already in use—but the combination of the elements and the construction he used was extremely effective.[21] From almost the moment the first quadricycle was completed, Ford began sketching out the improvements.

The first order of business was to change what was almost a totally wood frame to metal. For this, Ford employed a blacksmith he had hired at Edison. Another key change was the addition of a water jacket around the engine block to replace the air-cooling of the original. Before this, the engine had run so hot that drops of molten solder were deposited on the street.

Ford now had a team of three capable assistants to help remake his machine. Working nights and weekends, they assembled a vastly improved quadricycle—though Ford did little of the physical work. "I never saw Mr. Ford make anything," the blacksmith recalled. "He was always doing the directing." The end result was a stronger, more durable, better-running machine that could seat two—or three, if Clara was holding Edsel—while not being appreciably heavier.

Ford drove this new version extensively, occasionally as far out of town as Greenfield and Dearborn, often accompanied by Charles King, who seemed as pleased for Ford's achievement as Ford himself.

Work on the improved quadricycle also set the tone of Ford's approach to business, at least until he had grown so wealthy that his interests began to include broad national and international questions. For much of that early period, he slept as often at work as he did at home. There was always a cot at his disposal, even when his factories grew to be immense. He considered himself a family man and focused intently on Clara and Edsel—but he simply wasn't around that much.

His one lifelong passion that was neither work- nor family-related was birds. Ford often marked significant occasions in his life by how they coincided with the migratory patterns of local species. He endowed bird sanctuaries well before he had even considered other philanthropic endeavors. While he never publicly stated that he liked birds more than people, it would hardly be a surprise if that was the case.

Working for the Edison Company had proved a boon. Ford had availed himself of employees, shop space, and materials, all while performing his duties superbly and advancing rapidly. By 1896, he was earning more than $150 per month, heady numbers for those days. As a result, in August, Ford was chosen as a delegate to the Edison Illuminating Company convention in Manhattan Beach, then a posh resort area in Brooklyn, New York, where the founder himself would be present. Edison, the only other man to attain stunning wealth during the industrial age while also being credited as an inventor, was similar to Ford in temperament. He asked to meet the younger man when he was told that an employee of his had built a gas car that ran. They sat and talked, Edison asking a number of pointed questions about the machine's operation. "Young man," Edison is reported to have said, banging his hand on the table, although the source was the often unreliable William Simonds, "that's the thing. You have it. Your car carries its own power plant—it's self contained—no fire, no boiler. You have the thing. Keep at it."[22] Simonds went on to assert that Edison's comment was "a turning point in Henry Ford's life," coming "at a moment when he was disheartened, uncertain whether to follow a conventional pattern of a comfortable job and an assured future," or abandon all that to pursue his life's dream. Ford is reported to have said, much later in life, "The bang on the table meant the world to me," although the episode is conspicuously absent in *My Life and Work*.[23]

At any rate, Ford was ready to move on. He sold the quadricycle for $200 to a willing buyer named Charles Ainsley (or Annesly), who would be the first of tens of millions around the world to purchase a Ford vehicle, and then got to work on a new design, announcing his intention, for the first time, to produce a cheaper, lighter, more reliable car.*

At this point, Ford, although remaining at Edison, seems to have attracted outside capital, some from Detroit's new mayor, William Maybury—although none from Edison himself, who certainly could have afforded it. At this point, however, no contract was signed or agreement entered into. By July 1899, Ford had completed his second car, the one that R. W. Hanington would extol in his report, and one

---

* Ford bought the quadricycle back a few years later for $60, thus being perhaps the first man to demonstrate the depreciating value of used cars.

that would result in Ford acquiring even more capital from local men drawn to the idea of a simple, solid, reliable, and affordable car.

Ford took the money, but, to his investors' consternation, instead of working on his automobile for the masses, he spent almost all of his time building cars for a far different purpose.

CHAPTER 8

**SPEED**

Ford famously quipped that auto racing began five minutes after the second car was built. It took longer than that, but not much. If one accepts 1886, the year Karl Benz introduced his Motorwagen, as the dawn of the gasoline automobile age, and 1888, the year of the first sales, as the dawn of the industry, it took only six years for the first race to occur.[1]

From there, to meet the demands of the wildly popular new pastime of auto racing, the top speed of a gasoline-powered automobile had increased from approximately 15 miles per hour to more than 100 by 1904; six years after that, a Blitzen-Benz drove at more than 140 miles per hour. And while the view, commonly held in the United States, that the automobile was largely a creation of American ingenuity is fanciful, it was an American, albeit an expatriate, who made building a faster—and better—motorcar a matter of national pride and sent innovation off at a dizzying pace.

James Gordon Bennett Jr., freewheeling and larger than life, was a human catalyst: a man who invented nothing, perfected nothing, and personally participated in almost none of the events he sponsored, but whose vision and patronage flung automobile technology and then aviation to a level of early sophistication it could not have achieved without him.

Bennett's father founded *The New York Herald* and was one of the initial sponsors of the Associated Press. Bennett senior made the *Herald* such a magnet of controversy that he secreted a veritable arsenal in the walls behind his desk at the newspaper's offices on lower Broadway to repel the crowds that often gathered outside and threatened to storm the building. As a result, the younger Bennett was sent to Europe for his education, though he returned to serve in the Union Navy during the Civil War. When he took over the *Herald* from his father in 1866, he focused on the sort of breathless, splashy journalism that could always be counted on to sell scads of newspapers. Bennett, for example, personally sent Henry Morton Stanley to Africa to search for David Livingstone, a journey that was followed meticulously and melodramatically in the pages of the *Herald*.

But Bennett's greatest notoriety sprung from a series of outrageous personal incidents that were gleefully reported in every newspaper but his own. In the most celebrated of these, he arrived roaring drunk to either his own engagement party or a New Year's fête at the New York townhouse of the couple who were slated to be his future in-laws and proceeded, in full view of the guests, to urinate into either the fireplace, a grand piano, or a punch bowl, depending on which account one believed. To no one's surprise, the engagement was broken off, after which Bennett repaired to his three-hundred-foot yacht and sailed it to France, where he remained for the rest of his life. He didn't marry until 1914, four years before his death at age seventy-seven.*

In Paris, abandoning none of his eccentricities, he established a foreign edition of the *Herald,* which later evolved into the *International Herald-Tribune.*[2] With thousands of wealthy Americans then spending

---

* Bennett is buried at the Cimetière de Passy, where auto pioneer Marcel Renault and auto-racer-turned-aviator Henri Farman were also laid to rest. Avenue Gordon Bennett currently borders Stade Roland Garros (named for another famed French aviator, killed during World War I), site of tennis's French Open.

most or all of their time in Europe, the Paris paper was a great success. Bennett also continued to run the New York paper, relying on shuttling staff or communicating both news and orders via transatlantic cable.* Unwilling to pay the exorbitant usage rates demanded by Jay Gould's monopolists, Bennett created his own cable company, partnering in a cable-laying vessel that in 1912 was used to recover bodies from the wreck of the *Titanic*.

The one sport in which Bennett participated personally was yachting. He won the first transatlantic race in 1866, and then decided to offer a prize for his own yacht race—called, of course, the Gordon Bennett Cup—the progress and results of which would be prominently featured in the *Herald*. While the yacht race attracted some interest, seagoing contests aroused limited fervor, since spectators could view the boats only at the start and the finish. Bennett soon abandoned the yachting competition to seek a better idea.

In 1899, he found one. He combined his fascination with innovation, his love of adventure, and the constant search for new ways to sell newspapers in one grand sweep by sponsoring a Gordon Bennett Cup race for automobiles. The idea did not spring fully formed but rather was built on the wreckage of a previous scheme that Bennett could not coax to fruition.

In 1894, Parisian Pierre Giffard, who owned *Le Petit Journal*, offered a hefty prize, 5,000 francs, to the winner of a 78-mile Paris-to-Rouen "reliability test" for *voitures sans chevaux*. The purse would not necessarily go to the driver who recorded the fastest time but rather for the best performance by a "practical road vehicle." More than one hundred competitors sought entry, but Giffard's minions selected only twenty-one to take part—thirteen gasoline-fueled vehicles and eight steam-powered. All but one of the gasoline vehicles were built by either the Peugeot brothers or Panhard et Levassor and used engines

---

* At one point, a New York employee showed up at his door. When Bennett demanded to know what he was doing there, the employee told Bennett that he had summoned him. "Well, go home," Bennett said; having little choice, the man did.

licensed under the Daimler patent. While the basic engine design might have been the Germans', the race cars themselves were distinctly French. Émile Levassor had created a lightweight version of his front-engine road car whose sleek, aerodynamic lines made previous designs seem anachronistic.

Even had he not invited both Gottlieb Daimler and his son Paul to be guests of honor, that Giffard favored the gasoline cars was obvious. When a De Dion steam tractor chugged across the finish line first, it was not given the prize. Its bulk and weight, according to the organizers, rendered it "impractical"—it did, in fact, exceed the vaguely defined specifications in both categories—and so the prize was split between the second- and third-place finishers, a Panhard and a Peugeot. De Dion, a man one thought twice about insulting, was awarded an "honorary" second-place finish. He grumbled but accepted the decision. To win their 2,500 francs, the winners had averaged a heady 11.5 miles per hour.

The public acclaim that accompanied the Paris-Rouen test begat a far more arduous event the following June. For this race, 732 miles from Paris to Bordeaux and back, there would, in theory, be no subjective criteria—the car with the fastest time would be the winner. Among the patrons contributing to the 30,000-franc prize were Gordon Bennett and another American, an extremely wealthy teenager named William Kissam Vanderbilt II.

Once again, gasoline-powered vehicles predominated—only one steam car was entered—with Émile Levassor's high-speed, front-mounted-motor blueprint now used almost exclusively by the twenty-three entrants. Levassor himself had entered in a specially designed, 4.5-horsepower two-seater, capable of 18 miles per hour, on which he had fitted encased candles for headlights, making him the only entrant who could drive at night.* (All racers needed at least two seats because each driver was accompanied by a riding mechanic whose assignments

---

* Two years later, Louis Blériot would develop the first practical acetylene car lamp, the "Phare Blériot," which would make him a fortune and allow him to turn his attention to his real passion, aviation. On July 25, 1909, Blériot became the first man to fly an airplane across the English Channel.

included not only on-the-fly repairs and adjustments but also watching the rear for other vehicles.)*

The organizers had estimated that four days would be required to complete the circuit, but Levassor, driving almost nonstop, reached the finish line in two. His friend and fellow race car driver Marquis Gaston de Chasseloup-Laubat reported that Levassor "remained on his machine for fifty-three hours, and nearly forty-nine of these on the run."[3] After the arduous journey, Levassor seemed little the worse for wear. "He did not appear to be over-fatigued," Chasseloup-Laubat observed. "He wrote his signature with a firm hand; we lunched together at Gillet's, at the Porte Maillot; he was quite calm; he took with great relish a cup of bouillon, a couple of poached eggs, and two glasses of champagne; but he said that driving at night was dangerous, adding that having won he had the right to say such a race was not to be run another time at night."

But Levassor's satisfaction would be short-lived. Once again, the judges insisted on awarding prizes according to their whim, and Levassor was disqualified for using only a two-seater rather than the four-seat machine that the rules seemed to stipulate—although no one had thought to point that out to him earlier. The prize was awarded instead to a Peugeot that cruised into Porte Maillot a full eleven hours after the Panhard. In the true French spirit, however, the official result was ignored. In the press, Levassor was widely reported to have won, and when a plaque was placed at the site of the race's end ten years afterward, it was Émile Levassor in his "Number 5" who was featured, not Paul Koechlin, the driver of the Peugeot.

The Paris-Bordeaux race brought automobile travel to the front pages of American newspapers. The publisher of one of those newspapers, Herman H. Kohlstaat of the *Chicago Times-Herald*, decided it was time to bring the thrill of racing to the United States. Kohlstaat, who had amassed a fortune in baked goods and restaurants, was one of the breed of gentlemen newspaper owners that were common at

---

* Rearview mirrors would not be introduced until 1911, during the first running of the Indianapolis 500, when Ray Haroun, driving solo, mounted one on his racer.

the time. On July 9, 1895, he announced sponsorship of an auto race from Chicago to Waukegan and back, a distance of 100 miles, to be run that November 2. (Kohlstaat's original plan was to go all the way to Milwaukee, but the roads in southern Wisconsin were simply too primitive.) As *Horseless Age* announced:

> With a desire to promote, encourage, and stimulate the invention, development, perfection, and general adoption of motor vehicles, the *Times-Herald* offers the following prizes, amounting to $5,000, divided as stated: First prize—$2,000 and a gold medal, the same being open to competition to the world. Second prize—$1,500 with a stipulation that in the event the first prize is awarded to a vehicle of foreign invention or manufacture, this prize shall go to the most successful American competitor. Third prize—$1,000. Fourth prize—$500. The third and fourth prizes are open to all competitors, foreign and American.[4]

There would be an additional contest to come up with a name for the machines that would be racing. At the time, vehicles were referred to by any number of terms, including "horseless carriage," "motor carriage," "motor car," and "motor vehicle." The *Times-Herald*'s readers submitted a number of entries, of which, on July 15, "motocycle," the brainchild of the general manager of the New York Telephone Company, was declared the winner. It would not be for long, however—within months, "motocycle" had withered into disuse.

To Kohlstaat's great satisfaction, he received nearly one hundred entries. But virtually all of them were from aspirants whose "motocycles" were still works in progress, including Charles King, who intended to adapt the machine he had piloted on the streets of Detroit to endure the rigors of a long-distance race. Eventually, however, King realized that he would never have it ready on time. He so informed the judges and was told that almost every other entrant had issued a similar communication. So few vehicles—a total of two—would actually be prepared to race on November 2 that the judges were forced to postpone the event until Thanksgiving Day, a four-week delay that could be problematic in often intemperate Chicago.

The two that were ready to go—an American-built Benz, driven by its manufacturer, Oscar Mueller, and a Duryea, driven by Frank, accompanied by Charles—staged an "exhibition run" on November 2, "in order not to disappoint the public." A prize of $500 was offered, to be equally divided between them if they could complete the round-trip in less than thirteen hours. Mueller succeeded, but Duryea "was forced into a ditch by a careless farmer who swung his team of horses across the road, damaging the steering-gear and rear axle of his car and putting it out of the running." Mueller therefore claimed the entire $500, while the Duryeas frantically attempted to repair their vehicle in time for the actual race.[5]

As Thanksgiving approached, the postponement appeared fortuitous, as more than thirty entrants announced their intention to compete—a gaggle, according to Hiram Percy Maxim, who was present as an observer, of "the most astounding assortment of mechanical monstrosities,"[6] everything from the finely engineered two-cylinder gasoline automobile of the Duryea brothers to untried electric vehicles to hastily constructed motors attached tenuously to three-wheeled bicycle frames. To Maxim, the best-constructed vehicles were the Duryeas' and Mueller's Benz, which looked to him "like a machine shop on wheels."

But conditions proved even more dreadful than normal for late November in Chicago. The night before the race, a storm deposited six inches of "wet, sticky snow" on the streets—drifts running to two feet—and temperatures dipped well below freezing. Although the day of the race dawned "bright and clear" and "a large snow plow drawn by four horses was hard at work clearing a place for the start," the previous day's weather and treacherous roads took their toll, and only six vehicles made it to the starting line.[7] As a result, the course was shortened by almost half, with the run up the lakefront terminating at Evanston. King, who had been unable to meet even the extended deadline, was appointed an "umpire," one of whom was assigned to each vehicle, King to Mueller's Benz.

Charles Duryea and the winning car from Chicago

As the *Times-Herald* itself reported the next day, at the beginning of an enormous four-page spread, "Against tremendous odds, which perhaps demonstrated conclusively the practicability of the horseless carriage, the *Times-Herald* motocycle race was run yesterday. Through deep snow, and along ruts which would have tried horses to their utmost, six motocycles raced. Before half the course was covered three of the motocycles dropped out of the race, and the machine of the Duryea Motor Wagon Company, of Springfield, Mass., arrived first at the winning post at 7:18 o'clock, after more than ten hours' struggle through the snow."[8] The only other entrant to make it to the finish of the frigid, sometimes almost impassable course was Mueller's Benz, which arrived a full ninety minutes later, with Oscar Mueller slumped next to Charles King, unconscious from the cold.

It might seem that a race whose entrants were winnowed down from almost one hundred to six, of whom only two completed the course, was a failure. Precisely the opposite was the case. The Chicago race made an enormous splash, both for the event itself and for what Herman Kohlstaat wanted most—to prove the practicality of the automobile. Newspapers across the nation greeted the spectacle with enthusiasm, one offering a page-one headline that read, "Horse Is Doomed."[9] The significance of the race was affirmed by almost everyone who wrote about it:

> The contest in every respect was most novel, and the performance of the winning vehicle the most remarkable in the history of motor vehicle contests. . . . Thousands witnessed the fight of these vehicles against the fifty-four miles of slush which constituted the course from Jackson Park to Evanston and return. It was considered impossible that any motocycle would complete the course, and the prediction was freely made that not one of the contestants would make five miles. . . . These tests have been in progress for ten days and have been followed with great interest by hundreds of manufacturers from all parts of the United States. These tests have proved of great value. The Paris-Bordeaux race is worthless from a scientific standpoint, but the contest just closed may result in the establishment of reliable data concerning what many consider the vehicle of the future.[10]

Hyperbole notwithstanding, the Chicago race was a turning point. Between the prize money and the spike of interest in automobiles, automaking suddenly became an enticing business opportunity, as Charles King so noted when he returned to Detroit and spoke with his protégé, Henry Ford.

In Europe, the Chicago-Evanston run caused nary a ripple. Fifty-four miles, no matter the conditions, was not considered a serious competition. In races that mattered, France had firmly established itself as the center of both auto racing and automotive technology, and so it intended to continue. Shortly after the Paris-Bordeaux event,

Count de Dion and his fellows formed the Automobile Club de France, and the club's charter included organizing ever more competitive races—as long as French cars won—and taking whatever other steps were necessary to keep the French auto industry preeminent. City-to-city racing had gripped the imagination of the French public, as well as almost everyone else, so the club's first venture was to sponsor an event from Paris to Marseille and back, the first of its kind to officially be termed "Grand Prix."

The race began on September 24, 1896, and was divided into ten stages, five in each direction, the same format as would be adopted by the Tour de France bicycle race when it began in 1903. More than forty cars of every description—steam, gasoline, two-seat, four-seat, three-wheel, four-wheel, and even some categorized as "bicycles"— were entered, but Levassor, who had received more notoriety as a victim of injustice than he would have as a declared winner, was considered the favorite.

For the first four stages, Levassor did not disappoint. With his usual panache, he roared into the lead and seemed likely to stay there until, just outside Avignon, he swerved to avoid a dog in the road and crashed.* He was jarred but not, it seemed, seriously injured. Nonetheless, he was sufficiently shaken to turn the driving over to Charles d'Hostingue, who ultimately finished fourth. Panhard-Levassors also finished in first and second place.

Levassor was persuaded by race officials to be examined at a local hospital. There he was diagnosed with a concussion from which he was expected to quickly recover. He did not. Six months later, on April 14, 1897, Émile Levassor died, leaving behind a design that dominated racing for decades, and automaking in general for a century.

Death in Grand Prix racing, however, has never dissuaded public fancy. The Paris-Marseille affair inspired a spate of imitators across

---

* Levassor would not be the only racer to crash trying to avoid a canine, but it would be well more than a decade before barriers would be placed along racecourses to prevent both animals and humans from wandering out in front of the race cars.

Alexander Winton on a racetrack

Europe. Germany, Belgium, and Italy all held road races. Even the British finally got into the act, repealing the Red Flag Act. Within weeks, a race was staged from London to Brighton.

But the center of the automobile universe remained France. In 1899, the Tour de France covered more than 1,000 miles, won by a Panhard that averaged 32 miles per hour. With road racing becoming virtually a national sport, the French public demanded an even grander event. But automobile performance seemed to be butting up against the limits of technology. To maintain its unquestioned superiority, ACF members cast about for some splashy new way to hold an auto race. Gordon Bennett, who had long since lamented the laggard progress of America's automobile industry, decided to give it to them— and in the process spur American automaking.*

In May of that year, Alexander Winton had challenged Fernand Charron, then France's premier driver, to a match race. He offered to put up 20,000 francs to ensure Charron's participation, if the Frenchman would do likewise. When Bennett heard of the challenge, he de-

---

* Bennett's view of the Chicago race matched that of his adopted countrymen.

cided this was the opportunity he had been looking for. He offered to handle logistics, to act as intermediary, and to hold the stakes. He also assured Charron that regular dispatches would be sent around the world trumpeting the intrepid American's challenge of Europe's best.

Charron, who had won a Paris-Amsterdam-Paris run the previous year and a Paris-Bordeaux race just weeks before, agreed, assuming that Winton would travel to France, where automobilism was far more advanced. Bennett kept his word about publicity—the planned Charron-Winton race received regular newspaper coverage as far away as Australia. Charron deposited his 20,000 francs with Bennett, and Winton deposited an equal sum with a newspaper in New York, but not the *Herald.* Then Winton balked. In the first place, he said, he had planned on the race being staged in the United States, and in the second, his 20,000-franc offer was not meant to be a bet but was simply security against his not showing up.

The Frenchman took umbrage, as did Bennett. He was quoted in the *Herald* as saying, "I am very much surprised at the turn the proposed international automobile match has taken. It promised at the start to be a serious affair, but apparently it has stopped off suddenly."[11] Bennett issued a dispatch complaining that the race was "in a bad way" since "Winton declines to back up his challenge by any sort of bet, were it even a dollar." Bennett then dismissed Winton's challenge as a "humbug."

Charron then issued a counterproposal. Feeling "discouraged," he told the *Herald,* "I shall do my best to extricate Mr. Winton from his dilemma. Now I offer to pay his expenses up to the sum of 5,000 francs to come over here, and I will lay 50,000 francs against his 20,000 francs that I will beat him on any route he may choose in France from 500 kilometers to 1,000 kilometers."[12] Winton was to post his money, this time with Bennett, "as an ordinary sporting transaction." Charron made the 2½-to-1 offer because he had "such confidence in the good qualities of the French automobile."

The article then quoted Charron as adding a challenge that almost certainly came from Bennett himself. "New York newspapers which have taken up the interests of Mr. Winton so much in this matter will surely find money enough through their readers, among whom will be found persons who have confidence enough in Mr. Winton, and who will complete the sum in his behalf. The whole sum should be placed with the *Herald,* where my forfeit now lies, and where I shall pay in the stakes." It is also likely that Charron's stake was put up by Bennett, so the Frenchman never put up a franc of his own money.

But Winton again refused to cross the Atlantic. He claimed to be committed to a series of endurance runs in the United States, including the one from Cleveland to New York in May, after which he had deposited his good-faith money for the Charron race.* Charron, who had never been to America and spoke no English, then agreed to a race from New York to Chicago, to be held in August, the first major cross-country event ever held in the United States. The next day he decided against it, prompting one newspaper to observe, "If MM. Charron and Winton do not cease expending wind about that automobile race, there will not be enough left for their tires."[13]

But the wind did not cease. At one point Charron demanded the wager be 100,000 francs, lending even more credence to the likelihood that Bennett was the actual source of funds. Even Thomas Edison, who announced his own intention to build a car that would "cost less than a team of horses," joined the debate, predicting a rousing defeat for Charron because French automobiles were used to driving on roads as "flat as billiard tables."

In the end, the race never came off. As reported in *The Sydney Morning Herald,* "The Winton-Charron motor-car match has been declared off owing to the stakes not being large enough to tempt Charron over to America. . . . Although an American paper offered Charron £250 expenses if he would go across and meet Winton, who offered to put up a side wager of £800, Charron has held out for larger stakes which, not being forthcoming, will put an end to what would have proved an exceedingly interesting international contest."[14]

Bennett, a man accustomed to getting anything he wanted, was fu-

* In that jaunt, which Winton completed in a record-setting forty-seven hours, a reporter accompanying him referred to his vehicle as an "automobile." The name stuck and eventually all others faded away.

rious, but it did not take him long to come up with an even better idea, something far more auspicious than a match race. Although various manufacturers such as Panhard et Levassor often functioned as de facto teams, auto racing was officially an individual sport, the disadvantages of which had been accented all too acutely in the Charron-Winton fiasco. Bennett would correct all that and introduce national pride in the bargain by sponsoring an event in which automobiles would race under their nations' flags. To prevent any one nation—France—from overwhelming the others, a maximum of three vehicles from any one country would be allowed. Finally, to ensure that spectators knew which nations' entries were winning, each country's cars would be painted in one of their national colors. The French would get their first choice, blue, the Belgians yellow, the Americans red, and Germany white.* As a final inducement, the nation whose driver claimed victory in what promised to be a wildly popular and highly lucrative event would choose the venue for the following year's race.†

Bennett presented his idea to the ACF, which, after grumbling a bit about restricting France to three cars, agreed to organize the race. Bennett volunteered to donate the cup that would be presented to the winner. While the official name for the race was the Coupe Internationale, it quickly became known by the name of the trophy, the Coupe Gordon Bennett. To avoid subjective judging, another of Bennett's requirements was a strict set of specifications. Automobiles must be constructed entirely in the nation under whose flag they raced and must weigh more than 882 pounds. (A 2,200-pound maximum weight was added in 1902.) Each car must carry two riders who weighed at least 168 pounds each or ballast would be added to make up the difference. The initial Gordon Bennett Cup thus became the world's first modern automobile race.

---

* With red, white, and blue gone, the British, who did not participate until the following year, were forced to settle for green. British drivers groused, but over the years British racing green became one of the sport's most popular colors.

† When Bennett switched to balloon racing in 1906 and then added fixed-wing airplane competition in 1909, he abandoned the national team contest but continued the practice of holding the ensuing year's race in the country that the winner claimed as his own.

And only for modern automobiles. The sort of Rube Goldberg–type machines that had filed for entry in Chicago would have been laughed off the course in Europe. For Americans, that meant only superior technology—and superior finances—could qualify an owner as a participant. "If horse racing is the sport of kings," *Automobile* magazine observed, "then motor races must be the sport of millionaires."[15]

France soon announced its three-car team. Each of the French cars would be a Panhard with a vertical, 27-horsepower, two-cylinder motor encased in aluminum alloy, an arrangement that had demonstrated remarkable performance and durability. They were, however, stupendously noisy, even by the volcanic standards of the day, with an explosion followed by a vibrating metallic ring every three to four seconds. One of these detonations on wheels would be driven by Fernand Charron. Belgium announced that it would match France's three entries, and Germany entered a single Benz.

For a sport "in its infancy on this side of the Atlantic," *Automobile* added, the competition for Gordon Bennett's "international challenge cup . . . has been entered into . . . with a zest which promises the best of sport for all concerned." By that the magazine meant that the United States had entered with two cars, both Wintons, one to be driven by Winton himself, who had agreed—to Bennett's surprise and Charron's anticipation—to come to Europe for the event.

The course had been set from Paris to Lyon, a distance of more than 350 miles over public roads, which the public, the organizers knew, would not always leave to the automobiles. As the date of the race approached—June 14, 1900—problems began to surface. None of the Belgian cars had arrived (only one would), and one of the Wintons was forced to withdraw because of mechanical issues. Soon afterward, the German entry, which was to be driven by Karl Benz's son, Eugen, also withdrew. Then the Belgian car that did arrive had French tires, which prompted a protest that was quickly dismissed. No one wanted a match race between the Panhards, which were expected to do well, and the remaining Winton, which wasn't.

European opinion of the American entry proved correct. Seventy-five miles out, Winton broke a wheel and bent an axle, and he was forced to abandon the race. A bit farther on, one of the Panhards dropped out with transmission trouble, and the last of the Belgian cars retired after colliding with perhaps a half dozen dogs. That left only the two remaining Panhards to complete the course.

Charron finished first despite, with 10 miles to go, "coming into collision with a big dog, with the result that the main spring of the autocar was broken. He finished by holding the spring with his hand."[16] Léonce Girardot, in the other Panhard, came in more than ninety minutes later, because he had run off the road trying to avoid a team of horses and lost more than an hour waiting while a blacksmith made repairs to a bent wheel.

Horseless Age, which was desperately trying to spur American auto-making, tried to mask its disappointment at Winton's feeble showing by injecting a bit of xenophobia. "The race was less international than its name would imply, three of the five participants starting being French, so that, granting equal value to each of the racers, and applying the theory of probability, we should have reached the conclusion that France had greater chance of winning than of losing the cup race."[17] The article did not bother to mention that the French would have been favored even had they been forced to run on three wheels.

Charron's impressive closing sprint notwithstanding, with only two cars completing the course, as in the Chicago run in the United States, the race might have seemed a failure. There was little reporting in American newspapers, except the *Herald,* of course, and *Automobile* magazine, while charitably calling the race "tremendously exciting," also proclaimed it "a disappointment."[18]

But Bennett, like Kohlstaat, had touched something in both the drivers and the citizenry at large. Traveling 350 miles over often uneven, unpaved roads—not at all suitable for billiard tables—Charron had averaged almost 39 miles per hour, a remarkable achievement. In addition, the thought of national pride being tested on the open road by this remarkable new invention created a clamor that someone with Bennett's acute ear for publicity could hardly miss. By the time the next Gordon Bennett Cup race was run, it was one of the most eagerly awaited events in the world.

But the significance of Bennett's brainchild was more profound. For all the resistance that would still be encountered at the widespread use of this cacophonous, smoke-belching machine, the Paris-Lyon Coupe Internationale had somehow managed to be a turning point. Suddenly, the thought of what might be achieved infused designers and drivers with excitement, and fascinated the public. Automobiles remained impractical as vehicles for the common man, but the question now was simply for how long. The spark had been set; it awaited the right man to kindle it to flame.

CHAPTER 9

▰▰A ROAD OF ONE'S OWN

F ew men have exhibited a more instinctive feel for the nuances of public mood than Henry Ford. Although he had finally put himself into the position to manufacture automobiles, he realized he must pursue a different path, albeit with his investors' money. He would not yet build the cheapest, most reliable car; consumers were not ready for that. For now, he would build the fastest.

Much later, he claimed to have embraced racing only under protest. "When it was found that an automobile really could go and several makers started to put out cars," he wrote in *My Life and Work,* "the immediate query was as to which would go fastest. It was a curious but natural development—that racing idea. I never thought anything of racing, but the public refused to consider the automobile in any light other than as a fast toy. Therefore later we had to race. The industry was held back by this initial racing slant, for the attention of the makers was diverted to making fast rather than good cars. It was a business for speculators."[1]

In 1899, Ford, still an Edison employee, accepted the overtures of a group of those speculators and allowed them to organize the Detroit Automobile Company. The corporation was capitalized at $150,000, 10 percent of that paid in, with a dozen investors, including Mayor Maybury and a local lumber baron, William Murphy. Ford was granted a small amount of stock and a salary of $150 per week as "chief engineer." He was also given modern, well-equipped shop space on Cass Avenue to produce his marvels. Although this was the first corporation set up in Detroit specifically for the manufacture of automobiles, these were hardly the only men with a dream who had been swept up in the horseless carriage rage. As with many of history's great technological shifts—movable type, aviation, electronic data processing—scores if not hundreds of would-be tycoons were applying their varying degrees of talent in the rush to innovation. "All over the country small towns were being treated to volcanic eruptions of frightened horses when some local inventor rattled through Main Street in a noisy 'horseless' at the head of a trail of black smoke."[2] Less than two weeks after he agreed to be part of the new venture, Ford was offered the job of general manager of Detroit Illuminating. Instead, he quit.

But Ford had been premature. Of the team of assistants that had been instrumental in helping him transform his previous visions to quadricycle reality, only one was willing to leave his job and roll the dice in the new venture. Without his team, Ford couldn't even decide what product to produce. The Detroit Automobile Company turned out to be a scattershot affair, fabricating beautifully wrought bodies with no working parts to mount inside them, or finely tuned parts with no chassis on which to mount them. Fred Strauss, the assistant who did come to work for him, summed it up: "Henry just wasn't ready." When the company folded after eighteen months, it had failed to complete a single automobile. It had also cost its investors $86,000.

Ford's explanation was somewhat different:

> A group of men of speculative turn of mind organized, as soon as I left the electric company, the Detroit Automobile Company to exploit my car. I was the chief engineer and held a small amount of the stock. For three years we con-

tinued making cars more or less on the model of my first
car. We sold very few of them; I could get no support at all
toward making better cars to be sold to the public at large.
The whole thought was to make to order and to get the
largest price possible for each car. The main idea seemed to
be to get the money. I found that the new company was not
a vehicle for realizing my ideas but merely a money-making
concern—that did not make much money. In March, 1902,
I resigned, determined never again to put myself under orders.[3]

While it is certainly true that Ford chafed at taking orders from anyone, the idea that he was upset at the rapaciousness of his partners is
at best a half-truth. For one thing, the sort of men Ford described
were unlikely to sit still while Ford frittered away their cash. For another, Ford loved money, as long it was he who was making it.

The timeline was not inaccurate, however. Detroit Automobile did
last three years, albeit in two segments. After the company folded,
some of his investors were still convinced Henry Ford was the man to
bring the automobile to the people and great riches to them; they
bought up the remaining assets at a receiver's sale. With Ford's complete and enthusiastic approval—and promise to produce a working
automobile this time—these same men set him up at Cass Avenue
once more.

Their eagerness to get Ford back in the shop was not misplaced.
Enthusiasm for the automobile in the United States had grown; its
evolution into a mainstream consumer good seemed inevitable. In
August 1899, taking a cue from France, a group of automobile enthusiasts, many of them wealthy, had incorporated the Automobile Club
of America (ACA). "The objects ... are the formation of a social
organization or club, composed in whole or in part of persons own-
ing self-propelled pleasure vehicles for personal or private use. To fur-
nish a means of recording the experience of members and others
using motor vehicles or automobiles. To promote original investigation in the mechanical development of motor carriages, by members

and others. To arrange for pleasure runs and to encourage road contests of all kinds among owners of automobiles."[4]

The club sponsored a number of races, some for substantial purses. These contests always attracted a large crowd as well as heavy newspaper coverage, and they established Alexander Winton as the most famous and accomplished manufacturer (and driver) in the nation.[*] In the spring of 1900, the club announced that it would mount America's first automobile show, to be held in late fall in New York.[5] In addition to a large space for exhibitors, an oval track for test-driving the automobiles was laid against the inner walls of the arena. Every means of propulsion would be represented, as would every design employed in both the United States and Europe. (The Panhard would come in for particular scrutiny from American designers.)

The auto exposition, held only two months before the reorganization of the Detroit Automobile Company, was an immense success. As *The New York Times* reported, "With the glitter of polished nickel and the sheen of many-colored enamels, the first show of the Automobile Club of America, an exhibition dubbed by facetious onlookers 'the horseless Horse Show,' was opened last night in Madison Square Garden. From the hour the doors of the big building swung inward until midnight, a throng of spectators variously estimated at from 7,000 to 10,000 surged through the maze of narrow aisles."[6] More than seventy exhibitors brought "an almost endless variety of motor vehicles," which enthralled a cross-section of New York society. "All," assured the *Times,* "went away satisfied." *Horseless Age* added, "It is . . . evident from a review of the machines exhibited, that neither money nor brains are being spared in the contest to produce the most attractive and reliable machine, not for exhibition purposes alone but for general road work."[7]

In the end, the ten-day affair was reported on in every major newspaper and journal in the nation and attracted more than forty-eight thousand visitors, one of whom was Henry Ford. He walked the floor, perused his competitors' products, and met with builders, designers,

---

* Winton also set a number of speed and distance records during the same period, winning purses as lush as $5,000.

and moneymen. He returned home more aware than ever before of the public clamor for automobiles, and this time he very definitely produced one of his own. Unfortunately for his investors, it was neither the one he had promised nor one that could be sold to the public. But what it could do was go very fast.

The first thing Ford did was reassemble the team that had built the quadricycle. In a stroke of luck, Charles King had decided to go off and fight in the Spanish-American War instead of continuing in the car business, and thus Oliver Barthel became available just when Ford needed him. Ford persuaded Spider Huff to join him as well. To this crew, he added C. Harold Wills, a virtuoso designer and engineer, although still only twenty-two years old.[8]

Wills's hire epitomized an irony of Ford's legacy. His widely touted but vastly overstated near-genius as an inventor obscured an authentic near-genius for management. Throughout his career, and certainly in its first two decades, Ford was uncanny in his ability to choose just the right people to complement his talents and maximize his efficiency. And he didn't restrict himself, as so many other businessmen did, to those who looked like him, thought like him, or had the same out-of-business pursuits as he had. Spider Huff, for example, adept with the electrical components that Ford could never quite master, was a hard-drinking carouser—and that is putting it mildly—who would not infrequently disappear on a jaunt, sometimes for weeks at a time. But Ford, who during Prohibition would vow to close down his factories if alcohol was once more made legal, always welcomed Huff back without judgment and even paid his bills. To design and build his factories, Ford, the vitriolic anti-Semite, would consider no one but Albert Kahn, the man who could best bring Ford's vision to reality. And then, of course, there were the thousands hired to work on the floor of the Ford factories, judged only on their ability to fit the needs of the assembly line's mind-numbing repetition. The examples of Ford's insight into personal and corporate dynamics are endless, and without those astonishing instincts, Henry Ford would have been, at best, a minor footnote in the saga of automotive engineering rather than its headline.

Once the right staff was on board, Ford demonstrated a commitment to this venture that he had not to its predecessor. He set up his cot at Cass Avenue and spent a good deal more time at the factory than he did at home. As one biographer put it, "Ford put into the racer all the energy his backers urged him to devote to the car they wanted to produce."[9]

By summer 1901, Ford's team began to get results. The engine they produced, a horizontally mounted twin-cylinder opposed-piston version that was cooled with water coils, was capable of 26 horsepower. Oliver Barthel later insisted he had designed the car from "the ground up," but the racer bore all the Ford trademark touches—elegant design, extreme functionality, durable construction.

Ford had never built a race car before, so balance and stability could only be determined in road testing. The machine was so loud that Ford had it towed out of the city to see how it handled. While Ford and his assistants were running and fine-tuning their racer, an official of the Detroit Driving Club—the Automobile Club had spawned a spate of local associations—got together with Alexander Winton's sales manager and arranged to host an auto meet in Detroit in October. There would be a number of different events culminating in a 25-mile stakes race, for which the winner would be awarded a hefty $1,000 prize. Winton, driving his own car, would be the main draw.

This was the event Ford had been building toward—but even so, he didn't post his entry fee until the day before the race. He needn't have hesitated. The finished machine, which Ford called *Sweepstakes,* was a remarkably advanced product: a large, efficient two-cylinder engine with prototypical fuel injection, improved spark plugs (by now, only Daimler was still using hot-tube ignition), a 96-inch wheelbase for stability, and a steering wheel rather than a tiller. This last improvement was reportedly supplied by Winton, who sportingly gave Ford one of his new steering assemblies because he said that "somebody would get killed" using Ford's tiller mechanism. Ford later said that *Sweepstakes* tested at 72 miles per hour, which would have made it by far the fastest automobile on earth. (At that point, drivers were still trying to beat the "mile-a-minute" mark, or 60 miles per hour.)

The organizers had scheduled the event for October 10, a Thursday, at a horse track in Grosse Pointe, at the mouth of the Detroit River. The turns of the mile-long track were built up to a slight bank, to prevent the entrants from running off into the fence or the grandstand. Six thousand people paid to see the race that organizers optimistically billed as the "world championship," with eight entrants, including the hometown favorite.[10] In fact, while the race garnered immense local interest—the Detroit Street Railway Company ran special trains to the track and the city courts adjourned on the day of the meet—it was hardly a championship. Racing had become quite popular and any number of other events were run that fall, particularly in the east, where Henri Fournier had crossed the Atlantic to drive the newest spectacular French machine, the Mors, and was tearing up the tracks.*

The day began auspiciously for Winton. In a preliminary event, he covered a mile in a record-setting 1 minute 12.4 seconds, cutting almost 2 seconds off the previous mark. The next day, in New York, Henri Fournier—whom Ford had met at the automobile show—took an additional 6 seconds off Winton's record in his Mors.

By race day, the "world championship" seemed as if it would be anything but. Of the eight expected entrants, only three could make it to the starting line, and one of those was forced to retire with a cracked cylinder. Faced with a match race between Ford and Winton, the judges shortened the race to 10 miles, hoping to ensure that both—or even one of them—finished.

Ford had never before driven in a race. Despite the bank on the track, he was terrified of turning at speed, a justifiable sentiment in a car in which he had not installed brakes. Spider Huff rode with him. There is no report on whether Huff had a few drinks before the race, but he probably should have. He was charged with crouching on the outside running board, grasping two makeshift handholds, and leaning out, his upper body suspended over the track surface, in order to

---

* Émile Mors was the first man to employ a V-shaped arrangement in his motors. By the time Fournier arrived in the United States, Mors racers had eclipsed all others, save the Panhard.

prevent *Sweepstakes* from capsizing on the turns. Winton, an expert driver, rode with his sales manager, who in theory would have a good less to do.

In addition to being a more experienced driver, Winton also had what seemed a far superior machine. Although his car was about 600 pounds heavier, it generated almost three times the horsepower, a muscular 70 to Ford's puny 26, and despite its bulk it was a good deal tighter and more stable in the turns. As the ten-lap race began, although the crowd cheered lustily for the local entrant, it appeared that it would not be much of a contest. Ford's racer held up surprisingly well in the straightaways but, despite Huff's efforts, he consistently lost ground on the turns.

After 5 miles, Winton was substantially ahead. Although Ford's driving became more assured as the race progressed, by mile 7 he had failed to cut into Winton's lead. Then Winton's racer began to belch smoke. "The brasses on [his] machine became heated," the journals reported. In fact, the cooling system had broken down. Winton's sales manager/mechanician frantically poured oil on the gearing assembly, but Winton refused to decelerate and the overheating got worse. Ford began to make up ground. Eventually, the engine began grinding metal and Winton slowed to a crawl. Ford overtook him easily and won by almost a mile. His time was 13:24, impressive but hardly withering. Clara Ford remembered the crowd cheering wildly as her husband crossed the finish line in their native city.

Contemporary biographers generally attribute Ford's victory to superior design, which is technically correct. Winton's machine did, after all, overheat. But Ford had been lucky. Everyone's cars broke down in those days, including Ford's, and other than the flaw in the cooling system, Winton's racer was the better machine.

Most accounts of Ford's life also have the victory over Winton thrusting him into the spotlight, securing renewed financing, and establishing him as a first-rank automobile engineer. While this was true for the extremely limited universe of 1901 Detroit, the race did not engender anything but an occasional paragraph in national newspapers. The trade journals treated Ford and his racer with respect but hardly with unbridled enthusiasm. *Horseless Age* placed Ford's racer, "which won the race for its class at the Grosse Point track . . . among the gasoline machines which have lately attracted public attention in this country."[11] *Motor Way* did not mention the race at all.

But local accolades were sufficient to renew the faith of Ford's backers. Not six weeks after his defeat of Winton, a new Ford company, "builders of high grade automobiles and tourist cars," was incorporated. The new owners—Murphy and his chums—were much the same as the old owners. *Motor Way* wrote, "The Henry Ford Co., Detroit, Mich., was incorporated on November 30, for $60,000, for the manufacture of automobiles. They will occupy the old plant of the Detroit Automobile Co, at 1343 Cass Avenue, Detroit, of which company they are the successors. It is stated that all the defects of the first machines have been eliminated and the new carriages will be provided with greater power, with a reduction in the weight."[12] *Horseless Age* added, "The company will proceed at once to manufacture a popular runabout propelled by a two-cylinder 8 horse power motor and selling at about $1,000."[13]

Other than the capitalization—which was $30,500 paid in—and the company's address, nothing in either announcement was true. Having his name on the company did not make Henry Ford any more committed to its investors' goals, and once again he refused to adhere to the plan on which he and his partners had agreed. Instead, Ford found the perfect partner to help him to the next stage of his business, this time a man with no experience in either designing or even driving an automobile.

Among the spectators at the Detroit race was a twenty-seven-year-old Detroit native named Tom Cooper. Cooper, who had trained to be a pharmacist, had matinee idol looks and a chiseled physique, and happened to be just about the best bicycle racer on earth. He was a household name in both in the United States and Europe and one of the highest-paid athletes in America, outearning heavyweight boxing champ James Jeffries.

Cooper had become fascinated with automobiles and after *Sweepstakes*'s victory sought Ford out to talk about a racer. The meeting

went well, with Cooper passing along a number of design suggestions. Before a deal could be cut, however, Cooper inexplicably announced his intention to journey to Colorado to try his hand at, of all
things, coal mining.

Cooper's departure didn't change Ford's plans. He instructed his
assistants to set to work on the new racer anyway, this one bigger,
faster, and more powerful than its predecessor. When it sank in that
Ford was never going to do anything he didn't want to do, Ford Company investors finally balked. They forbade him to work on his race
car on company time and insisted that he build the car he had promised them. Ford merely took to working on the racer at night, mostly
with Harold Wills. Predictably, Ford's progress on the commercial automobile continued to lag and the components he did produce were
substandard. So, in order to either spur Ford on or replace him, the
now-seething board members engaged Henry M. Leland, the finest
precision toolmaker in the nation.[14]

Leland had been born in Vermont in 1843 and was the quintes-
sence of the flinty, laconic Yankee. He was tall, with ramrod posture
and a beard John Brown would have envied. At fourteen he was hired
as an apprentice in a tool shop, and he spent the Civil War working
with weaponry in the Springfield Armory in Massachusetts. After the
war, he moved to Providence, Rhode Island, where he got a job in a
sewing machine factory. He also worked for a time at Colt Industries.
Over the course of two decades, Leland became more and more adept
at building machine parts from the best materials at an extremely fine
tolerance; the resulting parts could then be employed interchangeably
in a company's product. In 1890, he moved to Detroit with another
fine-tool engineer, met a local financier named Robert Faulconer, and
founded Leland & Faulconer, which quickly established itself as the
preeminent precision tool firm in America and perhaps the world.

Leland, who "epitomized in singular fashion the march of machine
technology from the agrarian to the industrial era," could machine
parts to a tolerance of 1/100,000 of an inch, and his son and future
partner insisted he had worked as accurately as 1/270,000 of an inch.[15]
As the nineteenth century drew to a close, Leland had become expert

Henry Leland (right) and Robert Faulconer

in components for bicycles, sewing machines ... and gasoline-powered motors. He was first engaged to build Daimler motors for boats, but in 1899 he was approached by a man named Ransom Olds and asked to build engines and transmissions for automobiles. By the time Ford's investors approached him, Leland's reputation as an automotive engineer far exceeded that of the man whose name was on the Ford company letterhead.

Although each was an unstinting perfectionist, the contrast between the make-it-up-as-you-go, trial-and-error Ford and the methodical, punctilious Leland was acute. Predictably, they couldn't stand each other, though their skills were complementary and they might have made a superb team.

Leland wasted no time weighing in—he was critical of Ford's methods, his motor, and the practices in his shop. In order to be successful in marketing the automobile to a wide audience, Leland insisted, parts and components had to be engineered and fabricated so precisely as to be interchangeable. (Although Ford gave him no credit, this would become the first principle of assembly line production.)

The 1905 Cadillac

Although in theory the two men were to work together, Leland ensured there was no chance of that, probably with the board's approval.
Ford resigned.

The investors were relieved to see him go—in their eyes, he had
rewarded extreme forbearance by squandering large sums of their
money, by this time more than $100,000 of it. And in Leland they had
not only an able replacement but a man who took his commitments
seriously. Ford got some cash—less than $1,000—the drawings to a
racing car that had not yet been built, and the rights to a carburetor he
wished to patent. He departed with a record of two failed companies
and one no-decision.

"The Henry Ford Company," obviously, would no longer do as a
corporate moniker. To replace it, Leland and his partners chose the
name of the explorer who had founded Detroit. And so the Cadillac
Automobile Company was born. While the company never approached the vast profits that Ford would accrue in the coming years,
Cadillac established itself as the manufacturer of perhaps the finest-

made and most reliable cars in the United States, and returned a tidy profit to its investors in the process.

Tom Cooper's mining adventure lasted only a few months, after which he returned to Detroit to renew his race car discussion with Ford. Ford was taken with Cooper—although that would change—and they agreed to pursue the racing idea together. Details of the bargain they struck were never made public, but it is generally assumed that Cooper put up the money, or at least the lion's share of it, so that Ford could build him the fastest race car in the world. And that is what Ford proceeded to do.

Once again, Oliver Barthel was responsible for most of the basic design, which was revolutionary, although it was Cooper who suggested an extra-wide wheelbase and low center of gravity. Harold Wills drew up the plans and he and Ford spent long, cold nights in the shop refining them until they had just what they wanted.

Their product was a 10-foot-long stripped-down monster with a wood-and-metal frame. Its massive four-cylinder motor could achieve as much as 100 horsepower. Neither the engine, the carburetor, nor the lubricating system was shielded, so not only was the machine deafening, it also spewed oil that covered the driver from head to foot. To steer, Ford had installed what he called a "two-handed tiller," a horizontal bar with vertical extenders on either end, mounted crosswise on a post that rose from between the driver's legs. The driver would steer by means of the extenders, much as a bicycle racer might. The hand and forearm strength required just to keep so powerful a machine steady would be prodigious, to say nothing of keeping it from flying off in the turns. "Controlling the fastest car of today was nothing as compared to controlling that car," Ford wrote later. "The steering wheel had not yet been thought of. Holding the car in line required all the strength of a strong man."[16] (Ford had obviously forgotten that *Sweepstakes,* his own racer, had been fitted with a steering wheel donated by Alexander Winton.)

But the speed the racer could generate was unprecedented: all it needed was a driver sufficiently skilled—or foolhardy—to take the tiller and propel it to glory. And it wasn't going to be one of the builders. Ford drove his new creation on a test run and later described the experience: "The roar of those cylinders alone was enough to half kill a man. There was only one seat. One life to a car was enough. I tried out the cars. Cooper tried out the cars. We let them out at full speed. I cannot quite describe the sensation. Going over Niagara Falls would have been but a pastime after a ride in one of them." There would be no repeat performance. "I did not want to take the responsibility of racing [it] . . . neither did Cooper."

But Cooper thought he knew someone who would. "He said he knew a man who lived on speed, that nothing could go too fast for him."[17] Cooper's man was a former water boy on a railroad gang and kitchen helper in an insane asylum who had turned to bicycle racing, where he had acquired a reputation as a ferocious and fearless competitor. His name was Berna Eli Oldfield, but he went by "Barney."

Cooper wired to Salt Lake City, where Oldfield was engaged in some indeterminate pursuit. Oldfield agreed immediately and left for Detroit. "He had never driven a motorcar," Ford noted, "but he liked the idea of trying it. He said he would try anything once."

Neither Ford nor Cooper realized that they had engaged a man who would become the most famous racing driver in American history. "It took us only a week to teach him how to drive," Ford noted, with an uncharacteristic touch of awe. "The man did not know what fear was. All that he had to learn was how to control the monster."

Only Henry Leland could create machines that were truly interchangeable, but Ford had built two more or less identical models. One, painted yellow, he called the *999*, after a record-setting New York Central locomotive, and the other, painted red, was christened the *Arrow*, but was later referred to in the press and trade journals as the *Red Devil*. Under the terms of their deal, Ford owned the *999* and Cooper the *Arrow*. Oldfield did most of his driving on the *999* and quickly confirmed the wisdom of summoning him from the west.

For reasons never made totally clear, in early October 1902, Ford sold the *999* back to Cooper. Clara was pleased with the decision, declaring her husband "lucky to be rid of him. He caught [Cooper] in a number of sneaky tricks. He was looking out for Cooper and Cooper

Ford, Oldfield, and the *999*

only." She added a final, damning condemnation. "He thinks too much of low down women to suit me."[18] Despite the intensity of Clara's denunciations, however, there was no indication from Ford of dissatisfaction with Cooper's input or the partnership. And he certainly wasn't dissatisfied with Cooper's money. In *My Life and Work,* where Ford was happy to take shots at anyone he felt had wronged him—and the list wasn't short—the dissolution of the Cooper partnership is not mentioned at all.

Whatever the cause, the timing was curious. By the end of September, Oldfield was demonstrating the sort of open-throttle proficiency that would make him almost unbeatable. He drove *999* all out, even through the turns, which perhaps no other man would have had the skill or daring to do. And two weeks after the sale, on October 23, 1902, during the second running of the Grosse Pointe Sweepstakes, the *999* was scheduled to go up against Alexander Winton, who would sport a new and powerful machine he had called the *Bullet.*

Rain forced two consecutive postponements of the race. Finally, on October 24, the track was deemed sufficiently dry to begin the two-day event. As in the previous year, the first day belonged to Winton. His 2¼-ton *Bullet* completed 5 miles in 5 minutes 20 seconds, the last mile of which was 1:04.8, breaking Ford's record. Oldfield, in the equally weighty *999,* completed a 2-mile run in 2:13. Winton also triumphed in a 10-mile race that Cooper and Oldfield hadn't entered. In that victory, Winton kept the *Bullet* on track after another car, driven by J. D. Maxwell, collided with his during an aborted attempt to pass and then went somersaulting across the infield, "dashing the machine to pieces." Maxwell was thrown free—otherwise he almost certainly would have been killed.

The crash was widely covered in the press, but it was the next day's confrontation that thousands of Detroiters had waited to see. Although this time Ford and Winton would not meet in a match race, none of the other competitors, including a Benz, was considered a threat to the two main combatants.

As *Motor World* reported, "The Cooper racer, a huge, ungainly looking monster with no compensating gear, roaring and pounding in a fearful way, was driven wildcap fashion by Barney Oldfield, who tore off miles at a terrific clip, establishing a track record of 1.04⅕ and doing the five miles in 5.28."

Winton's improved racer was once again every bit as fast and powerful as Ford's creation—the *999* could not match the *Bullet's* time from the previous day—but Winton seemed cursed when racing against Ford-built machines. Oldfield, off the mark at full throttle and never braking, jumped to an early lead, but soon the *Bullet* was closing the gap. After the first mile, the Winton began to misfire and overheat. Oldfield pulled away, and eventually the *Bullet* was forced to retire. The Benz finished a distant second.

"It seems incredible," *Motor World* exulted, "but it is asserted by Cooper that Oldfield had never driven any kind of an automobile two days before [actually two months] and the ex–bicycle rider certainly showed himself a man of nerve. His performance was a hair-raising one, and local pride in his victory made his win popular."[19] Oldfield "was carried from his machine to the judges' stand on the shoulders of admirers who rushed out on the track by the hundreds."

Ford, who had not bothered to attend the race—it is a distinct possibility he thought the *999* would lose—was nonetheless happy to join in the celebration. In the same issue of *Motor World*, Ford issued a (paid-for) testimonial in an advertisement for the G & J Tire Company.

> GENTLEMEN—In reference to the automobile tires I ordered from you to be placed on my racer, I wish to state that the tires were placed on the machine the first of last June and I have not had to pump them up since that time. The machine entered the last races held here on the Grosse Pointe Track, October 25th, and being on the track with five other machines, it had to make some very sharp turns while passing some of the slower machines on the curves. The tires held the curves very well for such high speed. The machine broke the world's record, on a circular track, for five miles, the time being 5 minutes, 28 seconds. Yours respectfully, HENRY FORD.[20]

From there, Oldfield and Cooper barnstormed across the Midwest, racing against all comers—or if none were available, racing the *999* against the *Red Devil*, which often featured Spider Huff at the tiller. Oldfield would soon set world speed records for every distance from 1 to 5 miles, and six weeks after the race against Winton he came within a second of the mile-a-minute barrier.

Just how difficult and dangerous the *999* was for anyone other than Oldfield to control was pointed out in September 1903 at the Wisconsin State Fair. With Barney recovering from injuries suffered in a race in Detroit, a twenty-two-year-old would-be racer named George Day took the tiller in a match against Spider Huff in the *Red Devil*.

Day, who had been a car salesman and mechanic but had never before piloted a race car, nonetheless felt certain he could set a speed record. He wired his parents in Columbus, Ohio, to ask their permission to go against Huff. His parents refused, but Day decided to race anyway. The result was predictable.

> In making the turn around the north end of the track, Day's machine turned a complete somersault, crushing the

life out of the daring operator, and came to a standstill, a
wreck. Day lay on the track with a fractured skull, his collarbone broken and his left arm fractured in four places
and the flesh torn from his right hand. Blood gushed from
his nose, mouth, ears and eyes as he gasped a few expiring
breaths.[21]

Barney Oldfield went on to unprecedented fame. During the course
of his two-decade career, he had so many crashes, some at breakneck
speed or around hairpin turns, that newspapers eventually called him
"that specialist in averted suicide." With a flair for self-promotion and
the willingness, even perhaps eagerness, to risk his life, he became the
most famous man ever to pilot a racing car. As *Sports Illustrated* observed in a retrospective:

Even at his worst he was one of the most colorful figures
the sport has ever known, a square-shouldered, loud-
talking, lovable, brash ruffian with a strong flair for the dramatic and a canny knowledge of his public. He clenched an
unlit cigar stub between his teeth as he drove—and that
became one of his famous trademarks. He sent squads of
publicity men ahead of him with large circus-type posters
flamboyantly announcing the appearance of the "Master
Driver of the World."

He was the first American to drive a mile a minute in an
automobile; he claimed every world's record from one to
50 miles in the Peerless Green Dragon; he set a new mark
(131.724 mph) at Daytona Beach in 1910 in his powerful
Lightning Benz; he became the undisputed king of the dirt
tracks, winning hundreds of exhibition and match races; he
tamed the deadliest racing machine in America, the front-
drive Killer Christie, in which he set a new lap record at
Indianapolis in 1916 the day before the classic "500." Later,
with the treacherous Christie, which had brought near-
death to its inventor and injured many others who could
not master its wicked fishtailing rear end, he engaged stunt

Race between Lincoln Beachey and Barney Oldfield

flyer Lincoln Beachey in special exhibition matches billed as the Deadly Flying Machine vs. the Killer Automobile! In 1917, he went into semiretirement, the idol of his generation, having competed in over 2,000 events during his fabled career.[22]

Oldfield survived in the public mind long after he ceased to drive. "Who do you think you are? Barney Oldfield?" became shorthand for fast, reckless driving, and the term was used for decades.

At one point, Oldfield and Ford supposedly had this exchange, which Oldfield oft repeated but Ford did not. When Ford said, "You made me and I made you," Oldfield replied, "I did a damn sight better for you than you did for me."

Which man did more for the other is open to question, but what Barney Oldfield did do in the *999* was put Henry Ford directly in the path of George Selden.

CHAPTER 10

THE ONCE AND FUTURE CAR

The automobile saga overflows with incongruities. In one of the most glaring, the Selden patent was put into play only because of the failure of another technology, one that was originally seen as the future of motorized travel and which contemporary automakers are desperate to revive—the electric car. In fact, it was not George Selden who sought to enforce his patent on a "road-locomotive propelled by a liquid-hydrocarbon engine of the compression type" but rather a consortium of Wall Street opportunists who had gained control of a corporation known as the Electric Vehicle Company.

Electric Vehicle manifested the sort of evolutionary gestation common to companies in eras of technological upheaval. Even by the Wild West standards of early twentieth-century business, the company qualifies as a unique case study in both forward-thinking entrepreneurship and gross mismanagement. At the apex of the steep upward trajectory and equally precipitous fall of the electric automobile was a remarkable German immigrant named Isaac Leopold Rice.

Rice was born in Bavaria in 1850, but his family emigrated to Milwaukee when he was six, then moved to Philadelphia four years later.[1]

A chess prodigy and classically trained musician, young Isaac was sent to Paris and London for his schooling. As a teenager, he supported himself by teaching piano, a vocation he continued when he returned to America in 1869. Rice settled in New York and, in addition to teaching music and languages, wrote for local newspapers and published two books on musical theory, *What Is Music?* and *How Geometrical Lines Have Their Counterparts in Music.* Each was well received but hardly a boon financially. Deciding that he'd rather be rich than poor, at age twenty-eight Rice enrolled in Columbia College of Law, from which he graduated cum laude two years later. He established a practice that specialized in railroad law, immensely lucrative at the time, while also serving as a lecturer and librarian at Columbia's new School of Political Science.[2] In addition, he wrote scholarly pieces for other journals, including a scathing critique of Herbert Spencer's theories of "social Darwinism" in 1883 for the *North American Review.*[3]

Rice's railroad work was not confined to legal briefs. He insisted on investing in the companies he represented, and therein demonstrated a flair for creative financing that made him quite wealthy in only a few years. In 1884, he was appointed as sole attorney for the Brooklyn Elevated Railroad Company, which, after he supervised a financial restructuring, made him even wealthier. The following year, Rice married Julia Hyneman Barnett of New Orleans, one of the first women to practice medicine in the United States. Also in 1885, he founded *Forum,* a magazine that published highbrow articles on politics and finance, theater reviews, and political and literary commentary. Thomas Hardy, Jules Verne, and Henry Cabot Lodge would be among the magazine's contributors. Rice continued to publish *Forum* until 1910.

Although the demands on his time from the magazine and his various business dealings were extensive—he had resigned from Columbia in 1886 to work exclusively on corporate restructurings—Rice was never far from the chessboard. (He was never far from Mrs. Rice either: they quickly had six children.)[*] In 1889, he retired from the law

---

[*] Rice's children also led extraordinary lives. One founded the Poetry Society of America. Another, Marion Rice Hart, was the first woman to graduate from the

to play chess full-time and became a patron of the game. He was elected the president of the Manhattan Chess Club—the most important in the United States—after he helped pay to move the club to new quarters. There he played a long series of practice games with world champion Wilhelm Steinitz, who had won the title in a tournament at the club three years earlier. In 1895, while experimenting with a series of moves called the Kieseritzky Gambit, Rice discovered a variation in which a knight is sacrificed. To tout the Rice Gambit, as he modestly dubbed it, Rice paid some of the world's most eminent players, including José Maria Capablanca, Emanuel Lasker, and Mikhail Chigorin, to analyze his discovery—favorably, of course. He also sponsored chess tournaments with the Rice Gambit required in the opening. He ultimately spent some $50,000 on promotion.*

But the genteel world of rank and file was not sufficient to sate Rice's outsized intellectual energy. He missed the rough-and-tumble of business. While attending the Columbian Exposition in Chicago in 1893, he noticed the disproportion of innovations and gadgets that were electrical. So many entrepreneurs and inventors were rushing to electrical technology, it seemed, that the United States patent office had become swamped with more than three thousand applications per year. Rice also observed that the most sophisticated devices, in-

---

Massachusetts Institute of Technology with a degree in chemical engineering, and obtained a master's in geology from Columbia University. While working as a sculptress in Avignon, France, at age forty-five, on a whim she purchased a seventy-two-foot ketch and piloted it around the world. She served in World War II as a radio operator in the Signal Corps, often aboard a B-17, and became fascinated with airplanes. She learned to fly after the war and eventually made seven solo trips across the Atlantic, the last when she was eighty-three years old. She continued to fly alone, often for thousands of miles, until she was eighty-seven. She had no children and her husband divorced her when she "refused to be like other women."

* There were those who did not consider the Rice Gambit the result of incisive brilliance. In *The Middle Game in Chess,* grandmaster Reuben Fine wrote, "The story of the Rice Gambit is rather amusing. It begins: 1 e4 e5 2 f4 exf4 3 Nf3 g5 4 h4 g4 5 Ne5 Nf6 6 Bc4 d5 7 exd5 Bd6. Professor Rice, a New York amateur, had this position once and inadvertently left his knight *en prise;* then later he won the game. He was so impressed with his success that he immediately interested a number of the prominent masters in the move, which was easy enough to do because he had a lot of money."

cluding Otis elevators and Edison's Kinetoscope, were powered by a new, powerful, quickly rechargeable battery called a chloride accumulator, a lead-acid process that came to be known as "exide" technology, for "excellent oxide." The process appeared to have been patented and the sole manufacturer was the Electric Storage Battery Company of Philadelphia, a city Rice knew well. After some cursory investigation Rice was convinced he had uncovered a company ripe for just his sort of restructuring, and so he began to buy up large blocks of stock.

Electric Storage Battery had been founded in 1888 by a fast-talking promoter named William Warren Gibbs. Raised on a farm in Hope, New Jersey, Gibbs had dropped out of school to work as a grocery clerk, but he had somehow charmed Frances Ayres Johnson, the daughter of a wealthy Philadelphia merchant, and persuaded her to marry him. After the wedding, Gibbs moved to the city to make his fortune and used his father-in-law's connections to secure funding to purchase a gas company. After a year or two, however, Gibbs realized he had chosen a declining technology. He bought up some patents for lead-acid rechargeable batteries, purported to produce more energy for a longer period, although no one had thought to produce them commercially. Gibbs convinced some of his investors in the gas company that electricity would put them out of business and, even though he had put them into that business, cajoled them to fund the new venture. He then set out to build batteries to store power for electric lighting.

The market for chloride accumulators turned out to be much larger than even Gibbs had anticipated. Arrays of Gibbs's batteries were soon employed in a wide variety of industrial processes. In 1891, in a major coup, Gibbs sold thirteen thousand exide cells to the Lehigh Avenue Railway Company to power six of their streetcars. The horseless vehicles were immediately popular and sales boomed. But while revenues poured in, expenses were sucked out. Rather than build up the company's cash reserves, Gibbs began to buy up other companies to expand his reach. At the same time as he was trying to corner Philadelphia's electricity market, Gibbs learned that the patent controlling the exide process might not provide the exclusivity that he and his investors had thought. Patent examiners were, for the most part, ignorant of the mechanics of electrical power generation, and competing patents might actually have predated his.

At that juncture, Rice began amassing stock. He purchased sufficient shares to become a director—and also the company's lawyer—and soon after that gained control. His first act was to buy up every patent that might be a threat, and he spent $250,000 to do it, almost the equivalent of the company's 1894 revenue. But Rice also oversaw the purchase of a number of companies that used batteries, and thus provided a guaranteed market for his product.

For all his maneuvering, however, Rice was no mere stock manipulator. He saw himself as an inventor and a prophet and asked investors to put money behind him on that basis. Those who did were rewarded handsomely. Using hybrid processes from the patents the company owned, Rice oversaw improvements to the original exide product and fabricated the most advanced battery in the world.* He also came up with designs for containers, connections, frames, and switches, thus giving his battery more practical utility. Rice soon quadrupled the company's revenues, taking in more than $1 million, and Rice's batteries were eventually used in machine tools, telegraph offices, home appliances, and even player pianos. Exide generation remained the favored technology for the better part of a century.

But Rice's ambitions were yet more grandiose. In addition to the free-running electric streetcars that had become all the rage, he saw huge arrays of exide batteries powering ships, locomotives, massive telephone exchanges, and office buildings. While none of these came immediately to pass, in 1894 Rice heard of a newly patented device that would do quite well in their place. That year, an electric car was successfully test-driven by two Philadelphia engineers, Henry Morris and Pedro Salom.[4] They called their invention an "electrobat," and their journey down Broad Street required both a special permit and a

---

* The Exide brand was officially adopted in 1900, and so the Electric Storage Battery Company still exists as Exide Technologies. The company manufactures car batteries, but in 2013, with new technologies squeezing their market, filed for bankruptcy.

policeman to precede the vehicle for the protection of horses. Morris and Salom's vehicle was slow and immensely heavy—more than two tons, 1,600 pounds of which were primitive batteries. The wheels were steel to support the weight, and the front set was larger than the rear. Isaac Rice offered to help—and to invest—and the two quickly improved on their design. Soon Morris and Salom had produced a lighter and faster model, 1,600 pounds, of which only a third was exide battery. With the lighter weight came pneumatic tires and front and rear wheels of equal size. They soon had an even more efficient version, 800 pounds, with two 75-pound motors that could run at 15 miles per hour for 20 to 25 miles on a charge from 350 pounds of batteries.

With Rice in the wings, Morris and Salom entered the Electrobat II in America's first automobile race, the 1895 Thanksgiving Day jaunt up Chicago's north shore won by the Duryea brothers. The Electrobat II fared poorly in frigid conditions—as did almost everyone else. Aware that battery life was adversely affected by the cold, Morris drove so slowly to conserve charge that at times he hardly appeared to be moving. He and Salom had placed relays of charged batteries every few miles, but Morris never even made it to the first station. He turned around halfway and barely made it back to their home base before the battery gave out. But the race was a success for the Electrobat nonetheless. They won a gold medal for design and left Chicago convinced they had established beyond doubt both the technical and commercial feasibility of the electric car. Not that there weren't doubters. Hiram Percy Maxim, who rode in the Electrobat as an "umpire" (as had Charles King in the Duryea vehicle), returned to Hartford with "all my ideas as to the storage-battery-driven carriage confirmed."

But Maxim's was the minority opinion, and once back in Philadelphia Morris and Salom set about seeking commercial outlets for their invention. Quite clearly, the limited range of a single battery charge—no more than 25 miles—made the vehicle appropriate to cities rather than country roads. In January 1896, they incorporated as Morris and Salom Electric Carriage and Wagon Company. One of the stockholders in the new company was Isaac Rice. By early 1897, Rice had bought out Morris and Salom entirely. Morris and Salom never said why they sold their patent, but it was a terrible decision. Although they attempted other ventures—they formed the Electrical Lead Reduction Company in 1899, to sell battery components—neither was involved in a successful enterprise again.

Now president of the company—Gibbs was vice president—Rice wasted no time. In March 1897, he announced the introduction of a "public electric cab service," beginning with "twelve vehicles of the coupé, surrey, and hansom patterns, operated with electric storage batteries." The cabs would be "handsomely constructed and finished, and equipped with pneumatic tires." Side running lights and a reading light inside would provide additional touches of modernity. The hansom was fashioned so that "the up-to-date 'cabby' is seated on top of the battery box, from which point the various controlling levers are easily accessible to him. Under his seat is the so-called controller. From this device, which is simply a peculiar electric switch for connecting the battery with the motor for various speeds, a handle projects." Another lever was used for turning, with a treadle for braking, sufficiently effective so that "the vehicle may be stopped within its length even when running at full speed."[5] The idea was so novel that Rice would need the New York city council to grant a "special license . . . as there is no provision for public cabs without horses."[6]

Rice's hansom fleet would be the first use of motorcars for public transportation in the United States. By then, in most of America's major cities, overhead trolley cables had been supplanted by huge rows of exide cells percolating under the feet of a burgeoning number of urban commuters. This, the most successful experiment in mass transit yet undertaken in America, poured money into Rice's coffers—by the time he was ready to launch his first fleet of hansoms, he had achieved a virtual monopoly on storage batteries.

The linchpin of the system was the power and endurance of the exide cell, of course, and thanks to Rice's improvements Electric Storage Battery was producing batteries that had no equal: they provided "the greatest amount of output with the least weight, and combined low cost of production with high efficiency."[7] The life of an exide battery was "one and a half to two years and the cost of replacing the positive plates is far less than that which would have been required to keep a horse shod." With a range of up to 40 miles, a cab could do quite a bit of business on a single charge in the tight confines of New York City.

Like every plan Rice devised, the operating methodology for the hansoms displayed elegance and ingenuity. The cabs obviously could not waste precious battery charge cruising the streets for fares or even waiting, as did horse-drawn hansoms, at taxi stands. Instead, they were dispatched on call from a central charging station that was constructed at 1964 Broadway in a converted warehouse. As a result, most fares originated at restaurants, clubs, hotels, theaters, or the homes of well-to-do individuals, all of which were also the most steady and reliable sources of revenue. "Charging station" was a bit misleading as well. Batteries were not charged while sitting in the beds of the cabs. One of the elements of the battery's design was the ability to quickly remove and replace it in the vehicle. Thus, when a battery was discharged, the driver swapped it out at the charging station and returned to work while the first battery was again brought up to snuff.

Although at first blush this process might seem cumbersome, especially for an array that weighed 1,200 pounds, in practice it worked quite well. An electric crane was mounted on girders above the 16,000-square-foot "battery room." "The batteries are placed on stands arranged in eight long rows, and, corresponding thereto, the crane is equipped with eight electric hoists, one over each row. . . . The vehicle to have its battery removed, or a new battery loaded, is backed up to one of the two platforms so that the opened end of the battery compartment is against the loading table. . . . The further handling of the cab and batteries for loading and unloading is entirely under the control of the crane operator."[8] The mechanism was so well defined that a battery could be switched in less than four minutes, after which the cab would be in service for another 40 miles. Finally, to accommodate any driver who could not make it back to the charging station and had become stranded, a thirteenth cab was always kept in reserve to be used for road service.

The hansom cabs became a fad. "Many of the chappies and men-about-town are availing themselves of the opportunity to try the sensations of riding in a horseless vehicle. . . . Even aristocracy has been bold enough to overcome convention and step into a horseless cab," reported *Horseless Age*.[9] With the experiment working to his satisfaction, in September 1897, six months to the day after Rice introduced the New York fleet, he merged Electric Battery and Electric Carriage and Wagon to create the Electric Vehicle Company. The merged company, incorporated in New Jersey, was capitalized at $10 million, an immense sum at the time, and a thousand times greater than the $10,000 at which Morris and Salom had capitalized Electric Wagon. Rice then announced that he was ordering components for one hundred additional vehicles, this at a time when no more than fifty vehicles per year were produced in the entire nation. Alexander Winton, by then America's leading gasoline car manufacturer, would that year complete only four vehicles.

Producing one hundred vehicles presented quite significant logistical problems—Electric Vehicle did not build its own products but rather assembled motors, carriages, brakes, and other mechanisms purchased from outside suppliers. Building the charging stations required to service the vehicles was also a major undertaking. Suitable facilities had to be found, strategically placed to allow maximum flexibility; then each had to be constructed and staffed by highly trained personnel.

But Isaac Rice, like Henry Ford, had a singular eye for talent. When Morris and Salom incorporated Electric Carriage and Wagon, Rice prevailed on them to hire a young engineer named George Condict. He proved so adept that it is doubtful Rice's plan could have succeeded without him. (Rice may or may not also have anticipated Morris and Salom's departure, but Condict quickly and seamlessly assumed their responsibilities when they were gone.)

No one manufacturer of any of the components, except for the batteries, could begin to fill the entire order, so the cabs arrived with sufficient differences in specifications to make standardization impossible. And the initial order of one hundred vehicles was just the beginning—Rice planned to order hundreds and hundreds more. Any charging station, then, needed to be built to accommodate a variety of different machines. Condict, who had also designed the original station, "a marvel of modern mechanical engineering," created a layout flexible enough to allow for the sort of fast changes that the hansom fleet required.[10] Although building such a facility was obviously costly, the popularity of the electric hansoms created economies of scale in battery production that to some degree balanced out the expense.[11]

In 1898, Rice built his charging stations in Manhattan, and while he fell slightly short of his goal of one hundred vehicles, scores of electric taxis ferried passengers on New York streets. For quite a while, the electric cab was viewed as something of an oddity, a bizarre contraption missing a front appendage, although why proper New Yorkers felt more comfortable staring at a horse's rump than the streets on which they were riding is puzzling. Still, doubtless many did. "There is a seeming brazenness to the whole performance," wrote society columnist Cholly Knickerbocker. "I dreamed once that I walked down Fifth Avenue in my pajamas in the full tide of the afternoon promenade, and I almost died of shame before I awoke. Yesterday, I had something of the same feeling as I sat there and felt myself pushed forward into the very face of grinning, staring, and sometimes jeering New York." But Cholly eventually became inured to the lack of "the protection of a horse in front of me." He simply "returned the wicked glances of the bicycle ladies on the Boulevard, and when I got back to Fifth Avenue I was almost as much at home and felt almost as devilish as the other chappies whose faces were glued to the club windows."[12]

Early in 1899, the electric cab seized the opportunity to achieve wide acclaim, and in doing so, it set in motion a series of events that would doom electric automobiles for a century. February of that year saw a particularly vile stretch of weather plague New York City. Storms, both rain and snow, sometimes one after the other, left many of the city's roads impassable. On the eighth of the month, an unexpected blizzard descended on the entire East Coast and left New York streets "blockaded with banks of drifted snow. The snow on the sidewalks was drifted high over the boot tops of the struggling pedestri-

The electric taxi conquers the snow
William M. (William Manley) Van Der Weyde / Museum of the City of New York

ans. A high northwest wind lifted and carried along in the murky atmosphere particles of solidly frozen snow that cut and stung like so many needles."[13] The conditions played havoc particularly with horse traffic, as "truck horses slipped and fell or were stalled in freezing slush." Even worse, the fire department, which relied on horse-drawn wagons, was "greatly handicapped." With railroads also knocked out, the only vehicles that seemed capable of navigating through the ankle-deep frozen slush were Electric Vehicles' cabs. As a result, every taxi they could put on the street was full virtually every minute. The "whole rolling stock of the company in active operation [was] literally coining money."

Even better, every New York pedestrian who was forced to slog through the slush with frigid, sodden feet could see his or her more fortunate fellow citizens being transported to their destinations in comparative luxury. The streets were not cleared for nearly a week, just in time for a brief thaw, a rainstorm, and a return to subfreezing temperatures. Once again, the only public conveyances that could negotiate the ghastly conditions were the pneumatic-tired electric cabs.

By the end of February 1899, all doubts about the commercial potential of the electric car had vanished. Not one month later, the speculators arrived, led by the rapacious, charismatic Jekyll-and-Hyde financier William Collins Whitney.

Few men in the history of American business are more enigmatic. Patriarch of the great family fortune, Whitney was at once a political reformer and a political hack, a man whose sound management saved New York City millions and one whose stock manipulations bilked both private and public interests out of just as much, a generous patron of the arts and the epitome of Gilded Age greed. Dubbed "Warwick the Kingmaker" by Elihu Root, after the fifteenth-century English earl, Whitney was described by a muckraking journalist as "having wonderful mental gifts ... brilliant, polished and suave ... physically handsome, loved by most men and all women ... displaying those talents for diplomacy that made him the mastermind of presidential cabinets and the maker of American presidents."[14]

Whitney was born into a distinguished family in 1841, and although he would have been ideal officer material for the Union Army, he spent the war in school. He graduated from Yale in 1863, then studied law at Harvard, after which he joined a prominent New York firm. Whitney combined law and politics, helping to organize the reform-minded Young Men's Democratic Club, and then became, with Joseph Choate, one of the young attorneys Samuel Tilden employed to build the case that eventually brought down Boss Tweed. His own foray into elective politics was not successful: he failed in a run for district attorney in 1872. But when Tilden was elected governor in 1875, Whitney was rewarded for his loyalty with an appointment as New York City's corporation counsel. In his seven years at that post, Whitney helped recover a substantial portion of the loot that Tweed

William Collins Whitney

had appropriated from city coffers, estimated at as much as $20 million. He also oversaw agreements with private contractors and holders of city franchises, experience that he would later put to good use.

Whitney resigned in 1882, his reform credentials unblemished, and set to work to get Grover Cleveland elected president. He was one of Cleveland's most successful fundraisers and also demonstrated a deft touch in smoothing over party infighting. When Cleveland won, Whitney was appointed secretary of the navy, where he "achieved an enviable record in converting the existing navy of antiquated vessels, mostly wooden, into a modern navy of steel built economically and efficiently."[15]

When Cleveland was returned to office in 1892, Whitney had been so instrumental in his election that he was offered any job in the administration he wanted. But Whitney was finished with public service. He decided that he needed to work full-time on his ambition to become very, very rich.

Just because William Whitney had spent years in government rooting out conflicts of interest did not mean that he had none of his own. In fact, Whitney had spent much of that time investing in businesses that, with his insider's knowledge of New York politics, he knew could be exploited for sizable profit. In the 1880s, he teamed with a group of like-minded investors and set in motion a campaign to monopolize the surface trolley business, first in New York and then in major cities across America. The group's longer-term plans included similar acquisitions of gas and electric lighting companies. Although the syndicate had no formal structure and not every member participated in each of the deals, they operated sufficiently in concert to eventually be dubbed the "Whitney-Ryan trust." Other members included stockbroker Thomas Ryan—whose middle name was, appropriately, Fortune—and Philadelphia's Peter Widener.

They began in earnest in 1884, when "the transit situation in New York was an especially tempting one . . . some thirty independent street railways [that] operated largely on perpetual franchises, for which they paid practically nothing into the city treasury. Each company aimed only at cultivating its own traffic and never considered the convenience of the city as a whole."[16] As a result, in addition to often having to pay multiple fares and following a "zigzag course" to their destinations, riders were forced to endure cars that were "small, unventilated, shockingly filthy, and broken down."

His years as corporation counsel had left no one more acquainted with railroad law or better equipped to outflank city franchise regulations than Whitney. Widener, who was the son of an immigrant bricklayer and had made a fortune in, among other ventures, railroad speculation, was a force in Philadelphia's particularly dirty political culture. Ryan, also from a modest background, was a seasoned Wall Street operator who saw great potential in light rail. They shared high intelligence, unvarnished ambition, and the willingness to push hard against the letter of the law while trampling on its spirit.

"Whoever hoped to monopolize New York transit had to control Broadway," so Whitney began there.[17] At first, both Widener and Ryan were aligned with competitors for the franchise, but they soon banded together to ruin the franchise holder, Jacob Sharp—who in 1886 was indicted on twenty-one counts of bribery, a crime of which he was surely guilty, although so was everyone else—and then took over the Broadway and Seventh Avenue Railroad themselves. From there, the new partners spread their net, acquiring one surface and elevated rail franchise after another; in most cases, the licenses, worth millions, were granted "practically as gifts . . . even in the face of existing laws that apparently protected the city's rights." Those laws, which required that every franchise be awarded at a public auction, were circumvented by Whitney and Ryan on the grounds that the new franchises were merely extensions of existing ones, a claim that was transparently false. In other cases, where auctions were held, Whitney used his connections in government and the courts to obtain rulings disqualifying the competing bidders. A good deal of money obviously changed hands during these machinations, although neither Whitney nor Ryan was ever implicated. By the time the Panic of 1893 set in, the partners had achieved a virtual monopoly: only two of New York's horsecar railways were not under their control. (One of the two was the Third Avenue Railroad, the second-most-important franchise in the city, whose owner, Henry Hart, briefly outwitted the cabal before ultimately succumbing.) Whitney and Ryan then consolidated their purchases by forming the Metropolitan Street Railway Company, essentially a holding company, to which they leased most of the franchises.

The future of public transportation and public utilities, the syndicate agreed, was not in horse power, but they were undecided as to whether steam, compressed air, or electricity should be their technology of choice. They experimented with each, including installing underground steam cables to mechanize some of their franchises. They also decided to invest in storage batteries. When exide technology demonstrated itself superior to any other, the group bought up stock in the Electric Storage Battery Company, until they held a significant minority stake. At first they saw the devices merely as a means to store energy produced in surplus by generators during off-peak hours, power that could then be returned to the system during peak periods to supplement the generators' output, a process called "load leveling."

In 1898, when Isaac Rice's electric taxis first demonstrated serious potential, however, Whitney and his confederates altered their plans. "Since they were already experienced in the art of merger and stock manipulation, it was natural enough for these men to decide that electric taxicabs offered a useful adjunct to their traction interests, particularly with the battery patent offering monopolistic possibilities."[18] The syndicate bought even more stock in Electric Vehicle, bringing their total holdings to more than $1 million. But maneuver as they might, they could not wrest control from wily Isaac Rice.

After the February 1899 blizzard, however, Electric Vehicle became a Wall Street darling and the stock price soared, appreciating from about $20 per share to as much as $150 per share. There was no longer any possibility of Whitney and Ryan gaining a majority interest in the company without buying out Rice and even Gibbs, who had retained his minority interest. The parties met in March 1899 and settled on a price of $141 per share, an enormous profit to Rice and Gibbs. Rice would remain on as titular president, but his tenure with the company had effectively ended.

Just weeks after buying Rice out, Whitney traveled to Hartford, Connecticut, to meet with Albert Pope, who had recently initiated his expansion into motorcars. Pope and Whitney got along well—one monopolist to another—and on April 19, they came to terms on the most ambitious plan of expansion ever undertaken in American transportation.

The motor carriage division of Pope Manufacturing would be acquired by a new entity, the Columbia Automobile Company, which would then merge with Electric Vehicle and Electric Storage Battery (still technically the parent) to form the Columbia and Electric Vehicle Company, taking over Electric Vehicle's assets plus $1 million to be paid by the Whitney syndicate. The plan was to introduce taxicab fleets in every major city in America, projected at an astronomical twelve thousand vehicles. The new company would build its electric cars in Pope's Hartford factory, purchasing the batteries at a tidy 20 percent over cost from Whitney's Electric Storage Battery. The consortium also acquired some small electric automobile manufacturers. By 1900, the Electric Vehicle Company was, at least on paper, the largest automobile maker in the world.

The bicycle end of the Pope business was spun off into the Hartford Cycle Company. After a merger of more than a dozen smaller firms engineered by Pope and his cousins late in 1899, Hartford Cycle became a division of the American Bicycle Company. While American Bicycle fell victim to the declining market and declared bankruptcy in 1902, Pope once again demonstrated that he was a tough man to put out of business.

At his instruction, some of the bicycle affiliates had begun to make automobiles, almost all gasoline, and these operations were continued when American Bicycle was reorganized as the International Motorcar Company, which was soon changed to the Pope Motorcar Company, its principal factories located in Toledo and Indianapolis. Pope also converted the unused capacity of the Hartford plant to automobile manufacture. In 1903, he created the Pope Manufacturing Company to consolidate the Pope Motorcar Company and the remaining assets of the American Bicycle Company. He would manufacture automobiles until his death in 1909.

For Whitney's group, the Pope acquisition was merely the base of the pyramid. Soon after it was completed, they established the Electric Vehicle subsidiary as a holding company for the individual operating companies planned for each major city. (In May 1899, the first of these was obtained when Whitney and Widener bought control of "nearly all the surface and elevated railway lines" in Chicago, paying their previous owner, Charles Yerkes, "something less than $20,000,000.")[19] The following year, the parent company would again be reorganized and the Electric Vehicle Company would acquire Columbia, leaving Electric Vehicle as parent company for the entire organization.

These serpentine maneuvers were hardly affectations. With each assignment of subsidiaries or reorganization, the Whitney syndicate extracted profits, protected itself against losses that might accrue to ordinary stockholders, or insulated itself against any liability that could result from mismanagement or worse. Electric Vehicle eventually issued more than $20 million in stock, with authorizations for an additional $80 million in the various regional companies under its umbrella. With such intense dilution, especially for a company making modest profits, only a huge success would make public shareholders any money. Whitney and the rest, of course, had awarded themselves enormous blocks of stock, for which they had paid nothing, and they could sell at the very moment the speculative fervor that they had stoked was at its most intense.* Hiram Percy Maxim, no fan of either the electric car or his employer's new associates, later noted, "The scheme was a very broad one, promising all manner of possibilities in the way of stock manipulation. Whether it was intended to develop profits out of earned dividends, or by unloading the stock on the public, I will not venture to guess. In those days of wild finance, unloading upon the public was very fashionable."[20]

Maxim was equally vociferous when the mergers were being consummated. He told anyone who would listen that the deal as structured, attractive as it may have appeared, would end in disaster. But Maxim's was virtually the only voice of dissent within Pope's organization. In addition, he tried to convince his colleagues that gasoline, not electricity, was the future of automotive technology. Maxim was furious when Pope and the other senior executives dismissed his complaints out of hand.†

But Maxim's cavils looked silly in the face of the thousands of new automobiles dangled in front of Albert Pope's nose. In July 1899, Isaac Rice, still officially president of the new concern, announced that

> he had placed orders for $8,000,000 worth of electric carriages. This means 4,200 new vehicles, and this number will not begin to supply the big demand that is being made in all directions for the new-fangled vehicle. The delivery of the carriages will begin the latter part of this month and will go on regularly until the order is filled. The big order was given

---

* Whitney would make tens of millions of dollars by dumping his Metropolitan Street Railway Company stock. Upon his death in 1904, not a single share remained in his portfolio.

† Maxim would eventually strike out on his own, making his mark in a number of industries. He invented the car muffler and the gun silencer, pioneered a system of radio relays, and was active in aviation, astronomy, yachting, and cinema.

to the Columbia and Electric Vehicle Company, one of the subsidiary companies of the Electric Vehicle Company. It is said that all of the 4,200 vehicles could be put to instant use if they were finished now. The Electric Vehicle Company has a demand for more than it can supply at present.[21]

Other than the final sentence, virtually every word in that pronouncement proved to be false.

Whitney might have been reckless with stockholder money, but he had been a corporation counsel for too long not to be fastidious with his own. Early on, he inquired as to whether anyone had checked to determine not only whether the new venture would infringe on existing patents but also if there were any unrelated patents out there that it might be useful to buy up. Whitney heard that Pope's auditor, Hermann Cuntz, was purported to be something of a patent whiz, so he was assigned the task.

Cuntz soon reported back that Electric Vehicle seemed to be in the clear insofar as battery technology was concerned, but there was an obscure gasoline motor patent that, as Cuntz read it, might well control every automobile of that sort that had or would be constructed. It belonged to a man no one had ever heard of. His name was George Selden.

SELDEN REDUX

A fter the buyout, the fortunes of the erstwhile partners of con-venience, W. W. Gibbs and Isaac Rice, diverged.

Gibbs could not seem to do anything right. Within five years, he had declared bankruptcy, been accused of fraud, moved from his Philadelphia Main Line mansion to a tiny house, and forced his son to drop out of Harvard. The last of these had a serendipitous result, as the son, William Francis Gibbs, became perhaps the fore-most naval engineer in America, designer of the SS *United States*. The younger Gibbs later declared that he "never would have amounted to anything" had his father not gone bankrupt.

Rice fared a good deal better. He resigned from Electric Vehicle in August 1899, his final link with the company severed but his belief in the potential of electricity undiminished. One of Electric Storage Battery's other customers was a self-taught Irish-born engineer named John Philip Holland, a former music teacher in a parochial school, who was in the process of developing the first self-sustaining subma-rine. Holland, an Irish nationalist who began his quest in an effort to develop a weapon against the British navy, had been working on his idea for thirty years. He completed his first prototype in 1878—a one-man submersible powered by a foot treadle—and went from there to building machines of increasing sophistication for the next two decades. In 1893, with the Navy Department sufficiently interested in submersibles to offer $200,000 to the winner of an open competition for a workable design, Holland secured the necessary financial backing to form the John P. Holland Torpedo Boat Company and enter the fray. He won handily and was given a government contract, but by 1899, with war declared against Spain and the navy procrastinating, Holland ran out of money.

Even before his negotiations with the Whitney syndicate were concluded, Rice offered to step in. With the proceeds from the sale of Electric Vehicle, Rice purchased a controlling interest in Holland's company, a stipulation of the deal being that all patents held by Holland personally would be transferred to the corporation, which meant to Isaac Rice. Rice also bought out the Electro-Dynamic Company, which made the motors for Holland's submersibles, and combined the two in a new corporation, the Electric Boat Company. As with Morris and Salom, once Rice had acquired the patents he both put his own stamp on the design and marginalized the original owner. Holland, like Morris and Salom, was eventually forced out and remained bitter for the rest of his life toward the man he accused of stealing his company.[*]

In 1900, Rice used another part of the Electric Vehicle proceeds to purchase land at the corner of Riverside Drive and West 89th Street in Manhattan, on which he erected a four-story Beaux Arts mansion he called Villa Julia, after his wife. Rice designed much of the interior himself. Villa Julia took three years to build and included a sound-proof chess room in the basement cut out of solid rock.[†]

---

[*] In 1914, a year before his death, Rice sold his Electric Boat stock at a $2 million profit, roughly $4 billion in today's dollars. During World War I, Electric Boat built eighty-five submarines for the U.S. Navy. In 1952, the company was reorganized as General Dynamics, which today remains a major defense contractor.

[†] Villa Julia was to be torn down in 1980, but it was saved by Jacqueline Onassis as a historical site. It has since become the decaying home of Yeshiva Ketana, an ultra-Orthodox Jewish boys' school.

In 1906, to combat the increasing din from the spate of gasoline automobiles that had proliferated on the streets of New York, Julia Rice founded the Anti-Noise Society. That same year, Isaac Rice received a summons for the unlicensed use of an electric vehicle in Central Park.

Electricity might have been the making of Isaac Rice's fortune, but it was not going to add to William Whitney's. Within three years, Hiram Percy Maxim's prediction as to the limitations of electric vehicles was proven correct.

Whitney and his cohorts had taken on a project that needed more than clever financial structuring. Charging stations were costly and labor intensive, and for all the clean, quiet operation, batteries had severe limits in both power and charge—a 40-mile range for a new battery and only 18 miles after continued recharging, a process that took eight hours. That stunted range might have been manageable in large cities, but it was highly problematic almost anywhere else. The only way to make the venture succeed, then, was through continued innovation, particularly in battery life and efficiency; deft control of costs; and intelligent, hands-on management at all levels, from designing and building the charging stations to managing the drivers—just the sort of things at which Isaac Rice had proved particularly adept.

But the Whitney team did not buy into electric vehicles to laboriously improve an emerging technology. They were interested only in the sort of rapid expansion that could lead to equally rapid and highly profitable turnover. From virtually the moment they acquired the company, its allure began to wane. Daunting operating challenges aside, the Whitney group seemed to have vastly underestimated the effort involved in getting the vehicles built. Even to reach the initial quota of one hundred hansoms involved purchasing, machinery, and organization well beyond the scope of anything attempted in automotive technology to that date.

And although novelty was a strong selling point, getting the public to accept motor vehicles as part of their daily lives was hardly a certainty. Matters were not helped on September 13, 1899, when one of Electric Vehicle's taxis gained the distinction of striking and killing Henry Bliss, a real estate salesman, as Bliss stepped into the street at 74th Street and Central Park West, the first recorded death of a pedestrian caused by an automobile in United States history. Although Bliss's mishap was ruled an accident and would not in itself dim the enthusiasm of New Yorkers for their fleet of electric taxis, it proved a harbinger.

As the diseconomies of the electric engine manifested themselves, Whitney's group cast about for potential alternatives. Although the racing craze had gripped America, at that point gasoline remained a filthy, smoky, cacophonous power source, unacceptable to most of the wealthy patrons who purchased the bulk of private motorcars. "People seem to expect that automobiles should not only be horseless, but noiseless," *Automobile* magazine lamented in early 1901. There had, however, been sufficient improvements in the technology—and in sales—to pique the group's interest. So they called in Hermann Cuntz.

Choosing Cuntz was perhaps the only sound management decision that the Whitney group made. He turned out to be one of those remarkable hires more responsible for the success of a business than the CEO.

After Cuntz stumbled across the Selden patent, he had urged its purchase, but most of Whitney's group sniffed and proposed the company simply ignore it, as had everyone else. After all, it held no real invention and was for a laughably obsolete design. But Cuntz knew better. He was, as it happened, both a patent attorney and an inventor in his own right—he held a variety of patents for such devices as a gear cutter, a "hand and indicator" for watches that could be coated with radium and made luminous, and a snow-melting machine.

Cuntz once more insisted that, regardless of how primitive the described device, the patent appeared quite solid. In addition, with the concept of "pioneer patents" having been recently introduced into jurisprudence by the Supreme Court, he was convinced that the Selden patent held even greater profit potential than the electric motorcar. That finally won Whitney's attention. Outside patent attorneys were consulted, and they agreed that the Selden patent seemed to control the art. Whitney and his cohorts instructed Cuntz to purchase the license.

But by then there was competition. After nosing around a bit, Cuntz discovered that another group of Wall Street speculators had set aside $250,000 to acquire the Selden patent, though they had yet to contact Selden himself. Cuntz left immediately for Rochester to make a deal before Selden got wind of the other offer. Like everyone else involved, Cuntz was, at that point, unaware that Selden held *only* a patent. Once he realized that there was no product or facilities to acquire, Cuntz persuaded Selden to sell for $10,000 and a guaranteed $5,000 yearly stipend, against which a royalty of $15 per car would be applied. Although he did ultimately make hundreds of thousands of dollars, it appears that Selden never learned how cheaply he had given up his monopoly.

Securing Selden's patent, however, in no way meant that Whitney and his colleagues had abandoned their original scheme. Only the timing had changed. They remained convinced that they could still turn a tidy profit on electric vehicles by building—or appearing to build—a far-flung network of facilities and then selling their interests before the edifice collapsed. The Selden patent could be held in abeyance until that portion of the plan had been actuated.

But Whitney and his fellows had miscalculated. The complex web of subsidiaries that they had created to finance the deal soon came under scrutiny and was revealed—like Selden's road carriage—to have only paper assets with neither actual sales nor prospects. Investors and newspapers began to talk of fraud, and lawsuits were initiated by minority shareholders. The stock price plummeted.

Under increasing pressure, the Whitney group decided to utilize the Selden patent at once to demand license fees on gasoline motorcars that would, if nothing else, provide an income stream. Fully expecting gasoline car manufacturers to scoff at their demands, the Whitney group prepared legal briefs to enable it to quickly initiate infringement suits. So, just as he had never built the automobile for which he was granted his patent, George Selden, still in Rochester, would have no role in the landmark legal case that bore his name.

When undertaking infringement suits, the usual strategy is to attack the weak first—bring litigation against companies that lack the resources for a protracted legal battle—and then, when those have agreed to pay licensing fees, use the precedent to begin to stalk more robust prey. But Whitney's group did not have the time to let such a protracted scenario play out. Instead, their first suit was filed against a large supplier of engines, the Buffalo Gasolene Motor Company, and the second against the most successful of the gasoline automakers, Alexander Winton. If these two could be brought to heel, the thinking went, every other manufacturer was sure to follow.

The Winton Company, in particular, seemed a risky choice. By 1899, Winton had sold more than one hundred automobiles, making him by far the most successful manufacturer of gasoline vehicles in the United States. His exploits on the racetrack and in cross-country driving had left him a renowned public figure. Almost certainly Winton had not known of the Selden patent, and so he most likely saw the demand for licensing fees as the transparent dollar grab it was. As a result, when the Electric Vehicle Company initiated legal proceedings, Winton vowed to fight, as did Buffalo Gasolene. To help defer legal expenses, other makers of gasoline-powered cars agreed to fund a protective group, the Manufacturer's Mutual Association. As an opening gambit, each defendant filed a demurrer, essentially a motion that the case be dismissed out of hand.

Demurrers are pro forma and both motions were rejected, which was not a surprise, but the judges' rulings turned out also to seriously undercut the defendants' ability to mount a successful defense, which was a surprise indeed. Electric Vehicles' legal team, it seemed, had been extremely clever in choosing the venue for its suits.

Winton's motion went before Alfred C. Coxe, nephew and former law partner of notorious political boss and corporate apologist Roscoe Conkling. (Conkling had once claimed before the Supreme Court, somewhat successfully, that the Fourteenth Amendment had been enacted for the protection of corporations rather than freed slaves.)

Coxe had been appointed as a federal judge by Chester A. Arthur, a Conkling associate, and later became the protégé of another New York political boss, Senator Thomas Platt. Platt was known for courting monopoly power and would famously nudge a recalcitrant, trustbusting Theodore Roosevelt out of his way by persuading William McKinley to take him on as vice president in return for a promise to deliver New York's electoral votes. Buffalo Gasolene faced a similar situation in going before Judge Hazel, whose background and associations were similar to Coxe's.[1]

Rather than simply reject the demurrer and allow the cases to proceed to trial, both Coxe and Hazel went to great lengths in their rulings to assert that the Selden patent deserved pioneer status, meaning that the broadest possible latitude would apply. Such strong and unambiguous language established precedent and could not help but create a favorable atmosphere for the Selden interests if and when the cases were actually tried.[2]

Coxe and Hazel had therefore wholly changed the playing field. What the gasoline car manufacturers had likely considered a nuisance action was now a definite threat to their business. Whitney was sufficiently notorious that his adversaries knew not to underestimate him, but that he might hold the exclusive license to build gas cars was an unexpected cataclysm.

While the scales had tipped his way, Whitney's position was not all that strong either. Lacking the means to produce a gasoline automobile himself, he would be unable to establish a traditional monopoly—he needed manufacturers willing to actually build the cars or there would be no licensing fees to collect.

It turned out, however, that Electric Vehicle's lawsuits had provided the impetus for the perfect accommodation between the combatants. Many of the larger carmakers were more than happy to come to terms with Whitney—at the right price—if by doing so they could limit the licenses that Electric Vehicle granted and thus drive the smaller, independent operators out of business. The Whitney group grudgingly agreed to negotiate. When it began to appear that Selden's patent might enhance their profits rather than limit them, the gasoline faction withdrew support from Winton's defense and the Manufacturer's Mutual Association became a shell.

Unable to bleed the licensees, in early 1903 Whitney came to terms. Selected manufacturers—most from the MMA—were allowed to form the Association of Licensed Automobile Manufacturers (ALAM), which would pay modest royalties to the Selden group but would also be allowed to restrict membership and thus licenses to manufacturers of their choosing. To entice Winton to join them as well as to forgo any countersuit, ALAM agreed to foot the legal expenses of any automaker that had been the object of infringement proceedings. Winton, of course, was the only manufacturer that fell into that category. And so, in return for reimbursement of the more than $43,000 he had spent on lawyers, Alexander Winton became perhaps the most auspicious member of a trade group whose sole purpose was to inhibit the very sort of open-source innovation that had allowed the group's members to establish their own businesses in the first place.

The Selden patent had thus effectively been transferred to ALAM and, in exchange, the Whitney group had obtained the manufacturing facilities it lacked. Any maker of gasoline-powered cars that was denied admission by the ALAM executive board could be put out of business if and when an infringement case resulted in an adverse judgment. ALAM members had gone from victims to oppressors. Almost all of the independents sought to join; some were admitted, some not. One of those denied admission was Henry Ford.

CHAPTER 12

FORD BEGINS
HIS ALPHABET

Victory over Alexander Winton at Grosse Pointe once again provided the impetus for a new automobile company for Henry Ford. This time, both Ford and the Ford name would stick. As Ford told it, "The *999* did what it was intended to do: It advertised the fact that I could build a fast motorcar. A week after the race I formed the Ford Motor Company. I was vice-president, designer, master mechanic, superintendent, and general manager."[1]

In fact, Ford had been planning for months to move on from Tom Cooper to a new set of investors. As early as May 1902—three months before his breakup with Cooper—Ford had solicited a local coal baron named Alexander Malcomson as a potential new backer. Malcomson—who marketed his product under the brand name Hotter than Sunshine—was a popular, well-connected Detroit man-about-town, who happened to have a rich uncle who owned a bank. He was also a notorious speculator and almost always in debt—often to his uncle—despite the revenues that streamed in from his six coal yards. Malcomson wanted very badly to get into the automobile business—there were few businesses Malcomson did not want to get into—and when Ford presented his plan for a car that could be sold cheaply and in large numbers, Malcomson enthusiastically agreed to fund a partnership. (That Ford had presented the same idea to two previous groups of investors but failed to follow through dissuaded Malcomson not at all.)

In August 1902, before the *999* racer had even been built—and two months before Cooper had been accused of sneaky behavior by Clara Ford—Malcomson and Ford signed a memorandum of agreement. Ford entered the new business with a design for a production model, for which he provided the overview and Harold Wills drew the blueprints.

For a half interest in the new venture, Malcomson agreed to front the $3,000 Ford said he needed to start and to supply any additional financing the venture would require. What he did not divulge either to Ford or to those to whom he already owed money was that, to raise the capital, he would need to pledge all his credit. If Ford once again failed to produce, Malcomson stood to lose his coal yards as well as his automobile.[2] For his efforts, Malcomson would ultimately suffer the same fate as Ford's other partners and, like everyone whose money Ford needed, would earn Ford's lifelong animus for providing it.

As his first official act, Malcomson, although he did not know it at the time, made perhaps his greatest contribution to the new venture's stunning success, and it was not financial. In an attempt to keep news of this latest bout of speculation from his debtors, particularly his uncle, Malcomson opened the bank account of the new company in the name of his office manager, James Couzens. Couzens was also told to work with Ford, both to handle the business side of things and to keep careful watch on where the money went. Malcomson might be impetuous, but he wasn't stupid.

That assignment turned out to be a stupendous stroke of luck for Henry Ford, because if he had had the option he never would have hired Couzens. The two men were different in almost every way, and during their association their feelings for each other would range from mild antipathy to outright loathing. But each man brought to the company vital skills that the other lacked, and for more than a decade, they put up with each other and became immensely wealthy in the process.

Couzens was nine years Ford's junior and had emigrated as a teenager from his native Ontario to Detroit. There he found a job inspecting cars at the junction yards of the Michigan Central Railroad, where he would spend the next ten years.

Even as a laborer, Couzens dressed impeccably and conducted himself with sufficient seriousness to be considered aloof by his fellows. But his superiors appreciated his perfectionism and almost obsessive attention to detail, and he was eventually promoted to supervisor. In the new position, Couzens was to deal with shippers and suppliers, one of whom was Alexander Malcomson. In 1895, the coal man hired Couzens away at double the salary and made him office manager and chief clerk.

The two men worked closely together and eventually developed something of a father-son relationship—a mixed blessing for Couzens, since his own father had been bullying and could exhibit extreme fits of temper, traits that he again encountered at the coal company. But Couzens did not back down when Malcomson's ire got the better of him—Couzens would never back down from anyone—and when someone was needed to guard what might amount to Malcomson's last dollar, Couzens was tapped for the job without hesitation.

Couzens, by then married with three small children, had never appreciated the potential of the automobile, a view that did not substantially change when he met Henry Ford. But to Couzens, a business needed to be managed just so, no matter what the product. For his part, Ford never appreciated the necessity of sound business practices, although he thought he did. Their negotiating styles differed as well. Ford tended to be dry and acerbic, which was often merely offputting, whereas Couzens could be pugnacious and confrontational when the situation called for it (and sometimes when it didn't)—a useful trait for a small business trying to appear more successful than it actually was.

Soon after the August agreement was signed, Ford and Wills began to hire mechanics and craftsmen to build a prototype for the company's new car, which Malcomson intended to call the Fordmobile. Both he and Couzens had decided to market the maker as much as the car, a strategy with which Ford was in hearty agreement.

As the prototype began to take shape—Ford and Wills would produce the engine and chassis and subcontract the body, wheels, and other parts—Ford and Malcomson converted the partnership to a corporation. The November 1902 filing indicated a capitalization of $150,000 divided into 15,000 shares. The two principals split 6,900 of those shares and paid $3,500 for an additional 350, which left 7,750 shares to be sold to the public. The paid-in capital was to be used to finance production and marketing of the company's car.

Unfortunately, while the Fordmobile's name might have pleased its creator, its performance did not—the prototype was wrecked during a test run. Ford and Wills set to building an improved model; Couzens set about looking for investors.

For Couzens, a man who prided himself on overcoming obstacles, the chilly reception he received was maddening. Even with the market for low-cost automobiles beginning to ripen, it seemed no one was interested in investing in Henry Ford. After one particularly dismissive rebuff, Couzens left the man's offices and collapsed on the curb, frustrated almost to tears.[3]

Part of the problem was that, with automobiles becoming more predominant in the public consciousness, a good many crackpots and fly-by-night operators were entering the field, each promising investors vast returns but delivering only red ink, a scenario that had categorized both of Ford's previous ventures. Far more significant, however, was that by the time Ford & Malcomson was incorporated, another manufacturer was already quite successfully marketing the nation's first low-priced, mass-produced automobile, the curved-dash Olds, which would soon be immortalized in the popular song "In My Merry Oldsmobile."*

* The song, released in 1905, had lyrics that were quite racy for the time, with lines such as "They love to 'spark' in the dark old park." The chorus, which began,

Ransom Eli Olds, whose family ran a machine shop in Lansing, 90 miles northwest of Detroit, had cobbled together his first automobile, a steamer, in the summer of 1887. Still in his early twenties, he decided to test his creation on the city's streets at three in the morning. The resulting din prompted neighbors to leap from their beds. During the ensuing panic, "Civil War rifles and sabers were snatched from walls and attics."[4] The contraption soon died and had to be pushed back to the shop, but Olds persuaded his father to begin manufacture of those small steam engines, and the family sold 2,000 of them in the next five years. Olds soon moved on to gasoline engines, "Best Small Power in the World," advertised as "One and Two Horse Power, specially adapted for running Printing Presses, Sewing machines, Lathes, Ventilating Fans, Ice Cream machines, etc." The Olds product, readers of *Scientific American* were assured, was "Simple, Safe, Economical and Durable," requiring "no engineer or extra insurance."[5]

By that time, Olds had also produced an improved automobile, an odd hybrid of gasoline and steam. The vehicle became the subject of a highly favorable article, also in *Scientific American,* which called it "such a practical success" that "an engraving of its appearance" was included. "The boiler is upright," the magazine reported, "and placed between the two cylinders on the rear platform, both engines being connected so as to work as one engine. Just behind the seat are the water and gasoline tanks. The water tank is sufficient for a ten or fifteen mile run, while the gasoline tank is sufficient for a forty mile trip. Over the entire vehicle extends a canopy top, so that the general appearance of the rig is like an ordinary surrey."[6] Olds's new steamer was actually not all that practical, however. It lacked brakes and was so underpowered that on the slightest incline, Olds's wife had to follow on foot with a block of wood to shove under the rear wheels in case of a stall.

The following year, 1893, Olds visited the Chicago World's Fair, where he took a short drive in one of Gottlieb Daimler's cars and

"Come away with me, Lucille," also included, "You can go as far as you like with me."

from there directed his focus solely on gas power. By 1896, he had built a gasoline motor that he considered superior to the German's design; he was granted a patent, and the following year he founded the Olds Motor Vehicle Company.

Olds was obsessive, working sixteen to eighteen hours a day, even on weekends. When a design didn't work, he took it apart and examined it piece by piece to determine the cause and then create a successor that would perform better. He was particularly drawn to engines, but the factory Olds had established was not adequate to manufacture those engines in quantity. Olds "looked around his home town of Lansing and decided that among its twelve thousand residents there were not enough trained machinists to man a factory such as he had in mind. He must be nearer a larger supply of competent labor. Despite the fact that Lansing bankers had been more generous with him than bankers in general were inclined to be with prospective automobile makers, he needed a less timid source of capital."[7]

After briefly flirting with Newark, New Jersey, Olds returned to Michigan to seek the capital he needed to expand. He had acquired a reputation as a mechanical genius, so suitors were not a problem. Olds chose Samuel L. Smith, a copper and lumber magnate from Detroit, who offered him both financing and facilities if Olds would move to the city. In 1899, while Henry Ford was still frustrating his first set of investors by refusing to build a salable automobile, Olds and Smith formed Olds Motor Works, for which a factory was constructed on East Jefferson Avenue in Detroit, the first in the United States built specifically for the manufacture of motorcars.

With Smith's blessing, Olds began to design a variety of models and fabricate the engines to power them. Their first product of significance was a touring car priced at $1,250 that had difficulty attracting a market. While trying to decide where next to focus the company's energies, disaster struck. On March 9, 1901, the *Associated Press* reported:

> The Olds Motor Works, manufacturers of gas engines, automobiles, and other vehicles, was completely destroyed by fire this afternoon, entailing a loss of over $75,000, with

$45,000 insurance. The plant shut down at 12 o'clock noon for half a day, and fire broke out soon afterwards. It is supposed two tanks of gasoline in the building exploded and caused the fire. Two men at work on the third floor were compelled to jump for their lives. The entire season's output of the Olds works, which was stored in the large building, was destroyed.

The account turned out to be inaccurate, however. Before the fire had totally consumed the building, the plant's timekeeper had managed to push one of the cars out into the street, a small, single-cylinder runabout with a distinctive curved dash.[8] Working feverishly to repair the damage, Olds had the plant back up and running in two weeks. Two weeks after that, he told reporters that he intended to meet his previously announced target of ten cars per day. But rather than continuing to tinker, he adopted a strategy that Henry Ford would later claim as his own. "Olds [took] a page from history. Just as Eli Terry found that by standardizing and increasing production, he could reduce the price of his clocks from $25 to $5, so Olds found he could sell a car for $600 if he concentrated on a single model and made enough of them using efficient production methods to keep the cost down."[9] Ten cars a day turned out to be overly ambitious, but that first year, despite the March fire, Olds produced four hundred curved-dash runabouts and sold them all.[10]

He could have sold many more. By early summer, Olds realized he would soon overrun his capacity and not be able to fill all his orders. He particularly needed to increase production of engines and transmissions. For the first, Olds sought out Henry Leland. Leland had not previously worked with automobile components, but after a glance at Olds's blueprints, he signed a contract to produce two thousand single-cylinder engines. These engines soon acquired the reputation as the finest in the industry. For transmissions, Olds approached a pair of hard-drinking brothers, John and Horace Dodge, who were known for manufacturing excellently built bicycles, but who also had never before worked with automobile components. The Dodges, who had

1 CYL. CURVED DASH
OLDSMOBILE, 1905
GROGAN PHOTO COMPANY

Curved-dash Oldsmobile

grown up in poverty, "typically worked eighteen-hour days, slept in the shop, and rarely spent week nights with their families."[11] After a brief meeting, an agreement to build two thousand transmissions was concluded on a handshake. The Dodge brothers would also use their contract with Olds as a springboard to great wealth and success with Ford. As a result of the need to subcontract, Olds was forced to raise his price to $650, but the increase did little to quell demand.

From there, Ransom Olds revolutionized automaking. Remembering a visit to a musket factory where a gun was assembled by a series of workers, each performing a specific task, Olds decided to employ the same technique for automobiles. He set up an experimental production line soon after his factory reopened in 1901, and expanded it the following year. By 1903, the entire plant was devoted to pushing a single model through in numbers as great as the market would bear. By then, with Leland gone, Olds was once more producing his own motors. Raw materials, metal, wood, or fabric, would be delivered to the appropriate station to be machined, cut, trimmed, or shaped; finished components would be completed by degrees, tested, and then assembled until finally a finished car emerged at the other end of the factory.

A 1904 article in the *Detroit Free Press* described the Olds plant with words that might easily have applied to a Ford factory a dozen years afterward.

> Rows upon rows of special machinery are humming and buzzing away, bewildering the onlooker with their number. A great expanse of floor space stretches away before the visitor, along which are arranged these ingenious devices, each with its own peculiar work to do. Some bore out cylinders ... some finish the connecting rods and shafts ... every step in the process of turning out ... a modern car is carried out by a group of these beautiful machines.[12]

The process was an immense success, allowing Olds to build—or assemble, in the case of subcontracted components—thousands of curved-dash runabouts at a time when most automakers could barely turn out one hundred cars in a year. Fabrication translated to sales, and Olds—an ALAM member—would sell an unheard-of four thousand cars in 1903, the year Henry Ford was just beginning production.

Olds's influence extended to the city that would become automaking's hub. In an evaluation of early car manufacturing published in 1921, *Motor World* wrote, "It was Olds' success in Detroit that fixed the center of the automobile industry in that city. It is equally true that the Olds Motor Works was the first to reach quantity production by applying the progressive system of assembly to the manufacture of a single model gasoline-engine driven vehicle, and the first to popularize the automobile with the American people, taking it from the classification of rich man's toy to that of every man's servant."[13]

Ransom Olds was also the first to grasp the value of marketing to the masses. In 1901, soon after the plant reopened, he decided to exhibit his runabout at the November auto show at Madison Square Garden in New York. Rather than ship the car by railroad, Olds assigned twenty-one-year-old Roy Chapin to drive it from Detroit to

New York, where Olds himself would be waiting. Chapin was the son of a Lansing attorney and had originally been hired as a photographer, but he showed such talent at the tiller that he was soon assigned to test-drive Olds's new models.*

Chapin set out on October 29 on what would be an arduous seven-day adventure. The roads across New York State were so bad that Chapin was forced to drive on the Erie Canal towpath, prompting some very unkind words from the muleskinners who claimed right-of-way. When car and driver arrived covered with mud at the doors of the Waldorf Astoria, the doorman refused to believe that Chapin was there to meet a guest of the hotel. Chapin's odyssey did not garner the headlines Olds had hoped for—local newspapers ignored the story—but the little grime-encrusted runabout was a hit at the auto show, and Olds was able to announce that he had landed a deal with a New York dealer to sell one thousand cars in 1902. (The actual number turned out to be 750, still massive for a single location.)

With his success, Olds became the fulcrum on which automobiles moved permanently to gasoline power.

> Of the 2,500 motor vehicles counted in the United States Census of Manufactures for 1899, the vast majority were steam and electric-powered carriages produced in New England plants. By 1900 steamer sales had inched past electrics, with the young industry producing 1,681 steam, 1,575 electric, and 936 gasoline vehicles. Steamers maintained this lead through 1902, at which point the three engine types held roughly equal shares of the market. Not until 1903, when the Olds Motor Vehicle Company's curved-dash Oldsmobile led the industry with 4,000 sales, did gasoline-powered carriages become dominant.[14]

---

* Chapin would found the Hudson Motor Car Company in 1908 and eventually accepted the thankless job of secretary of commerce under Herbert Hoover in August 1932.

By the time Ford, Wills, Couzens, and Malcomson were preparing to design and market a low-priced car, Ransom Olds had provided them a clear business model. Still, Ford needed money, and it did not appear that any local financiers would step forward to provide it. To make the company's future even more problematic, Couzens informed Malcomson that when all the bills came due, Ford would have spent $7,000, more than double the amount that Malcomson had agreed to provide as front money.

Couzens suggested that, rather than becoming a manufacturer, the company subcontract out the entire car, component by component, so that all that would be necessary in its own factory was assembling the finished automobile. The idea was not new—almost every small and medium-sized auto company was an assembler, and even Olds had yet to fabricate his own transmissions. While such an approach involved paying more to a supplier than the variable costs of producing a component themselves, it saved an enormous amount on fixed costs—plant size and machinery—which could allow a good bit of the accounts payable to be covered through sales.

Malcomson took Couzens with him to meet with John and Horace Dodge. In less than a year, thanks to Ransom Olds, the Dodges had not only expanded their tool works but also established themselves at the forefront of automobile machinists. Couzens extolled the virtues of Ford's and Wills's new motor, but before the brothers would work for Ford, "Horace Dodge examined the plans for Ford's new automobile and improved the design of the engine and rear axle considerably."[15] Malcomson then offered the brothers a contract to build 650 chassis—engines, frames, and transmissions—at $250 each, or $162,500 worth of business.[16] This was a much larger and potentially much more lucrative deal than the Dodges had made with Olds. Still, the Dodges would be forced to spend a good deal of up-front money for the machinery to produce the product, and so they did not sign on until Malcomson agreed to advance them $10,000—$5,000 when they had finished retooling and $5,000 when they actually began production. It would turn out to be a wholly inadequate sum. The Dodges would spend $60,000 before they ever saw a penny in return.

Similar deals were struck for other components—wheels, bodies, tires, upholstery—bringing the total commitment to approximately $350,000. The only potential flaw in this plan was that Malcomson had no cash on hand, not even the $10,000 deposit for the Dodges, and, with his credit stretched like a guitar string, no prospects of raising it. His plan was to essentially kite his bills: to gain payment for the cars after they were assembled but before they were delivered, and then turn around and pay his bills with the proceeds. At $850 per car, he computed happily, he would walk away with a profit of $95,000 in the first year. This strategy was risky and extreme even to someone with Malcomson's creative view of credit, relying as it did on maximal sales volume and almost perfectly timed movement of money.

Not surprisingly, it didn't work. Malcomson was soon in full flight, creditors, especially the Dodges, reaching for the back of his shirt collar. The coal baron finally broke down and confessed the entire scheme to Uncle John—John S. Gray, president of the German-American Bank of Detroit—who was waiting for his nephew to make good on a previous loan with which he had bought out a competing coal supplier.

Banker Gray was, of course, appalled. But Malcomson, for all his rashness, had not gotten where he had without some substantial business acumen. He convinced his uncle that Henry Ford's automobile had immense profit potential and that Gray should front the $10,000 to the Dodge brothers; he promised to pay Gray back personally if the venture went under. That, in turn, persuaded a local carpenter, Albert Strelow, to invest an additional $5,000 and supply the premises where the vehicles would be assembled. From there, Malcomson abandoned the notion of funding the new corporation with one large investor and instead went to a series of smaller ones.[17]

Thus, unlike Henry Ford's first two ventures—three, if one counts the *999*—the Ford Motor Company, as it would be called, was bankrolled by a diverse, ad hoc group of twelve mostly ordinary people, some of whom put their life savings into the enterprise. Horace Rackham and John W. Anderson, the young lawyers who drew up the incorporation papers, each invested $5,000, Anderson only after begging the money from his tight-fisted father. Vernon Fry, a dry goods merchant and a member of Malcomson's church, also put up $5,000, as did Charles Bennett, a Malcomson acquaintance who was president of the Daisy Air Rifle Company. The Dodge brothers were persuaded to forgo the $10,000 they were owed and take shares in the new company instead. They would work exclusively for Ford until 1914 and help make each other fortunes.[18] John Gray decided to leave his $10,500 in and accept stock in lieu. (He had added $500 on his own, to ensure he would be the largest stockholder, the better to keep an eye on his money.) James Couzens, no longer a skeptic, wanted in badly but had only $400 in the bank. Malcomson, however, agreed to advance him his $500 bonus and accept a promissory note for $1,500. Couzens took that money, his own $400, and $100 from his schoolteacher sister, and bought shares in the company.[19]

The willingness of this diverse group to ignore Ford's record of antagonizing investors and back his enterprise earned neither his gratitude nor his loyalty. While he would never actually cheat anyone, Ford maintained the fervent belief that investors were at best a necessary evil, to be dispensed with, if possible, the moment there was no further necessity. He remained determined to make his own decisions and not allow other people's money to dictate the new company's direction. Ironically, for the first time his intentions matched those of the men—and woman—who had put up the money, and he finally dedicated himself to building the automobile that he claimed had been his vision since the quadricycle. Had that been the case with the first two ventures, there might have been no cause for their dissolution.

With twelve investors in hand and only $28,000 of actual paid-in capital, on June 16, 1903, the Ford Motor Company was incorporated. (It was Malcomson's idea to take his name off, not Ford's.) John S. Gray was president—at his insistence, although it didn't hurt to have a banker on the letterhead—Ford was vice president and general manager, James Couzens was secretary and business manager, and, in something of an irony given his proclivities, Alexander Malcomson was treasurer. As the company's affairs played out, however, Gray and Malcomson had virtually nothing to do with the running of the company, either in product development or in financial management. Couzens, although without the title, became the actual treasurer of the company.

Ford later claimed that the vision he would bring to fruition in 1908 with the Model T was already fully formed when the Ford Motor Company was incorporated in 1903, and, Olds's success notwithstanding, that it was unique and original. To buttress this argument, Ford pointed to the very first advertisement the Ford Motor Company unveiled, for which he had approved the copy himself:

> Our purpose is to construct and market an automobile specially designed for everyday wear and tear—business, professional, and family use; an automobile which will attain a sufficient speed to satisfy the average person without acquiring any of those breakneck velocities which are so universally condemned; a machine which will be admired by man, woman, and child alike for its compactness, its simplicity, its safety, its all-around convenience, and—last but not least—its exceedingly reasonable price, which places it within the reach of many thousands who could not think of paying the comparatively fabulous prices asked for most machines.[20]

But, in fact, the idea to mass-market lower-cost automobiles was neither new, obscure, nor confined to either the Olds or the Ford company. The same month Ford would sell his first automobile, and a full five years before production of the Model T, a long, remarkably prescient syndicated article, "This Is the Age of the Auto," ran without byline in newspapers across the nation.

> The automobile is no longer an experiment, and motoring is no longer a pastime or a luxury. The old coaching roads

and coaching inns will once more be thronged with travelers. We shall know the land we live in—its rural interests, its beauties, its antiquities. The man who has a business in the town will no longer be dependent upon a slow and rare service of trains. Therefore thousands of the town dwellers of today will be the country dwellers of tomorrow. This will bring into the market at good prices a great number of country places unlettable and unsalable today. There will soon arise, in consequence, an irresistible demand for better roads.

This, however, will be but a minor factor in the coming development of motor traffic. The motor vehicle for business purposes will soon be universal. A few years hence we shall look back with a smile to the practice of the railways and large firms in using horse-drawn vans. Commercial travelers will take their samples through the country in suitable motor-cars. Agriculture will be one of the chief industries to benefit by the coming revolution. I am even inclined to go a step further and hazard the opinion that the motor vehicle will kill the railway.[21]

The trade magazines, of which there were by this time more than a half-dozen, also regularly carried articles on the potential of the automobile—and other gasoline-powered vehicles—for business and on the farm. So while it was not Ford's unique vision that attracted investors to his idea, his plans did contain an element that seemed a significant improvement on what was available from his competitors. "The cornerstone of the edifice was the engine. It was primarily because of their faith in the engine that the experienced Dodge brothers, in the teeth of a strong bid from Olds, had signed the vital contract of the new business."[22] But what Ford never admitted publicly was that the Dodges had corrected a number of flaws in Wills's initial design.

Ford's engine would have two cylinders, set horizontally opposite each other, to Olds's one. This is not to say Ford's machine would be

Ford Model A, 1903

superior. While Olds's one-cylinder motor would not be able to reach the two-cylinder's 8 horsepower or top speed of 28 miles per hour, its performance was more reliable. Each machine featured a transmission with two forward gears and one reverse gear, but Ford's became notorious for transmission bands that slipped regularly, thus leaving the car without power. The Ford car was also prone to overheating, while the Olds was not.

Work had been proceeding apace, and just weeks after the Ford Motor Company became a legal entity, completed "running gear"—motors, frames, transmissions, and axles—began to arrive at Strelow's from the Dodges.* From there, the remaining components were attached and the car was painted. (During testimony in a later lawsuit, Ford would be forced to admit that "the Dodges had made the entire Ford car except the body, wheels and tires.")[23] The only problem was that while the vendors were producing, they were not being paid, because not all the investors had as yet deposited their money and no one had bought a Ford automobile. Couzens stalled as much as he

---

* The problems with the transmissions on the Ford cars were due to a design flaw, not faulty fabrication at the Dodges' plant.

could and remitted funds when he had to, but by July 11, after less than one month in existence, the company's bank balance stood at $223.65. But on that day, Strelow paid in his $5,000 and Ford Motor survived.

Instead of naming the new model, Ford decided that since anything he produced would be constantly improved, he would use succeeding letters of the alphabet. Four days after Strelow saved the company from insolvency, the first Model A was sold, to a Chicago dentist named Ernst Pfennig. (Doctors and dentists were, by far, the professionals who most often availed themselves of the new technology.) Pfennig bought the standard model, $850, without the optional "tonneau," a detachable rear seat, that would have added $100 to the price. The car was shipped to him on July 28, 1903.[24] Other sales followed, and soon the survival of the company, at least in that pivotal first year, was no longer in doubt.

Ultimate success, however, would rest on the reception the Model A received in the trade magazines. Despite being exceptionally light at only 1,250 pounds, containing a number of new features such as an improved carburetor, and being billed by the company as "the most reliable car in the world," the Model A was, in truth, neither better built nor more reliable than its competition.* Nor was it cheaper. The Oldsmobile was priced $100 less than Ford's model even though Olds, as a licensed ALAM member, was paying royalties on each sale. So if significant flaws were exposed in the trades, word would make its way into the popular press and doom the Ford car.

But Ford's runabout, and particularly its engine, received raves. *Cycle and Automobile Trade Journal* wrote:

> The first one of the first lot of 650 Ford automobiles was placed on the road early in June, 1903 . . . the latest repre-

---

* Ford constantly inveighed against weight being synonymous with strength. "Excess weight kills any self-propelled vehicle," he wrote later in *My Life and Work*. "There are a lot of fool ideas about weight. It is queer, when you come to think of it, how some fool terms get into current use. There is the phrase 'heavyweight' as applied to a man's mental apparatus! What does it mean? No one wants to be fat and heavy of body—then why of head? For some clumsy reason we have come to confuse strength with weight."

sentative of the American type of two-cylinder driven vehicles, which is unquestionably destined to hold a high
place among the leading forms of self-propelled carriages.
The two opposed cylinder motor has advantages in the way
of balance and frequency of impulse delivered to the
motor shaft, which produce distinctively smooth running
and strong hill climbing, and there is no possible room for
doubt as to the pronounced success of this form of motor
for driving low-cost and high-duty vehicles of the runabout and detachable tonneau class.[25]

Horseless Age added that when the motor ran at high speed, about
1,000 rpm, it was "remarkably free from vibration and noise."[26]

Cycle and Automobile Trade Journal also indicated that, although its
technology was not new, the Ford machine and not the one-cylinder
Oldsmobile was the future of low-cost automobiles. "Since the Ford
wagon is the latest to be driven by two opposed cylinders, it should
be among the best of its kind, as its designer had the vast advantage
of a number of highly successful examples in the work of his prede-
cessors, as well as in his own previously constructed two-opposed
cylinder driven wagons, to aid him in selecting the elements and determining the detail forms of his latest motor, the last of a series of
conspicuously speedy wagon drivers produced under his direction."[27]
For contrast, the ad on the inside front cover of the journal was for
a Winton 20-horsepower four-seater touring car, much more luxurious than the Model A but with a price of $2,500.

The significance of the Ford Motor Company—new, undercapital-
ized, and hastily thrown together as it may have been—establishing
itself as a participant in an expanding market for low-priced automobiles was not lost on those for whom it would be competition, most
prominently ALAM members Olds and Packard, a newer manufacturer.

Packard had been started in Warren, Ohio, by Col. J. W. Packard, a
quick-tempered manufacturer of wire and cable. After purchasing a
Winton in 1899, Packard thought it terribly flawed and decided that he
could do better. He told the equally quick-tempered Winton as much,

and Winton challenged him to try, so Packard did. Packard's car, a one-cylinder runabout, aroused the interest of his friends, most of whom agreed that the new automobile was superior to Winton's model, and by 1901, Col. Packard was in the automobile business, with his brother as his partner.

The following year Packard licensed a group of dealers, and his 12-horsepower machine with tonneau sold briskly, even though the price was not substantially below what Winton was charging. One of the purchasers was a man from Detroit named Henry Joy, whose late father had been president of the Michigan Central Railroad, where he had once engaged a young lawyer named Abraham Lincoln. Joy stopped in Warren on his way home from New York for a chat with Col. Packard, who, it turned out, was so pleased with his car business that he had decided to expand, assuming he could raise the necessary capital. Joy put together a group of investors with himself at its head, moved the company headquarters to Detroit, and engaged a young architect named Albert Kahn to build a new factory with reinforced concrete—the first of its kind. With the Warren plant continuing to operate, the Packard Motor Car Company entered the industry as a force.

Although Packard continued to produce its one-cylinder model, Joy, himself a rich man, wanted also to build cars that other rich men would want to drive. He suggested a luxurious model with a price tag in excess of $7,000. Col. Packard, whose success had been based on reducing both the complexity and the price of the machine, thought that idiotic, but Joy nonetheless turned much of the company's efforts to producing a four-cylinder, 25-horsepower touring car.

Despite the diversion of resources, Packard's Model F runabout— Packard, not Ford, was the first to use letters to denote their automobiles—remained popular, and Joy finally grasped that it would be sound business to exploit its potential. Henry Joy was not a man to do things in a small way, and he decided to launch a publicity stunt so grand that Packard would explode into the marketplace and leave both Olds and Winton far behind. When Frederic Smith, who by then had effectively taken over Olds Motor from his father (and from

Olds), heard about Joy's plan, he was determined to match it with a similar venture of his own.* Each of the two Brahmins accepted the necessity of slugging it out—as gentlemen—but neither man was prepared to accept an additional competitor in the market for smaller cars, especially an arriviste such as Henry Ford.

In mid-1903, as it happened, Henry Joy and Frederic Smith were also the most powerful voices on the executive committee of ALAM. To these men, the notoriety Ford had garnered from his race cars made him a target, someone to be squashed, not encouraged. The man who had beaten Alexander Winton and built the *999* just might be able to produce a car that cut drastically into their companies' profits. What was more, Smith was none too pleased that Ford had stolen the Dodge brothers out from under Olds, which now meant out from under him. As a result, from the outset, Ford's ability to gain entry into what amounted to a private club encountered quite serious obstacles. Nor would the presence of John Gray as president of the company provide a lever—the men who had faced down William Whitney were not about to be cowed by a local banker.

Ford had been aware of the Selden patent since 1900, and although no record of his early impressions exists, his later pronouncements and his antipathy toward the patent system in general make it fair to say he didn't think much of it. It is a virtual impossibility that he viewed Selden's unbuilt machine as controlling an invention of the sophistication of the automobile. Still, in February 1903, Ford met with Hermann Cuntz at an automobile show and let it be known that he would be happy to operate as a licensed manufacturer and pay the appropriate royalties. He was apparently either unaware of the antipathy in which he was held by ALAM board members or so willing to compromise in order to gain a license that he would accept any conditions to gain entry.

* As a result of Frederic Smith's ascension, Ransom Olds would eventually run into the same trouble Ford had with Malcomson—a key investor who did not share his vision. Smith insisted Olds produce a more expensive model, and when Olds refused, Smith forced him out. Ransom Olds went on to form the REO Motor Company (taken from his initials), which achieved only modest sales for the remainder of the decade.

Cuntz seemed courteous and receptive but, in a surprise to no one outside Ford & Malcomson, Ford was soon rebuffed, although not yet in a manner that would cause confrontation. At that point, ALAM was continuing to portray itself not as an oligopoly, whose purpose was to restrict competition and safeguard profits, but rather as a trade organization, whose primary goal was protecting the public interest. As such, board members insisted that the decision to grant or withhold licenses to "the flower of the industry" was based on strict criteria of capitalization, manufacture, and performance. The association "will not try to shut out reputable and established manufacturers who build a reliable vehicle," they proclaimed in the trade magazines. "It will license all such, but it will license no unreliable upstarts. In this way, the association will protect the public and be a boon to all purchasers of gasoline automobiles."[28] Those lofty sentiments notwithstanding, the association was never terribly precise as to what terms such as "reputable," "established," and "reliable" actually meant. In fact, the standards under which a firm was granted or denied membership often seemed arbitrary.

In a prime example, one of the few specific requirements ALAM was willing to enunciate was that a manufacturer must actually build its cars. Mere "assemblers" would be excluded because of the ease of simply cobbling together an inferior product with a poorly thought-out design from an ill-conceived conglomeration of parts.

Two weeks after he deposited $5,000 to purchase his Ford shares, John Anderson, the young lawyer who had entreated his father for the money, reported a "chance encounter" with Frederic Smith. The two knew each other well, so Anderson inquired about the licensing association. "Smith told him that the ALAM had been formed for the purpose of stabilizing the industry and barring fly-by-night operators and mere assemblers." When Anderson replied that Ford was an assembly plant and asked what they were to do, Smith replied, "Well, we are disposed to be fair. We will take an inventory of their stocks, machinery, and equipment, whatever they may have, give them a fair value for it, and then they quit business."[29] The only problem with Smith's altruism was that, to some degree, virtually every carmaker was an assembler, including his company, Olds. In fact, up until a few weeks prior to their conversation, Olds had been assembling components delivered from the Dodge brothers.

Although he must have been getting a sense that the game was rigged against him, after Ford Motor had been incorporated in June Ford tried again, this time submitting a formal application for membership in the Association of Licensed Automobile Manufacturers. At Smith's and Joy's instigation, an official and dispassionate investigation of Ford's business was ordered. John Gray assured the board that he was happy to put up the $2,500 initiation fee and that the Ford business, regardless of a current lack of actual factory space, was sure to be a going and growing concern. Smith, many years Gray's junior, later said, "Mr. Gray put their case so simply and fairly that I had a guilty feeling of sassing my elders."[30] However, that did not stop him from turning Gray and Ford down. If the Ford Motor Company persisted in manufacturing automobiles, it would do so in violation of the Selden patent and most assuredly be the subject of an infringement suit.

There is more than one account of what happened when Ford and Couzens received the news, but the most popular—and most colorful—was that James Couzens leapt to his feet and bellowed, "Selden can take his patent and go to hell with it!" Ford, who supposedly was sitting in a chair tilted back against the wall, leaned forward, stood up, said to Smith, "Couzens has answered you," and moved for the door. Smith, once more with a pretense of affability, said, "You men are foolish. The Selden crowd can put you out of business—and will." At which point, either Ford or Couzens leveled a finger in Smith's direction and sneered, "Let them try it."

Whether or not this exchange actually took place, the spirit of the reaction of Ford and Couzens is accurate. Both men were combative and, in the fashion of those who often bullied others, became furious when such behavior was aimed at them. Neither of them likely needed additional motivation to make their venture a success, but Frederic Smith and his cronies nonetheless provided it.

The attempt to join ALAM was a blunder, one of the rare occasions when Ford's marvelous instincts failed him. The last thing he needed—or should have wanted—was to cede initiative, to compromise with a group of men whom he was capable of outthinking and outmarketing. But Ford was saved by an even larger blunder: Smith and Joy denied him entry.

Even as he was shown the door by Frederic Smith, the future glimmered on the horizon. Ford began to sell cars, eventually more than one thousand in his first year. At a profit of $150 per car, the company was actually able to declare a stock dividend in 1904.

CHAPTER 13

MAN AND DOG
OVER THE ROCKIES

W ith great fanfare, Henry Joy announced his plan: "I want to have people crying out for Packard machines," he told *Automobile Quarterly* in spring 1903.

In Europe, cross-country car races regularly drew hundreds of thousands along the route, so many that spectators often spilled onto the roadway, leaving only a narrow channel for the racers to squeeze through. A race from Paris to Madrid, to be staged in May, had attracted a stunning international array of drivers and automobiles and was receiving unprecedented publicity, even in the United States. Joy thought to have Packard undertake an equally spectacular journey of endurance on this side of the Atlantic. But instead of a race, Joy would send a Packard Model F across the United States, "with the purpose of demonstrating the ability of the American moderate powered automobile to negotiate the all but impassable mountain and desert roads and trails of the Far West."[1] This was a feat no one had yet achieved and only one man, the redoubtable Alexander Winton in 1901, had seriously attempted. Winton had succeeded in traversing only California and then was forced to abandon the slog when his automobile became mired in the desert sands of Nevada. No one had ventured the journey since, as it seemed doomed due to the lack of adequate roads, particularly in the West. In fact, for much of the terrain between Chicago and California, there were no roads at all.

The Packard would travel west to east, thus guaranteeing maximum exposure when it completed the run in the nation's media capital, New York City. Logistics were daunting since, in addition to the absence of roads, there were no service stations—indeed, no way at all to acquire gasoline outside of major cities, unless it had been shipped previously to predetermined points. Navigating to those points would present an additional challenge because without roads, there were no road maps (although the Union Pacific Railroad map would be put to good use), and the topography, which featured quick descents from 11,000-foot mountains to searing desert, often lacked recognizable landmarks. So Joy, for whom this was a personal as well as commercial crusade, planned with extreme care.*

To drive the Model F across the United States, he chose E. T. Fetch, known as Tom, who was employed at the Warren, Ohio, factory as a test driver and either foreman or plant manager as well. To motivate Fetch not to abandon the journey during times of trouble, Joy arranged that Fetch's payment for the job would be divided up and waiting for him at the same ad hoc depots at which Joy would deposit stores of gasoline and spare parts. A route similar to the one on which Winton became marooned in the sand was chosen, but Fetch would carry lengths of canvas to roll out and lay under the wheels to allow the car to traverse the most inhospitable tracts of soft sand. (Joy also arranged to have an expert mechanic parallel the car's route on a train, an aspect of the plan that he took pains not to publicize.)

To ensure maximum exposure, Joy solicited the trade journals to publish dispatches that Fetch would send whenever he was able to locate a telegraph office. Fetch would attempt to take photographs as well. Marius Krarup, editor of one of the newer weeklies, *Automobile* magazine, thought that was a fine idea, but he had a better one. Kra-

---

* In later years, Joy would undertake the journey himself, in a Packard touring car.

rup offered to ride with Fetch, writing stories of their adventures; an accomplished photographer, he would also keep a detailed visual record of the journey.*

As soon as Frederic Smith got wind of what Joy was planning, he rushed to engage a top driver, Lester Whitman, and a mechanic, Eugene Hammond, both Pasadena-based, to take an Oldsmobile across the country as well. There was no way for the Olds drivers to complete preparations in time to leave before the Packard, or even at the same time, but since the odds of Fetch and Krarup completing the journey were not all that favorable, they were willing to dispatch one of their "Merry Oldsmobiles" weeks after Fetch and Krarup had departed.

To compete in the publicity battle, Smith thought to add some wrinkles to Whitman's trip. For example, he would play up that the Olds weighed only 800 pounds, a good deal less than the Packard—and Ford's Model A. He would also note that it cost only $650, much less than the competition, and was unique in that it had been mass-produced. In another clever bit of marketing, by carrying a single letter, the Olds would become the first automobile to deliver mail coast to coast. Like the men in the Packard, Whitman and Hammond would file both stories and photographs with the trade magazines, and since the most widely read journals, such as *Horseless Age,* were not keen on publishing a competitor's work, they were guaranteed more exposure than a number two would ordinarily receive.

It took the Olds seventy-one days to cross the nation, an incredible feat for a car so light and with only 4.5 horsepower. To prove that the car wasn't spent, Whitman and Hammond left New York City almost immediately for Portland, Maine, where they arrived eight days later. Although they lost twelve full days to breakdowns and were forced to employ a team of horses to tow them 35 miles to a blacksmith's shop after one breakdown in the Nevada desert, Whitman and Hammond demonstrated that the Olds was a sturdy, remarkably well-made automobile that was capable of providing years of reliable service to the average driver at low cost. Almost certainly, that demonstration, which

---

* The photographs turned out to be stunning, possibly the best ever taken depicting early automobiles crossing dreadful terrain.

was featured prominently in their advertising, helped Smith sell those four thousand curved-dash runabouts the following year.

All the same, nothing could make up for not being first. In sending the Olds off so long after the Packard, Smith had bet that the Model F would not make it all the way to New York. It was a bet that he lost.

The Packard set out from San Francisco on June 20.[2] The Model F that Fetch drove had been modified only slightly—the fenders had been removed, and it had been fitted with extra gasoline tanks and an additional low gear for negotiating mountains. In addition to the canvas, Fetch took along a pick and shovel and log chains to get the car through ruts. The car weighed 2,200 pounds stripped and almost 3,000 when laden with equipment. Finally, Fetch thought his chariot should have a name, and since they would initially be following the Southern Pacific tracks, he chose *Old Pacific*.

Fetch detested the route, "straight through the Rocky Mountains and on to Denver," which he believed was chosen by an advertising man Fetch later called a "dumb fool." In fact, Packard's general manager, Sidney Waldon, had chosen the route, but he didn't disagree with Fetch's assessment. "I didn't understand the difficulties and consequently selected the wrong route from San Francisco to Emigrant Gap, Reno, Lovelock, Winnemucca, around the north end of Great Salt Lake, and from Salt Lake City told them to go right through the center of Colorado. Like a dumb fool, I was thinking from the standpoint of publicity, with pictures of the mountains and canyons, but what I sent them into was something terrific."[3] Clearly, Waldon was not using "terrific" in the positive sense.

It took the Packard a full month to arrive in Denver. But the route, as hoped, provided a plethora of opportunities for publicity. A series of regular press releases were issued, such as this one that appeared in *Horseless Age:* "The Packard Motor-car Company reports that E. T. Fetch and M. C. Krarup, who have undertaken to run a Packard automobile from San Francisco to New York City, have reached Wadsworth, Nev. in their progress eastward. This is the first time that an automobile has succeeded in crossing the Sierra Nevada Mountains." They would also cross the Rockies; at 11,000 feet, the Packard set a record for altitude. There were no bridges built to accommodate automobiles, so Fetch had to use more than a little creativity to nudge the Packard along the tracks on railroad bridges. He also learned that the appearance of good fortune could be deceiving. More than once in the early weeks of the trip, Fetch found what appeared to be a well-groomed main road, only to learn after following it, sometimes for miles, that it led only to the entrance of a mine or some wealthy rancher's spread. Asking directions was equally knotty, as few of those encountered on the trail had ever been more than a day or two's horse ride from their homes.

The journey was immensely challenging. Extremes of temperature and altitude were exacerbated by bad food, no bathing facilities, fatigue, and a series of impediments that seemed to have been drawn from a Greek saga. Fetch and Krarup were called upon to use all the skills they had learned and some that they had not, like road construction. When they finally reached Colorado Springs, Krarup wrote of the terrain they had just traversed. "Nevada is awful, but Utah is the worst I ever saw. We carry a pick and shovel along, and we found it necessary in more than one instance to use them when we had to build roads ourselves, cutting along the sides of hills." But a bit farther along, Krarup decided he wasn't keen on Colorado either. "It rained and the water made the alkali roads like soap, making steering impossible. . . . The strain going down into the gullies on the machine was awful and I was afraid something was going to break, but *Old Pacific* stood it all." *Almost* all. At one point the car had to be pulled by a team of horses from a buffalo wallow, but other than that it ran the entire course under its own power.

The wisdom of allowing an editor of one of the minor journals to accompany the expedition became questionable, as reports in the more important publications could be less than enthusiastic. For example, *Horseless Age*'s deadpan report of *Old Pacific*'s arrival in Denver, not published until two weeks after the event, was hardly what Frederic Smith would have hoped for. "The arrival of the Packard transcontinental car from Colorado Springs on the afternoon of July 20 stirred Denver to a more than ordinary interest in automobile affairs . . . a circuitous route was followed through the principal streets to the Packard agency, giving all the population an opportunity to realize that the most difficult and perilous portion of an unprecedented motor-car performance had been successfully finished."[4]

Fetch and Krarup remained in Denver for two days, talking with Packard representatives and taking a well-earned rest. Each had a bath. After Denver, they would not travel on a surfaced road until they reached Illinois.

Still, they covered the eastern two-thirds of the nation in the same amount of time as it had taken for the western third. When *Old Pacific* reached Tarrytown, New York, on August 21, it was greeted by two hundred automobilists who formed an escort to lead Fetch to the finish, "bending all the 8 mile-per-hour speed limits," *Motor Age* noted. A long article in the *New-York Tribune* marked the Packard's arrival in New York City proper.

> The end of the long journey was marked with a good deal of ceremony, and the two men were hailed joyously by a large throng of horseless vehicle enthusiasts, who met them at One-hundred-and-sixty-third-st. and Jerome-ave. and, acting as their escort, brought them down through Central Park, over the Brooklyn Bridge and through the Coney Island Boulevard to a hotel at Sheepshead Bay, where a dinner befitting such distinguished explorers was given by the manufacturer of the car they used. Before the dinner was served, however, the car was run down to the ocean, and its wheels submerged in the deep, thus completing literally the journey from ocean to ocean, as at San Francisco the same formality was gone through.[5]

Motor Age added, "The entry into New York was a triumphal procession, with the brilliant lamps on the machines shining through the dark and all the occupants were singing."

Although the mechanic who had been made available to Fetch and Krarup in the West had come in handy—he left the expedition in Denver—*Old Pacific* had completed the journey requiring no major repairs. When Packard's hometown newspaper, the *Warren Tribune,* reported on the trip, it noted that the completion "demonstrates the superiority of the Packard machine over all other models, and this will be worth all the thousands of dollars it has cost the company." As for Fetch, his sentiments were a good deal more prosaic. When asked to address the hundreds who had come to celebrate his arrival, he merely said, "Thank God, it's over."

The Packard's successful arrival in New York ensured that the Olds, still on the road, would not be feted as the first automobile to cross the United States. But besting the Olds would not reap Henry Joy the publicity bonanza he sought. As it turned out, Fetch and Krarup weren't the first to cross the nation either. To Joy's and especially Col. Packard's chagrin, a Winton, of all things, had beat them to it. Even worse, the driver of that car was an amateur, a physician—and he did it with a dog.

In mid-May 1903, while Henry Joy was carefully planning the Packard's trip, Horatio Nelson Jackson, a physician from Burlington, Vermont, was enjoying a vacation in San Francisco. He happened into a men's club where, over cigars, a discussion on motorcars turned into a wager. Perhaps inspired by Phileas Fogg, one of his fellows proposed to bet Jackson fifty dollars that an automobile could not complete a trip across the country in less than ninety days. Perhaps also inspired by Fogg, Jackson accepted.[6]

Within a few days, Jackson had purchased a slightly used 20-horsepower Winton touring car; named it *Vermont;* hired a mechanic, Sewall Crocker, to accompany him; and stocked up on supplies. On May 23, 1903, more than a month before *Old Pacific's* departure, the *Vermont* took off for New York City. Unlike either of the other two drivers who would follow him or Winton, who had preceded him, Jackson headed north, willing to add more than 1,000 miles to the journey to avoid the Nevada desert. He carried three "cyclometers" to measure distance, but two would be lost on the trip. Much of the territory in northern California, Oregon, and Idaho lacked railroads, and so Jackson quickly and often became lost. They also lost most of their cooking equipment, which dropped off the back of the car after being inadequately packed. Days later, after finally reaching a town, Jackson was forced to wire back to San Francisco for tires, springs, and other parts, which would be dispatched by stagecoach.

After more delays and a number of fits and starts, Jackson and Crocker reached Idaho. It had been almost three weeks since they departed. There, a local man offered them a third member of their team. As Jackson wrote to his wife, "We were stopped by a man and asked if I didn't want a dog for a mascot. As I had been trying to steal one we were glad to get him so accepted the present (consideration $15.00). So Bud is now with us." Bud was soon fitted with his own pair of goggles, of which he became so fond that he would refuse to begin a day's journey without them. As the trip progressed, pictures of Bud began to make it into the newspapers, and he would become the most famous dog in America.

Other than Nevada desert, the Winton encountered all the difficulties that plagued the other cross-country vehicles. Jackson, Crocker, and Bud followed trails, rivers, mountain passes, alkali flats, and the Union Pacific Railroad tracks across the rugged terrain. A number of photographs were staged of the automobile in impossible locations, such as perched on boulders with no apparent means of extricating itself. The blacksmith shop became a popular spot, as there seemed always to be an axle, wheel rim, spring, or transmission part that required repair. Fortunately for Jackson, repairing an automobile part required no special training; for many of the blacksmiths, the *Vermont* was the first automobile they had ever seen.

> The sensation created throughout the country by the passage of these first transcontinental tourists can only be imagined. Whole cities turned out to greet the dust and mud-laden Balboas of the motor-car. Schools were dismissed, and business suspended completely. In Oregon and Idaho, the Winton tourists met many people who never had even heard of a motor-car. Some of them thought the car was an engine that had run off the railroad track and was going wild across their ranches.[7]

One incident, also described in *Motor Age,* epitomized not just what it was like to drive across the United States in 1903 but the degree to

Bud at the wheel
University of Vermont Special Collections

which most Americans outside the big cities were unfamiliar with the automobile.

> They were out of sight of human habitation for days at a time. The only signs of life were the occasional emigrant and his family traveling in his prairie schooner. One of these, when he saw the strange object approaching "at lightning speed," and apparently without any method of propulsion, was seized with terror and jumping down from the seat he hastily unhitched the horses and turned them loose. The whole family then got in the wagon and were on their knees praying when the motor-car came to a stop. They thought the judgment day had come and they were lost. It took considerable talking to reassure them, according to Dr. Jackson's account of the trip.[8]

As Jackson and his crew, often described as "tourists" in the press, neared the center of the country, where telegraph lines were more plentiful, word of their impending arrival reached both cities and small towns, and the *Vermont* was regularly gawked at by entire families who had sometimes traveled for days to witness the miracle for themselves. Jackson had begun the trip strictly as a private venture, without publicizing his departure, so the Winton Company had not received word of the endeavor until Idaho, when Jackson wired to request replacement parts. As the trip gathered momentum—and finally cleared the wilds of the West—Winton sent representatives to meet the travelers as they arrived in cities such as Omaha, where local newspapers would trumpet the amazing achievement of man, dog, and automobile.

After sixty-three days on the road, which included nineteen lost to rest, breakdowns, waiting for parts to arrive, or hoisting the *Vermont* up and over rocks and mud holes, the expedition reached New York. It had cost Jackson $8,000, spent on hotel rooms, gasoline, tires, parts, supplies, food, and the Winton. Jackson told *Horseless Age* that he estimated that he had covered 5,600 miles and that the *Vermont* "traveled on its own wheels every foot of the way. The only times when it did not also run by its own power were a few occasions when horses or a block and tackle were used to draw it across streams or out of miry places. The total of the distances overcome by these methods was said not to have exceeded a quarter of a mile."[9]

The three sets of travelers were hailed as heroes and were credited with inspiring an entire generation of automobile enthusiasts. In particular, their journey made people think about long-distance auto travel as an alternative to railroads. When the Winton, the Packard, and then the Olds chugged into New York, the automobile had been transformed in the minds of many Americans. And what Henry Ford seemed to recognize more than anyone else in the business was the degree to which that transformation would translate into a desire for ownership.

CHAPTER 14

▥ VILLIE K. COMES HOME

s impressive as was the trip across America, the other major
cross-country adventure in 1903 promised to lend even
greater worldwide acclaim to the burgeoning field of automobilism.

The Paris-Madrid race had been the brainchild of Automobile
Club de France. They sent emissaries to flatter Spain's King Alfonso
into supporting the endeavor, which then allowed them to enlist the
Spanish automobile club as a co-sponsor.[1] The race was sanctioned in
February, with the start date eventually set for May 24—a Sunday, to
ensure maximum public turnout—with the first race car leaving at
3:45 in the morning. The course would be 800 miles, divided into
three stages: Versailles to Bordeaux; Bordeaux across the Pyrenees to
Vitoria, Spain; and Vitoria to Madrid. Entrants would be divided into
classes based on weight.* The ACF promoted the event as the largest,

---

* The top class was 1,443 to 2,220 pounds; next was 888 to 1,443 pounds; then
555 to 888 pounds ("motorette"); and finally less than 555 pounds ("motor bicycle"). Actual weights were in kilograms, of course, with the entrance fee based on
class.

most prestigious, most challenging test of man and machine ever undertaken and predicted that hundreds of automobiles would participate and millions of spectators would line the roads to watch them pass.

The notion of commandeering such an immense stretch of public thoroughfare did not appeal to everyone, nor did the prospect of the series of accidents that seemed inevitable on roads clogged with racing machines. When ACF officials first announced their plan, the French premier, Émile Combes, and most of his ministers were in opposition. But the French auto club was not without resources and impressed on skeptics that forgoing such an opportunity to trumpet the preeminence of the French automobile industry would be tragic, even criminal. As for safety, the race was quite manageable, they insisted, particularly if local and national officials would lend suitable numbers of army personnel and gendarmes to help along the roadsides. The left-wing Combes was dubious—particularly since the members of the French auto club, almost all conservative, were hardly his political allies—but, with national pride at stake, he ultimately agreed.

Within weeks of the announcement, the genius of the idea seemed manifest. Entries poured in, particularly in the top class. The very best automakers in Europe—Mercedes, De Dion, De Dietrich, Panhard, Mors—would be sending, or in some cases building, their fastest, most durable, most aerodynamic, and most technologically advanced machines to compete in the most arduous road race ever undertaken.* Some of the racers were rumored to be capable of top speeds approaching 100 miles per hour, a mark that would have seemed preposterous just two years before. The Renault brothers—known for breakneck, accelerator-to-the-floor driving—had designed a lighter-weight car that would go almost as fast.

* Gottlieb Daimler had died in 1900. Emil Jellinek, an Austrian industrialist who had purchased a number of Daimler automobiles, then made a sizable investment in the company, particularly in vehicles for racing. He named the team Mércedès, after his twelve-year-old daughter. (The diacritical marks were soon dropped.) Mercedes and Benz merged in the 1920s and the first Mercedes-Benz was marketed in 1926.

Piloting those lightning machines would be the most celebrated drivers in Europe: Fernand Charron, now driving a car of his own manufacture; Henri Fournier; René de Knyff, winner of Paris-Bordeaux in 1898 and the Tour de France in 1899; Henri Farman, who later become one of France's most celebrated aviation pioneers; Marcel and Louis Renault; Charles Rolls, who would create his own famous brand of automobile and die in a plane crash in 1910; and Charles Jarrott, winner of the 1902 Circuit des Ardennes.

Although a number of American drivers also registered, all would drive European cars. Neither Ford nor Winton considered attempting the race—the Europeans were simply too far ahead. One of the American entrants was William Kissam Vanderbilt II, "Willie K." to his friends, only twenty-five, great-grandson of the Commodore, Cornelius Vanderbilt. Willie K. had become so captivated by automobile racing during the family's frequent trips to Europe that, in addition to driving, he had begun sponsoring automobile races in France while still a teenager.

Willie would compete in the Paris-Madrid in his 80-horsepower Mors. The Mors epitomized the vast gulf between European and American automaking. In 1902, when Henry Ford was building his powerful but crude *999*, Émile Mors was already employing a V-engine, pneumatic shock absorbers, a steel chassis, four-speed transmission, and rear-wheel brakes. For this race, he had designed an aerodynamic wedge nose, which would set a standard for decades to come.

By early May, 280 vehicles had entered, and safety, both French and Spanish officials agreed, had indeed been manageable. "M. Tampier, the official timekeeper of the A.C.F., was officially appointed to examine the roads and report on them, with a view to enabling the racing committee of the Spanish and French Clubs to cho[o]se definitely the route for the Paris-Madrid motor-car race. M. Tampier, therefore, is the best authority on the question of the roads, as he has been over every inch of them carefully. He tells me that as far as Bordeaux the route is in an excellent condition, incomparably good."[2]

And on these incomparably good roads, great things were expected:

The first stage will be the classic route from Paris to Bordeaux—straight and even, without serious hills. The distance is 362½ miles, and was covered in 1895 in about 24 hours, in 1898 in 15 hours, in 1899 in 11 hours 43 minutes and in 1901 in 6 hours 11 minutes, the present record. Presuming it is reduced to well under six hours by machines many of which are claimed to do 80 miles an hour on the level, some of the racers will be starting from Paris two hours after the leader arrives at Bordeaux.[3]

Outside the racing community, the Paris-Madrid had kindled all the excitement the organizers had hoped for and then some. The day before the start, *The New York Times* reported:

All the Americans are leaving Paris to-day en route for some point of vantage whence they can view the great Paris-Madrid automobile race, which starts from Versailles tomorrow, and every Parisian possessor of the humblest automobile, or the still humbler bicycle, will do likewise. It is estimated there will be an exodus of at least 100,000 people. The weather is magnificent. Every town in the neighborhood of Paris on the route of the race is already crammed to the last stretch of its accommodation. No such great motoring event has happened so far in the history of Paris.[4]

As midnight approached, "Versailles presented a scene of extreme activity, the gaily illuminated cafés packed with people. . . . 5,000 automobiles were crowded in the thoroughfares, many of them decorated with Chinese lanterns. Many of the contestants arrived during the evening, their huge machines trembling and groaning."[5]

Most of those who had come to witness the start had never seen a racing automobile or the men—and one woman—who drove them. The woman was the remarkable Camille du Gast, who had also driven in the previous year's Paris-Berlin race, finishing thirty-third in a field of one hundred. For this race, her 30-horsepower De Dietrich was decked with flowers, and at her arrival a great cheer rose from the crowd.* The scene was unforgettable for all who witnessed it. "The cars are denuded of all ornamentation, most of them reeking with oil and giving off foul vapors. The drivers wore rubber coats, drawn high and tight around the throat, and had their faces and heads completely enveloped in a mask. They did not wear goggles, but heavy plate glass was fixed in the mask, forming a miniature window. The contestants sat very low to minimize the resistance to the wind."

As the ACF had requested, ten thousand soldiers and police had been called out for crowd control along the route, and as the start approached, an honor guard lined the road from Versailles with bayonet-tipped rifles raised in salute. At 3:35, a cannon was fired and Charles Jarrott, who had drawn the first position, rolled to the line. Ten minutes later, the cannon fired again and Jarrott was off, to the cheers of the one hundred thousand spectators who had poured into Versailles to celebrate the historic event. For three hours, machines large and small, automobiles and motorcycles of every description, tore off the line at one- or two-minute intervals, the last not beginning the race until the rays of the morning sun had replaced the lanterns and electric lights.

The race had also caught the fancy of high society. Among the luminaries listed in the society pages were the Duchess of Marlborough and Mr. and Mrs. John Jacob Astor, as well as Biddles, Mellons, and others from the cream of the American and European elites. Many had paid for fancy viewing stations, and some had even constructed pavilions overlooking the track. Refreshments were served by retain-

---

* Camille du Gast, the widow of a wealthy Parisian department store owner, was also a crack shot and an expert fencer and horsewoman, raced toboggans and motorboats in addition to automobiles, traveled in balloons, and was the first woman to use a parachute. She also became a concert pianist and accomplished singer. When she was seventeen, she was reported to have been the nude model for a painting, after which she sued and won a defamation case. She was not done with scandal, however. In 1910, she successfully confronted a gang of men who had been hired by her daughter to kill her so that the daughter could inherit her fortune.

ers as the rich waited to experience the breathless excitement of the race.

What they witnessed was a bloodbath.

Moments after the cannon sent Jarrott on his way, the dazzling ignorance of the sponsors became manifest. The road was too narrow, the surface too dusty, and the complement of soldiers not nearly sufficient to hold back the crowds. Willie Vanderbilt could not even start until the crowds that had surged in front of his car were shoved out of the way. Jarrott, in the lead, tried slowing his De Dietrich to 40 miles per hour to avoid the spectators who jumped from the path of his car only at the last moment, but the lower speed merely caused the crowd to linger longer in the road.

The frustrations of getting up to speed pushed the drivers to more aggressive driving in those sections in which they could maneuver. In one case, a soldier dashed onto the course to push away a toddler who had gotten loose from his parents and wandered into the path of an oncoming two-ton racer; the soldier was killed. Another driver would die after striking the inevitable dog. Drivers crashed because they were blinded by the clouds of dust thrown up by other racers who had just passed. In the mishmash of sizes and shapes, underpowered vehicles were run down or sideswiped by more formidable machines.

In the end, only 110 of the 224 vehicles that began the race arrived at Bordeaux. Louis Renault, in his lightweight racer, crossed the line first—despite running over "three or four dogs"—with an adjusted time of 5 hours 40 minutes. But Renault's joy would be short-lived. He soon learned that his brother Marcel had been terribly injured, with two broken legs and a fractured skull, when his car overturned after hitting a tree.

And Louis, despite arriving first, was also not the winner of the stage. Fernand Gabriel, in an 80-horsepower Mors, starting from position 168—Renault had been number 3—had incredibly weaved his way through the dust, animals, spectators, and wreckage to finish with an adjusted time of 5 hours 13 minutes, shattering all previous records. A Mors had also finished second in the heavy-car class, with a Mercedes third and a De Dietrich fourth. Panhard could do no better

Marcel Renault (driving) moments before his crash

than fifth. Camille du Gast finished forty-fifth after stopping to help a fellow driver who had crashed and would have died without her assistance. Before she pulled off the road, she had been racing in the top ten.

But the news focused a good deal more on those who had not finished than on those who had. Scores of accidents sent both drivers and spectators to hospitals or the morgue. At least five drivers or riding mechanics were killed—including Marcel Renault, who died two days later—and more were maimed, some when their cars struck a variety of obstacles, others after their vehicles flipped over and caught fire.

Joseph Pennell, a reporter for *The London Chronicle,* described the scene from Chartres:

> As the cars fell—there is no other word for it—down the slopes and approached the narrow bridge, jumped with a bound across it, and flew with a scream up the rise beyond, one could see by the twitch of the wheels, not half of which was caused by the road, how agonizing was the strain on the driver, forced to make his way through the endless, uncontrolled crowds which littered the road from Paris to Bordeaux.[6]

Pennell did not have kind words for the soldiers overwhelmed by the crush of humans and animals that either lined the course or strode across it.

> Though on the stretch of eight kilometres between Char-
> tres and the first village there were from 5,000 to 10,000
> people and 500 to 1,000 cars, no attempt was made to con-
> trol the crowds, mostly made up of peasants and people
> from Paris who knew nothing about automobiles. The
> horse-drawn traffic was stopped during the race, but the
> fools on bicycles and the imbeciles on motors careened
> about and drew up anywhere all over the road and only
> escaped killing themselves and the racing men by the sheer
> dumb luck which is said to protect drunken men, children
> and fools.

Even as the last vehicles were leaving Versailles, it had become clear that the race was a debacle. Original reports had scores dead and hundreds injured, although the numbers quickly shrank. Still, the injuries were horrific and unprecedented.

> Long before the time when news of the first arrival in Bor-
> deaux set experts figuring out records, the total of the day's
> casualties had been summed up as follows: Dead.—Pierre
> Roderiz, Mr. Barrow's machinist; Nixon, Mr. Porter's ma-
> chinist; Normand, M. Tourand's machinist; Dupuy, soldier,
> at Angouleme; Gaillon, cyclist, at Angouleme; unknown
> peasant woman, at Ablis. Injured.—Mr. Barrow, pelvis and
> thigh broken, amputation likely; M. Marcel Renault, fatally
> injured (since dead); Mr. L. Porter, cut and bruised; Mr.
> Stead, overturned, badly injured; Mr. Stead's machinist,
> head cut open; Lesna, champion cyclist, broken knee-cap;
> Georges Richard, chest crushed, ribs broken; Henry Jean-
> not, Mr. Richard's machinist, shoulder fractured; E. Chard,
> head cut open; Tourand, severely bruised; Gaston Raffet,

boy, skull fractured, leg and arm broken; Marcel Renault's machinist, severely bruised; Mme. Chayscas, both limbs cut off.[7]

Charles Jarrott, whose number one start had allowed him to avoid the carnage, lost his lead when he slammed into an immense mastiff, which he carried across the front of his car for a couple of miles before it fell off, nearly every bone in its body broken. He later surveyed the course on his return to Paris. "I marveled, not that several had been killed, but that so many had escaped. Cars in fragments, cars in fields, some upside down, others with no wheels."[8]

Willie Vanderbilt, as it turned out, had been lucky, although he didn't see it that way.

> Further up the street was another car with a huge gash in the tire of one wheel, the other tire down, and the whole twisted and bent, in the hands of a dozen workmen. Walking away therefrom was a being with part of a cap over one ear and part of a pair of goggles over the other, plastered with mud and oil, in the rags and tatters of what had once been a suit of clothes. It opened its mouth and said in a voice choked with tears, and in the American language: "I don't mind breaking down again; but it makes me so very angry." It was Mr. Vanderbilt, and he had been in a ditch.[9]

A cracked cylinder had sent him spinning off the road—and perhaps saved his life.

The slaughter was so great that, over the objections of the ACF and many of the drivers, the race was terminated at Bordeaux. French officials, to be certain there would be no more deaths, ordered that all remaining race cars be towed by horse to the rail station and then shipped back to Paris. The ACF and the Spanish auto club made one last attempt to have the race restarted at the Spanish border, but Spanish officials refused.

French ministers, from Combes on down, were unanimous in their denunciations of the spectacle, and blamed the French auto club for so grossly underestimating the dangers. After an emergency meeting, they announced a ban on races on public roads. The ACF, in turn, was incensed at the government for failing to take the proper precautions or supervise the police and soldiers who were often little more than spectators as the cars roared into view.

In the wake of the tragedy, trade magazines fell over themselves decrying the excesses of an event that they had previously extolled for the challenges it offered to automobile and driver. An editorial in *Automobile Topics* was typical: "No more Paris-Madrid, Paris-Vienna, Paris-Berlin, or Paris-anywhere else. The annual saturnalia on wheels has gone, never, I hope, to return. It has died hard, and claimed its victims wholesale in dying. It was a species of mid-summer madness which should never have been allowed to reach the stage it did."[10] *Motor Car Journal* added, "The avalanche of fatality which rushed down the route of the Paris-Madrid race has struck a note of horror throughout the world, and will do much to stem the tide of the reckless daring that threatened to overwhelm the motoring community. . . . The result of this neglect was disaster, a disaster which threatened and still threatens, to injure materially the motor-car industry."[11] *Horseless Age* had a rather more xenophobic observation:

A more sudden change of public opinion has seldom been witnessed than that in France on May 24. The hundreds of thousands of people lining the road near the start in the small morning hours of that day were for the most part deeply impressed with the importance of the event they had come to witness, and the conversation centered on such subjects as the progress of practical science, La France once more taking the lead of the progress of the world, etc., but before the day was over these same people were clamoring loudly for the Government to stop the race. The French are naturally an impulsive race and one that easily forgets its lessons.[12]

Public disgust, it was widely predicted, would cast a pall over automobile sales for years to come.

In fact, the aftermath of what was widely termed the "Race to Death" saw both racing and automobiles catapulted to unprecedented popularity. Almost overlapping the condemnations were demands for more events. Paris-Madrid was an anomaly, it was argued. Such recklessness would never again be permitted. Sound policies could make for safe—or at least safer—racing. Orders to purchase automobiles increased, both in Europe and in the United States.

And of course, as automakers were quick to point out, however reckless the actual racing may have been, the need to create a successful racing machine had been the goad for improvements in motors, carburetors, cooling systems, brakes, suspensions, tires, control systems—in fact, there was no aspect of automotive design that had not benefited from the very sort of event that the French government, among others, wanted to ban.

Against pressure from the public, auto clubs, and automakers, naysayers soon began to backpedal. The trade magazines switched bandwagons, with the most immediate beneficiary of the new forgiving attitude being the Gordon Bennett Cup, scheduled to be run in Ireland in early July. (Britain had won the honor of hosting the 1903 race by virtue of Selwyn Edge's victory the previous year in a race from Paris to Innsbruck, Austria, where he had been the only competitor to finish. But road racing had been declared illegal in England, so the venue was changed to County Kildare.)

Rationalizations in support of the contest began only days after the Paris-Madrid dead had been buried. "But where the Gordon Bennett race differs from the Paris-Madrid is in the fact that it is really a race," *Automobile Topics* observed:

> A limited number of cars of estimated even quality, under the charge of the ablest drivers their respective countries can produce, testing their speeding power under the most careful police regulations, is altogether different from the mad chase of two or three hundred vehicles of every shape

and design, big racers, light cars, motorettes, and motorbi-
cycles, all mixed up indiscriminately, and all tearing like fu-
ries over a roadway which no human power could prevent
becoming a dust fog after the first 20 cars have started.[13]

The magazine added a cynical postscript in its next issue:

The statement from Paris that French manufacturers are
up in arms against the suppression of road racing is not at
all surprising. Without the annual speed parade from Paris,
the French automobile loses easily one-half its prestige.
Think of the hundreds and thousands of dollars worth of
free advertising which has been annually showered on
these machines. Where home-made [American] cars could
not get next to reading matter with their names in print,
foreigners have been given headlines at the top of the column in the very royal box of the daily paper's make-up, the
cable column. Will they surrender this merely at the bid-
ding of a premier or a president of the Republic? Nev-
vaire!! So I quite look forward to seeing "A bas Loubet!"
and "Conspuez Combes!" among the battle cries of automobilists in gay Paree before many moons.[14]

There were dissenting voices, albeit not many. *Horseless Age* noted:

About the only comment on the horrors of the Paris-
Madrid race by those who support road racing as an essential to the prosperity of the automobile industry is that
much nonsense is being written regarding the event—
which amounts simply to an evasion of the question. Some
consider, however, that to make road racing thoroughly
safe in the future the most competent drivers should be
selected in eliminating trials and the main race reserved for
these. This argument may sound plausible, but isn't it a fact
that most of the drivers involved in recent catastrophes—

Zborowski, Renault, Barrow, Stead—were among the best known men in automobile racing circles?"[15]

But logic was not going to overwhelm the thirst to see automobiles speed through the countryside, so on July 2, drivers from France, Germany, Britain, and the United States took off on the first of three and a half laps of a 98-mile figure-eight course that had been cleared of traffic and was guarded by 7,000 soldiers and police.

Notwithstanding the lack of success that had prompted American automakers to forgo the most prestigious European races, there was no choice but to again enter a team in the Gordon Bennett. Bennett was an American himself, after all, and the owner of a major newspaper, in which he could easily question the patriotism of automakers too timid to take on the Europeans. So Alexander Winton again entered his two automobiles, one of which was a redesigned *Bullet*. But this time he was not alone; another carmaker, also based in Cleveland, sought to qualify. Peerless Motor Car was new to the sport—until two years before, the company had been best known for making clothes wringers.

In 1900, the Peerless Manufacturing Company hired Louis Mooers, a twenty-eight-year-old engineer from Watertown, Massachusetts, to get them into the car business. Peerless had, a few years before, begun to manufacture bicycles as well—Mooers was running a bicycle factory when they hired him—but automobiles, the company decided, were a growing market and bicycles a declining one. Mooers's first design was a single-cylinder, 5-horsepower motorette powered by a De Dion–Bouton motor. Soon Mooers was designing his own two-cylinder motors, working up to 40 horsepower, and the company reincorporated as Peerless Motor Car. In 1903, Mooers created a four-cylinder, 80-horsepower behemoth. He mounted the cylinders vertically, copying Panhard, Mors, and the other successful Europeans.

Mooers was a talented engineer who "believed that racing not only advertised the brand, but motivated better innovations," and his design was quite advanced.[16] He employed a bevel-gear drive, with direct drive on high speed; also of the universal shaft. Each of the four cylinders is of steel with a cast explosion chamber. Both inlet and exhaust valves are mechanically operated. There are two systems of ignition; one a jump spark, placed directly over the inlet valve, the other a contact spark, placed alongside the inlet valve. Both can be advanced or retarded by the operator at will from the seat. The car is equipped with sliding-gear transmission. Ball bearings are used throughout the machine wherever possible in order to overcome friction. The engine, including flywheel, weighs about 700 pounds, and the car, complete, about 2,200 pounds, aluminum being used wherever possible to reduce the weight. The wheel base is nine feet. The front wheels are 34 inches in diameter, with four-inch tires, and the rear wheels 34 inches in diameter, with 4½-inch tires.[17]

But the road to the Gordon Bennett would have hazards even beyond those experienced by the Paris-Madrid drivers. The American auto club had decreed that potential entrants in the race must establish their bona fides in a qualifying run, which was to be held in Nassau County, Long Island, in April. Resistance to automobiles on public roads had grown in New York, however, and the state legislature had passed what came to be known as the Bailey Law, a horse-friendly decree that sharply restricted motorists' freedom on New York roads, establishing very low speed limits—usually 8 miles per hour—and under some conditions prohibiting access entirely.[*] In addition to local law enforcement, private vigilante groups had sprung up to ensure that New York's thoroughfares were safe from the mechanical menace. The American team might not, therefore, be able to make its qualifying run without incident.

Garden City, L.I., was the place chosen for the farce, and a tip to this effect was conveyed to Messrs Mooers and Owen

---

[*] One of the provisions, requiring numbered registration plates on the rear of an automobile, was later declared unconstitutional.

[in the Winton] on Monday, with instructions to keep it secret as they valued their chances of ever seeing the Irish course. An inkling of what was coming off was also allowed to reach Mr. Shattuck's lately-discovered political allies, the Long Island Protective Association, under pledge of the strictest secrecy, of course. As a result, two of the hired sleuths of this motorphobic organization were conveniently posted behind a hedge when Messrs. Mooers and Wridgway [the riding mechanic] hove in sight on their way to the rendezvous on Monday afternoon. There was the usual flutter of a handkerchief, followed by the indistinct tintinnabulation of a tomato can signal bell, and forthwith Mr. Mooers found himself under arrest, while the pair of sleuths, congratulating themselves on having earned their little four dollars a day apiece, went their ways rejoicing and were seen no more during the "trial."[18]

Mooers was eventually released and allowed to complete the trial, in which his racer, which he called the *Peerless,* after the company, was given leave to join the American team.

But in Ireland, the *Peerless* turned out to be far less than that. Winton also, although widely reported to be a victim of "bad luck," had a woeful showing. Camille Jenatzy, in a Mercedes, won for Germany, while the three French entries, René de Knyff and Henri Farman in Panhards and Fernand Gabriel in a Mors, were the only other cars to complete the course. Charles Jarrott broke his collarbone when his Napier overturned, and another British driver, J. W. Stocks, drove off the course and crashed into a fence.

Winton's first entry, the *Bullet 2,* could not start and was discovered to have been filled with dirty gasoline. The car ran poorly even afterward and retired less than a third of the way into the race. The other Winton, the original *Bullet,* lasted a bit longer but eventually quit when it was hopelessly outdistanced by the other competitors. Louis Mooers fared just as poorly, going out with engine trouble before he had completed a second lap.

Thus once again, Gordon Bennett's desire to use racing in Europe to advance American automotive technology had come to naught. Winton, in particular, seemed snakebit. In his losses to Ford, as well as in major races, automobiles that had performed admirably, sometimes brilliantly, fell victim to one or another mishap—even though these were the same machines that had amassed an impressive array of speed and endurance records. And every failure in the Gordon Bennett merely pointed up American cars' inferiority to European machines. Neither Peerless nor Winton would participate in future Gordon Bennetts, and for the 1904 race there would be no American entrant at all.

Louis Mooers would continue to build racing cars, but he would emphasize track rather than road events. He would hire as his driver the greatest track racer of them all, Barney Oldfield.*

Henry Ford, on the other hand, had again played it just right. Not only had he known when to get into racing, he had known when to get out. He had refused to build a commercial car when he knew that he needed the publicity that came with winning on the racetrack, and he knew when to resist the temptation to continue to race after that phase of his career had exhausted its usefulness.

But if the Gordon Bennett Cup had failed to spur America to produce better cars, Willie Vanderbilt thought he knew something that would. Going against conventional wisdom—and what would be a shrill chorus of dissent—Willie K. decided the only way to use road racing to promote automobiles in the United States was to stage the event itself within the United States. Late in 1903, therefore, he returned to America to bring speed and racing glory to our shores—with a road race to be called, of course, the Vanderbilt Cup.

---

* Mooers built Oldfield an enormous racer called the *Green Dragon*, and watched as Oldfield set a series of speed records—all on a track rather than on the road—and gained immense fame for both himself and Peerless Motor Car. The company would stay in business until the 1920s, building luxury automobiles.

CHAPTER 15

COLLISION

A lmost fifteen thousand gasoline automobiles were sold in the United States from autumn 1903 through summer 1904, more than had been sold in total since the automobile was introduced in the 1890s.* The majority of these were not luxury vehicles, such as Wintons, Cadillacs, or Peerlesses, but rather modestly priced automobiles—Olds, Ramblers, or Fords—aimed at a segment of the market that had been largely ignored until the curved-dash model had caught on the year before.† What was more, the largest seller of steam-powered automobiles, Locomobile, with fifteen hundred cars sold in 1902, announced that it would switch exclusively to gasoline in 1904.

---

* The September-to-August model year for automobiles had been established de facto almost from the moment automobiles were available for sale.

† Rambler, built by Thomas B. Jeffery Company of Kenosha, Wisconsin, also produced a $750 touring car that enjoyed a burst of popularity between 1902, when it sold some 1,500 machines, and 1909, when its sales numbers topped 3,000. Jeffery was also not an ALAM member, although, unlike Ford, the association had wooed him regularly. But Jeffery, who had successfully fought infringement suits as a bicycle manufacturer, was a confirmed lone wolf, unwilling to be part of any organization.

These figures belie the notions that automobiles were almost exclusively playthings of the rich and that, before Henry Ford's democratizing, early automakers failed to recognize the market for their product among the common folk. While the initial purchasers of lower-cost machines were often professional men, automobiles, at $650 to $850, were no longer out of the reach of much of the upper middle class. A far greater impediment to sales than cost was the lack of good roads outside—and in many cases, inside—city limits.

The broadening and deepening of automobile demand, then, was not an arcane phenomenon that Henry Ford alone perceived but an immense opportunity of which everyone involved in the design and manufacture of motorcars was aware. And since most of those manufacturers of any size were members of the new trade organization, protecting that burgeoning market, carving it up only among those already at the table, became a priority. As a result, in the summer of 1903, ALAM began to turn up the heat.

ALAM began a campaign aimed at enlisting public support for an organization that, as anyone with a basic knowledge of economics was aware, would result in increased prices. In the June 6, 1903, issue of *Automobile Topics,* for example, a column written by someone identified only as "Man on the Road" was little more than a press release.[1] Noting that he had previously been opposed to such an organization, and that "anything tending to a monopoly or trust would decidedly hurt me individually," he wrote that it had been his "good fortune" to have made a "fairly close study of the manufacturing conditions in the automobile industry," and "in the light of a better knowledge of conditions as they exist, my ideas have entirely changed, and I believe the association to be a necessity."[2]

Man on the Road went on to justify his change of mind by a desire to protect the consumer, observing that "the demand for machines has been so large that even the best equipped and largest factories have been and are now weeks behind on their orders," which would result—using unusual economic reasoning—in a *decline* in prices, which would, in turn, encourage fly-by-night assemblers to dump shoddily built machines on the market. As an aside, Man asserted that these rattletraps would inevitably be constructed of cheap imitations of patented components, though this, of course, was the actual crux of the argument:

> Take, for instance, such a concern as the Winton, or Olds, and suppose they own a patent on some one small but essential part of a complete machine. Now, suppose that 10 or 20 other concerns, each building a comparatively small number of machines, decide to use this device. They may do so for months, and not be molested, not because they have a right to do so, but because the older and larger makers positively cannot spare the time from their regular business to get after and teach the smaller maker that in reality he is dangerously near to being a thief; and it is here that the association can and will do its greatest work.

This appraisal was disingenuous, of course, since, as Man on the Road almost certainly knew, the only genuine threat to ALAM emanated from automakers such as Henry Ford, innovators who were employing either new ideas or new formulations of old ones. In many cases, the independents held their own patents. Few would be exposed to infringement suits on components. Only the overriding breadth of the Selden patent could protect ALAM's oligopoly, a point conspicuously absent from the piece.

As a result, unless ALAM could obtain a favorable ruling in the courts on the Selden patent, innovations were certain to eventually shatter its hold on the market. Although ALAM's twenty-six members were, for the most part, the largest and wealthiest in the industry, automaking in the United States remained an entrepreneurial enterprise. Fully 502 companies were formed to build automobiles between 1900 and 1908, and 200 of those remained in operation by the end of the decade. Most were small and the vast majority, almost 90 percent, felt they had little choice but to pay the auto trust. Eventually more than $2 million would be siphoned from the independents.[3] But of the independents that would not knuckle under, none presented a greater risk than Henry Ford.

In June—one month before he would ship his first automobile, but with legal action inevitable—Ford (and another independent, Marr Autocar) hired Ralzemond Parker, "the leading patent attorney in Detroit."[4] Parker thought the Selden patent claims ridiculous, or at least represented to his clients that he did. He did warn them that the fight would be long and expensive—possibly costing $40,000 in fees—but if they were willing to stay the course, they would ultimately prevail. While the costs were daunting, particularly to a company that had almost no money, this was precisely what Ford and Couzens wanted to hear. Both were spoiling for a fight, and long odds just made it that much more compelling. The other stockholders went along, and Ford and Couzens enthusiastically agreed to give Parker a more or less free hand to fashion their defense.

But before the courts came the advertising. ALAM began running ads in newspapers and magazines such as *Harper's*, informing "Users, Agents, Importers, Dealers, and Manufacturers of Gasolene Automobiles" that the Selden patent "controls broadly commercial forms of gasolene automobiles" and that the licensed manufacturers are "pioneers" who have "commercialized the gasolene vehicle by many years of development and at great cost." The last line warned that "the basic Selden patent and all other patents . . . will be enforced against all infringers." The notice conveniently omitted that the Selden patent could not be said to control anything until the courts agreed that it did.

Ford responded in kind. In an ad directed to the same list of recipients, Ford promised, "We will protect you against any prosecution for alleged infringement of patents." The copy went on to assure buyers of Ford cars that the Selden patent "does not cover a practicable machine, no practicable machine can be made from it, and never was." Then, borrowing an untruth from its founder, the ad asserted, "Our Mr. Ford made the first Gasoline Automobile in Detroit and the third in the United States." Finally, in a turn of the knife that Ford must have approved personally, the ad read, "Mr. Ford, driving his own machine, beat Mr. Winton at Grosse Pointe track in 1901. We have always been winners."

Ford's notice did not specify how he would indemnify buyers of his automobiles if his company went bankrupt either fighting the coming lawsuit or losing it. But what it did do was establish to the ordinary American that here was a man unwilling to be cowed by big money. Thus, when Henry Ford chose to defy ALAM, he became a hero not only to his fellow independents but also to small business owners and working people across America. No man who intended to sell his products to those very same segments of society could have asked for more.

By autumn, ads run by ALAM members—Winton, Cadillac, Locomobile, Peerless, Olds, and the rest—included a postscript, "Member Association of Licensed Automobile Manufacturers," and the automobiles that rolled out of their factories contained a metal plate that read, "Licensed Under Selden Patent, No. 549,160. Patented November 5, 1895," against the backdrop of Selden's never-built vehicle.

At the end of August, ALAM even trotted out George Selden, who until then had been only a spectral presence, and had him interviewed for the *Hartford Courant*. The reporter claimed to have merely run into Selden at the Hotel Heublein and there put questions to him. The newspaper then dutifully printed a series of misstatements and distortions, without once questioning their veracity. "We have now six good and sufficient grounds on which the court would award an injunction— viz., five decrees and the public acquiescence," Selden asserted, although no decrees had yet been issued. "In truth," he added, although it was no truth at all, "on a motion for a preliminary injunction on my patent as it now stands, the only question the court would consider would be that of infringement, and on this question all parties have agreed that it is impossible to build a gasolene automobile without infringing."[5]

Ford and Couzens matched each escalation. A letter, dated September 28, 1903, which appeared in *Horseless Age* and other trade journals over Couzens's signature, but had likely been written by Ralzemond Parker, stated,

> So far as our plan of action is concerned for the future it is extremely simple. We intend to manufacture and sell all of

the gasoline automobiles of the type we are constructing that we can. We regard the claims made under the Selden patent as covering the monopoly of such machines as entirely unwarranted, and without foundation in fact. We do not, therefore, propose to respect any such claims, and, if the issue is forced upon us, shall defend not only ourselves but our agents and customers to the fullest extent, and this, too, without regard to whether or not we join any combination for the purpose of defending against said patent.[6]

The letter did not mince words as to what the Ford camp had thought of Selden's interview. "In taking this stand we cannot conscientiously feel that Mr. Selden ever added anything to the art in which we are engaged. We believe that the art would have been just as far advanced today if Mr. Selden had never been born; that he made no discovery and gave none to the world." Finally, Parker went on to point out that George Selden's contention—which had also been, by implication, ALAM's—that the legal issues had been all but settled by Judges Coxe and Hazel was utterly false, and that those rulings bore no relation to the court case to come. In this he was technically correct, but from a practical standpoint—de facto, if not de jure—precedent had been set with those rulings.

It is debatable whether either of these missives swayed the undecided, but they established clear battle lines and, of greater significance, continued to position Henry Ford as a major player in automobile manufacture, a status he could not possibly have achieved based solely on his company's performance. Of the seventeen hundred Model As that he would sell that model year, virtually all of them were purchased *after* ALAM threatened its prospective buyers. ALAM, in attempting to isolate Ford Motor and squeeze it out of business, had succeeded only in elevating the company in the public eye. Ford and Couzens clearly understood the value of being perceived as the small independent, willing to wage the noble fight against a powerful bully. In another release picked up in newspapers and trades, Ford proclaimed, "We are fighting this matter single-handed, and have not joined any association whatever, nor do we anticipate doing so."[7]

The print campaign was merely the opening round of what would be an eight-year slugfest, a classic contest in which the heavy puncher needed an early knockout because as the fight went on he grew weaker while his more deft opponent grew stronger.

Finally, on October 22, 1903, war was officially declared when attorneys for George Selden and the Electric Vehicle Company, standing in for ALAM, filed suit in federal court in New York City against the Ford Motor Company for patent infringement. There had been intense speculation as to whether Thomas Jeffery of Rambler would be included in the complaint. Rambler, after all, sold as many cars as Ford and was the other independent that cut substantially into ALAM's lower-priced market. But in yet another decision that seemed prudent at the time but would prove disastrous, the suit named only Ford and C. A. Duerr, Ford's agent in New York. Thomas Jeffery's reputation for never backing down, it seemed, had successfully deterred ALAM and Electric Vehicle's boards.

The reaction in the industry was mixed. On the one hand, ALAM seemed to hold all the cards—it was the biggest and most powerful consortium in the business, with a patent that had survived its first court tests—but the independents were also producing cars that people seemed to want to buy, and in growing numbers. And, of course, the ultimate legal resolution was uncertain. No one wanted to commit to the side that ended up losing.

The trade magazines, for example, used firm language to say absolutely nothing. *Horseless Age* wrote:

> As stated in THE HORSELESS AGE some weeks ago, the institution of this suit was inevitable, and it was only a question of time. The association apparently pursued the policy of diplomacy in securing recognition of the validity of the Selden patent to the very last, for rumors were rife to the effect that an important concern outside the fold was about to institute suit against the association for alleged intimidation of its

agents. On the other hand, a prominent member of the association, located also in Detroit, is reported to have threatened to withdraw from it unless proceedings were instituted at once against the manufacturer who is made defendant in the present suit. . . . Now that the fight has begun we believe we voice the sentiment of the entire body of automobile users in this country and of the greater number of agents and manufacturers, both licensed and unlicensed, in saying that it is to be hoped that the fight will be short and decisive and that it will be settled once for all whether George B. Selden actually made a new and useful improvement in means of road locomotion of such scope as to entitle him under the law to the tribute of the entire gasoline automobile industry, or whether the patent was unjustly granted or does not cover the modern gasoline road vehicle.[8]

The lawsuit was not Ford's only problem. Members of Ford Motor's board of directors, especially the quixotic Malcomson, wanted the company to switch direction after one season of moderate success and produce a higher-priced luxury car. It hadn't taken long for Malcomson to forget that the very point of hiring Ford was his promise to produce a *lower-priced* car. Ford—as later events would prove—thought Malcomson an idiot, but he didn't have an alternative with which to bargain. The Model A had already acquired a reputation for overheating, even when being driven steadily on a flat road. As the car began to deteriorate under day-to-day use, it became less and less likely that those seventeen hundred sales could be repeated in the 1904 model year.

"Here, then, was Henry Ford's situation," wrote longtime Ford employee and future head of production Charles Sorenson. "He had in Wills a chief engineer who was a perfectionist; in Couzens, a dragon at the cashbox; in himself, a man with a strong stubborn hunch for a cheap car for the average man, yet unable to describe its execution; and a board of directors out of sympathy with his aim and driven almost to hysterics by the groping and fumbling toward a low-cost car. For Ford merely had the idea; he had no picture in his mind as to what that car would be like, or look like."[9]

Ultimately, Malcomson forced Ford to produce a $2,000 luxury car, the Model B, with four cylinders instead of two, an engine positioned in front of the driver instead of underneath the seat, and a rotating shaft drive instead of the Model A's chain. It was appointed with all the upscale touches that the cheaper models weren't—padded, tufted leather upholstery, a polished wood body painted "a rich dark green," and a brass steering wheel, steering post, and trim. The motor was rated at 20 horsepower, with a top speed of 40 miles per hour. The Model B was a drastic change in design and tooling that took a good part of 1904 to effect, and so it was not introduced until October. Although the sales brochure described the Model B as "a touring car of light weight and great power," sales, while respectable, were hardly brisk.

But Ford had not ceded authority entirely. That second year, the company also designed and produced a Model C, a vastly improved Model A. The C, which was not introduced until December 1904, had the stronger engine, redesigned cooling system, upgraded transmission, superior handling, and enhanced reliability that were necessary to compete with Olds and Rambler. Many of these improvements were fashioned by Wills, drawing on the work he had done designing the detested Model B. The Model C was slightly more expensive than the A, priced at $850 as a runabout, $950 with tonneau. Doctors, who had already established themselves as a prime market, were specifically targeted in Ford's brochure.

> To The Doctor: You need not be told the value to you of a few hours saved. Every doctor knows that, and today thousands have taken advantage of the time and money economies of the automobile. No longer experimental, the motor car has taken its place among the necessities of existence. The Ford stands first and foremost as the ideal doctor's car. With every quality found in other cars it is conceded to be the easiest riding car of its type known. To

the physician whose steadiness of hand and brain and nerve are all important, this is food for thought. The Ford stands for economy, reliability and simplicity. Its past successes vouch for it.

Ford's automobiles, of course, were no more reliable, no more elegantly designed, and certainly no less expensive than those of its competitors. And by the end of 1903, while the company was generating sufficient cash flow to keep it afloat, under ordinary circumstances Ford cars would hardly have garnered special acclaim. But the notoriety the company and its eponymous chief engineer had received from its enemies, as well as the constant growth in demand for automobiles engendered by the glamour of racing, virtually guaranteed that Ford products would continue to remain prominent in the eyes of consumers.

Ford was not a man to miss a chance to help fortune along. In order to successfully fight off ALAM he was going to need money, quite a bit of it, and that meant he needed to do everything he could to maximize sales. No one was more aware of the publicity that speed engenders, so on January 12, 1904, Ford once more took the tiller of his *Arrow*—which he had sworn he would never again do—and drove across a frozen Lake St. Clair. He was so nervous about the *Arrow* becoming stuck with the throttle open that he recruited Spider Huff, who like Oldfield was afraid of nothing, to ride on the running board, prepared to choke off the fuel supply if the powerful engine could not be brought under control by the driver.

It was a terrifying ride. The ice, which seemed smooth as polished marble when viewed from the bank, was actually fissured and uneven, not the ideal surface on which to drive a glorified drag racer with no brakes. "I shall never forget that race," he wrote in *My Life and Work*. "At every fissure the car leaped into the air. I never knew how it was coming down. When I wasn't in the air, I was skidding, but somehow I stayed top side up and on the course."[10] But the terror seemed worth it when Ford was told he had set a new measured-mile land speed record of 91.37 miles per hour. He and Huff celebrated by building a fire on the frozen lake and cooking themselves a muskrat for dinner.

Ford's feat was reported in newspapers across the nation. Unfortunately, the publicity boon was diminished less than one month later when Willie Vanderbilt, in a 90-horsepower Mercedes, broke Ford's record by tearing across the speed flats at Ormond Beach, Florida, at 92.3 miles per hour.[11]

CHAPTER 16

WILLIE K.'S ROAD

William Kissam Vanderbilt II was a man raised to believe he could do or have anything he wanted, and what he wanted least was a humdrum life. From age nine, when his father chartered an enormous yacht to take the family on a luxury trip down the Nile, to his sponsoring France's first road race when he was just sixteen, to yachting, race driving, playing the new sport of football, or simply traveling the world in luxury, Willie K. never lost the conviction that what were immovable obstacles for most people were merely twigs to him.*

When he returned from Europe, Willie repaired to Deepdale, his sprawling estate on the aptly named Lake Success, where he and his wife—herself the daughter of a senator and a partner in the Comstock silver mine—became tabloid fodder and from which Willie

---

* That category did not include his father, however. At one point he was forced to take a job at the New York Central Railroad, of which William K. Vanderbilt I was chairman. His desk was placed near his father's in what wags termed "the multimillionaire's division." Willie K. could not be kept at a desk, however, and so, while he remained an officer of the railroad, even becoming its president during World War I, he was never what one would call active in its management.

Willie K. at the wheel

launched his many high-speed sojourns in the *White Ghost,* his 33-horsepower Daimler. Local residents were so terrified of the 65-mile-per-hour machine that they prevailed on Hempstead town officials to enact a 6-mile-per-hour speed limit, which Willie simply ignored. "Arrest me every day if you want to," he is reported to have said. "It's nothing to pay fines for such sport."[1] Eventually, Willie had an even faster Mercedes racer shipped from Europe, which he called *Red Devil*—a popular moniker for fast automobiles—and settled in to promote the United States' first great international road race.

The plan was suitably ambitious; the notion that he could not simply get local officials to close any stretch of public thoroughfare he required did not occur to him. The original course, therefore, which he announced in February 1904, was 180 miles, beginning at Sag Harbor, near the eastern end of Long Island, then through Bridgehampton, Southampton, "over the Shinnecock Hills, following the south road through the Hamptons and Quogues, then through Bellport and Patchogue to Bayshore and Babylon, and then following the Herrick Road from Massapequa to Brooklyn." The automobiles would then return east, "where the road would be extended on the north side to Jericho Turnpike through Huntington to Greenport and Port Jefferson."[2]

The impossible logistics of closing so much public road and then monitoring it to ensure that the Paris-Madrid disaster was not repeated might have eluded Willie K. but was painfully obvious to everyone else. Even the Automobile Association of America, which had agreed to co-sponsor the event, could not sign on.*

Willie persevered, continuing to insist the race be 250 to 300 miles. But he was also no fool. However long the course, he wanted America to reap the benefits of racing without the free-for-all insanity that plagued open European road events, so he fashioned a set of rules similar to Gordon Bennett's.

> Only ten drivers from any one country can compete. Challenges must be made prior to March 15 of the year in which the race is to be run. The race will be run each year as scheduled, rain or shine, and will be open only to members of clubs affiliated with the Automobile Association of America or the Automobile Club of France.... During 1904 and 1905 the race must be run in the United States. Subsequently it may be held in the country which holds the cup. The entry fee will be $300 for every car entered, and of this $150 will be returned to the owners of those cars starting.... The cars in the race will carry numbers, to be drawn by lot, and these numbers will indicate the order of starting. The entries will be restricted to cars weighing between 881 pounds and 2204 pounds, and each car shall carry in addition to the driver, one passenger, to weigh not less than 132 pounds. The contestants will be required to start on time, and all time lost in getting under way will be counted against them.[3]

* The AAA had been founded in 1901 when nine local clubs recognized the need for a national organization and banded together to press for better roads and laws to protect automobilists. It was far more egalitarian than its forerunner, the Automobile Club of America, whose members were virtually all among society's elite. A number of ACA members who had resigned rather than mix with the hoi polloi were in a snit that Willie K., one of their own, was willing to rub elbows with AAA members.

For the winner, Willie ordered a silver loving cup—the Vanderbilt Cup—which was wrought to the standards of the man for whom it was named. Three feet tall, fashioned from 30 pounds of sterling silver mounted on an ebony base, the 10.5-gallon cup was embossed with an image of Willie K. at the wheel of his Mercedes, setting the speed record at Ormond Beach.

By June, Willie K. was finally resigned to the route he had chosen not being approved, so—reluctantly and with some irritation—he shortened the course to a 30-mile triangle, which would be traversed ten times, thus preserving the 300-mile distance. The roads on the triangle were almost entirely in Nassau County, just east of the New York City line, but one corner spilled over into Queens, where Jericho Turnpike met the newly constructed Hempstead Turnpike. The shortest leg was north-south Route 107, running between Massapequa and Hicksville. The shape of the course left three severe turns for drivers to negotiate, but a straighter run was out of the question. Nassau County was then largely agricultural, and farmers in particular were none too keen on the automobile, which spooked their horses and terrified their livestock. In fact, after the Nassau County board of supervisors finally, on August 23, approved the closing of the appropriate public roads, a series of legal actions were filed that threatened the October 8 start date until just days before the event was to take place. As it was, the organizers were forced to create "control stations" at Hicksville and Hempstead, where the cars would stop to be inspected during each lap, then be escorted by bicycles over railroad tracks. The time in the control stations would be deducted from a driver's total and not count in average miles per hour, a provision that would prove a good deal more controversial than it first appeared.[4]

Local officials were vehement in defending their decision to allow the race. They insisted a slew of dollars would be raked in from the thousands of spectators who were expected to witness the event—and they were right. More than fifty thousand visitors arrived, filling every hotel and inn, many of which charged "Waldorf-Astoria prices" for the privilege of a bed and a roof. The luxurious Garden City Hotel, located almost in the center of the triangle—the very same hotel in which Louis Mooers had been registered before his arrest during the Gordon Bennett trials—was forced to turn away guests who, in calmer moments, would have been treated like royalty. That this deluge of humanity, most of whom had never witnessed an automobile race, might well create precisely the conditions that had doomed Paris-Madrid was pointed out by only a few malcontents.

If Willie Vanderbilt had been correct about the interest his spectacle would engender among Americans who had never seen such an exhibition, he was equally correct about the enthusiasm of drivers and manufacturers to compete in it. Eighteen cars would race, numbered 1 to 19—there was no 13—with Panhard, Mercedes, De Dietrich, Fiat, Renault, and Clement-Bayard represented.* The drivers were an equally impressive lot, the best-known being Paris-Madrid winner Fernand Gabriel, Albert Clement, and George Heath, who had been tearing up the European circuit. Heath had been born only miles away in Astoria, New York, but had lived most of his life in Europe, and at forty-two was the oldest racer. He captained the three-car Panhard team. The six French cars ranged from 60 horsepower for the Renault to 90 for the Panhards. The two Fiats were also 90 horsepower, and four of the five Mercedes cars featured 60 horsepower, with the other a 90-horsepower machine. The Mercedes racers were all privately owned by Americans, some of whom would drive their cars in the race.

By contrast, the five American cars—except for the 75-horsepower Simplex and a 70-horsepower Pope-Toledo—seemed vastly underpowered. A Royal Tourist generated 35 horsepower, a Packard just 30, and another Pope-Toledo an impossibly skimpy 24. While the race received enormous national publicity from late summer on—another reason the courts would have been reluctant to enjoin its running—no one gave the Americans much of a chance.

In terms of stimulating interest in American automobiles, how-

* Panhard and Renault were added to the ALAM suit against Ford after they had announced their intention to compete in the race but before they had shipped racers to the United States. Each sold passenger cars in America, however, using licensed agents in New York.

ever, the apparent overmatch had little effect. In its August edition, *Cycle and Automobile Trade Journal* observed, "Now that the Vanderbilt Cup race is to be held in the United States, there is no doubt but that American makers will give more attention to the building of racing cars; in fact, several new claimants for racing honors have already appeared, and there is a chance that America may figure in future races for the James Gordon Bennett.... As we have repeatedly asserted, America can only hope to win in international races through experience gained in similar races."[5] As both Vanderbilt and Gordon Bennett knew from watching the French, the Germans, the Italians, and even the come-lately British, building more competitive racing cars unfailingly led to building more efficient and reliable commercial vehicles.

More publicity was generated on October 3, five days before the start, when Herbert Lytle, who would later be described as one of the most daring race car drivers in the country—a euphemism for "reckless"—crashed the 24-horsepower Pope-Toledo during a practice lap. Lytle was unhurt, flung forward over a picket fence, as was H. C. Anderson, a mechanician riding on one of the running boards. But Harold Rigby, another mechanician, riding on the other board, was thrown between the fence and the 2,000-pound automobile, his chest crushed. As the result of what *Motor Age* termed "a peculiar accident," Rigby died at 3:00 A.M. in a local hospital from a punctured lung.

Rumors began to swirl about that the accident had been caused when the car, traveling at high speed, encountered a farmer who "would not yield a bit of the road and forced Lytle to dash into the fence." The organizers moved quickly to debunk this account. "They were going not faster than 20 miles an hour.... Lytle had passed the farmer, and a furlong or less further on, the steering knuckle broke." Lytle was not about to be dissuaded by the death of a teammate. "The car can easily be repaired. Lytle will drive it in the race."[6]

The controversy faded almost as quickly as it had arisen. As in Europe, the specter of death had only increased the fervor of the public.

On race day, the start time for the first car, a red Mercedes driven by Albert Campbell, was set for 6:00 A.M., avoiding the middle-of-the-night start of Paris-Madrid, but still early enough to ensure that all eighteen cars would finish in daylight. Neither the Long Island Railroad nor local police considered the impact of tens of thousands of eager race fans jamming the train station—only one ticket booth would be open the day before the race—the trains themselves, the woefully inadequate roads for those arriving by automobile, and even public toilet facilities, of which there were few.

For the wealthy, of course, the experience was somewhat different. As they had at Paris-Madrid, the well-to-do "treated the race like any other society outing, bringing along their servants and setting up camp kitchens behind the grandstand. Breakfast was served on china plates at 7:00 A.M., one hour into the race. A second informal repast was arranged for 9:00. Throughout the morning, coffee, bottled beer, mineral water, and Scotch whiskey were delivered to the well-heeled spectators by their liveried staff."[7] As *Motor Age* noted, "The grand stand when the race was fully under way contained almost as notable a representation of wealth and fashion as ever graces the golden horse-shoe of the Metropolitan on opera night."[8]

For the remainder of the horde of visitors, however, it was a raucous scene, with revelers drinking, carousing, and making life generally miserable for residents, except those residents with something to sell. Hay wagons doubled as taxis, and farmers' parlors served as way stations, all at outrageous prices. The owners of the two roadhouses along the two-mile route from the train station to the racecourse stayed up all night preparing food and drink, and were so mobbed that they sold out before sunrise. It was as if, *The New York Times* observed, "Nassau County had been invaded."[9]

But a swarming bevy of fans exuded frenzied anticipation as well, a mood that was absorbed by the plethora of newspapermen sent to cover America's first international road race. Willie Vanderbilt had been hoping for the sort of coverage that attends only the most important sporting or society events, and that was what he got. The race would have everything—speed, suspense, the closest finish ever in a major automobile event, and another death.

Albert Clement takes a turn

The cars went off at two-minute intervals, each with a roar that both deafened and intoxicated the thousands of spectators jammed together at the start/finish line. When the last of the racers had departed, William Wallace in one of the Fiats, the eerie silence at first prompted an odd disorientation and then curiosity among the onlookers. Mimicking the observers at Paris-Madrid and other road races, some began leaning forward, trying to catch a glimpse of the first car to complete a lap, and then, when others did the same, wandering onto the course for a clearer line of sight. When the first car did come into view, Fernand Gabriel in the De Dietrich, the crowd was shooed back to their seats, only to pour back onto the course when the big racer had passed.

One-third of the racers were out by the end of the second lap, five with mechanical problems and one because of a crash. Tobacco heir George Arents, an amateur who had not felt the need for a practice run, blew a front tire on his Mercedes while speeding at perhaps 90 miles per hour on a straightaway. "Anxious to stop the car quickly, so as to lose as little time as possible in replacing the damaged tire, Mr.

Arents applied the brakes suddenly and so strongly that the left rear wheel was completely wrecked, every spoke breaking off short. The vehicle wheeled about sharply and overturned in the centre of the road. Mr. Arents, who was at the wheel, was thrown clear of the machine and landed head first upon the macadamized roadway."[10]

Arents suffered severe head injuries from which he was not expected to recover, but after two weeks in the hospital, he ultimately survived. Carl Mensel, his riding mechanic, however, "was caught underneath the overturned machine and received a fracture of the skull and probably internal injuries as well, from which he subsequently died." Although newspapers the next day reported that the fatality "cast a pall over the grandstand," news of Mensel's death was not made public until well after the race ended, and other reports provided firm evidence that the holiday spirit in the grandstand was undiminished.

After Arents and Mensel were removed to Nassau Hospital, the Mercedes was quickly hauled from the track—by a team of horses—and the other racers continued on. Georges Teste, in a Panhard, forged ahead with a 71-mile-per-hour lap, the fastest of the race, a lead he held until he was forced out with either a cracked cylinder or a failed clutch. (It was the nature of early automobiles that the precise reason for breakdowns was often a matter of speculation.) The next two laps claimed another Mercedes and the 70-horsepower Pope-Toledo.

In the meantime, George Heath and Albert Clement were staging a classic duel. Heath, proclaimed across the United States as "the American," although he would remain in Europe for virtually the rest of his life, took the lead after Teste's Panhard dropped out. Unlike his teammate, he drove at a steadier pace, attempting to maintain both his position and the well-being of his automobile.

That strategy seemed ill-conceived when, in the eighth lap, he blew a tire; while he repaired the damage, Albert Clement—the "Boy Racer," only twenty-one years old and the son of the car's designer—sped past him into the lead. Heath's prospects diminished further when, as he took the road with a new tire, he was told he was still first and drove conservatively to avoid additional damage. (Heath, like most of the racers, had begun the race with two spares. He had blown a tire earlier, so if another one failed, he would have no means to replace it.)

Clement, in his "long, rakish, blue car," continued to hold the lead as the ninth lap concluded. Only his "ears and the tip of his nose were visible from the thick folds of his automobile hood, and the car was emitting a tremendous amount of smoke and gasoline odor, showing that the motor was working to do its best out on the course."[11]

Each time he passed the grandstand, thousands cheered wildly, prompted from an unexpected quarter. "Enthusiasm was beginning to make itself felt by the time the hours wore on past noon and the race narrowed down to Heath and Clement. Mrs. W. K. Vanderbilt, Jr. was the main factor in it. Nothing could suppress her delight in the proceedings. She led the applause; she led the cheers; she jumped up on a camp chair and waved anything that came handy whenever a racer came by."

It was not until he was about to begin his final lap that Heath realized he was running second. He had no choice but to let his 90-horsepower machine out full, aware that running at top speed would greatly increase the chance of breakdown. But the Panhard held together and Heath crossed the finish line at 1:08:45 in the afternoon. He had averaged 52 miles per hour for the 284 miles of the course, control station segments deducted from the total driven. The spectators crowded onto the track in front of the grandstand, peering up the road for signs of Clement. Mrs. Vanderbilt, "still standing on the chair, pulled her watch out, bent over, and looked up the road, calculating the time." Clement had started ten minutes after Heath, so, assuming similar time at the control stations, he had to beat that margin at the finish line.

He did not. After final calculations, Heath was declared the winner by a mere 1 minute 28 seconds, by far the smallest margin of victory ever in a road race. Clement was livid, chasing after Willie Vanderbilt, who was also the referee, complaining that he had been excessively detained at one of the control stations. A news photo shows him, face black from oil and dirt, yelling at Willie K., who is staring stolidly straight ahead, goggles perched on the brim of his cap. Clement's protest was denied.

After Clement's arrival at the finish line, spectators poured onto the course, and Vanderbilt and AAA officials decided to halt the race to prevent accidents. The order of finish from three on down would be determined by the position of the remaining cars when the race was halted. The good news for Willie Vanderbilt had not ended. Herbert Lytle's 24-horsepower Pope-Toledo was in third place and the Packard in fourth. Two American cars had finished ahead of Mercedes, De Dietrich, Fiat, and Renault.

The Vanderbilt Cup race became the most widely and enthusiastically reported automobile story in American history, surpassing even the cross-country jaunts of the year before. In the evening editions of October 8 newspapers, or morning editions of those published the next day, a Sunday, it garnered front-page headlines from New York to California, with most of the features accompanied by gaudy descriptions of the race and the racers, and copious numbers of photographs.

For example, the Richmond, Virginia, *Times Dispatch* led with a four-column headline, "Heath Gets Vanderbilt Cup. Driver Killed, Owner Dying."* *The Washington Times* trumpeted across two columns, "Records Fall Before Winner of Auto Race." Similar headlines appeared in the West, in such newspapers as *The Spokane Press* and the San Francisco *Call*. Perhaps the most lurid was in the *St. Paul Globe*, which featured two front-page stories. One read, "Death Sits Behind Arents' Chauffeur in Mad Race," and the other, "Vanderbilt Cup Is Baptized in Blood."

The New York newspapers had both the most extensive and the most exuberant coverage. The New York *World* devoted four pages to "The Great Race"; across two of them lay the headline "Speed-Mad Automobilists Dash Along Today in Deadly Race." *The Brooklyn Daily Eagle*'s opening paragraph told the story of the race precisely as Willie

---

* Arents's recovery had been ensured soon after his arrival at the hospital, but it took a while before the initial reports of a probable fatality were updated.

Vanderbilt would have wanted: "A blur of dusty gray streaked past the judges' stand on Jericho Turnpike this afternoon, and a Long Island boy on a French machine had won the most thrilling race the modern world has ever seen. It was a finish that stilled heart beats and held thousands breathless."[12]

Even the staid *New York Times* could not resist the allure of sensationalism. After a lead column story on page one, the *Times* devoted all of pages two and three to the contest. Its opening paragraph almost matched the *Daily Eagle*'s in rapture and outdid it in verbiage. "When, with a deep rumble growing into a roar and terminating in a whizz, Heath, the American, in his 90-horsepower Panhard machine, at 1:08:45 o'clock yesterday afternoon flashed across the finish line of the 284-mile course of the international automobile race at Westbury, L.I., the cheer that the well-groomed crowd on the grand stand let out marked the first real excitement of the great contest for W. K. Vanderbilt, Jr.'s cup."

Not everyone was so taken, of course. Among the naysayers, none was more strident than an editorial writer in that same edition of *The New York Times*. Taking issue with his own paper's news coverage, and epitomizing a point of view rooted in the past and about to be swept aside in an avalanche of auto sales, he bristled:

> The race was utterly futile, proving nothing of interest and value to any one concerned in promoting "sport" or the mechanical development of the practical and useful motor vehicle—unless it be that the type of road locomotive capable of making high speed is an overorganized piece of machinery, too complex and too frail to be of any use for the pleasure of normal persons or the benefit of humanity. . . . [R]oads suited for speeding them do not exist and their employment on common highways is an outrage upon everything moving which cannot go as fast as they do or may not want to go in the same direction.[13]

He then demonstrated an equally profound ignorance of human nature.

The worst enemies of the automobile are those who are making it odious in abusing public patience by misusing highways to the inconvenience and danger of others. A road race such as that in Nassau County, L.I., will encourage gross violations of law everywhere and create a popular antagonism to the automobile and those who use it which will not be overcome in a long time.

In fact, after Horatio Jackson's *Vermont* and George Heath's triumph, the automobile had already become indelibly part of the American culture. Few things stoke demand for a product more than associating it with glamour and excitement, and by October 1904, cars had glamour enough for anyone. A race of a different sort had begun, and Henry Ford was in the thick of it. The question had passed from whether or not a lower-priced automobile would ever be a runaway success to which one it would be and when.

CHAPTER 17

PALACE COUP

enry Ford had a hound's nose for publicity, yet the man who had made his name racing had either chosen or been forced to sit on the sidelines in the Vanderbilt Cup. Both the *999* and the *Arrow* were fast and powerful, but neither could have survived a lap on the twisty, uneven Nassau County roads. Ford's attempt to steal some headlines by setting a speed record over the ice had gained him notice for less than a month.

Even so, by early 1905, the economy was booming and the clamor for automobiles was booming right along with it. "Demand was outrunning production. . . . The automobile, once little more than a fashionable novelty, was becoming a necessity for thousands of business and professional men. . . . Numerous manufacturers, inundated with orders, hired additional batches of men and began working their assembly floors in two shifts."[1] What was more, in what seemed a vindication of Alexander Malcomson, with the burst in GNP came a soaring demand for larger and more expensive automobiles, in the $2,000 to $2,500 range. An automobile had come to be viewed as a symbol of success and prosperity, and consumers believed—

inaccurately, as it turned out—that larger, heavier, and more expensive meant better-made. Manufacturers had therefore begun to add "luxury" features, many of which protected passengers from the elements—tops, for example.

Despite the market trend, Ford continued to be convinced that the future lay in lighter and less expensive, mass-marketed automobiles. In February 1905, Ford tried to split the difference and introduced a third model, the F, an improved, more luxurious Model C.* The engine had been retooled, with a larger cylinder head but slightly shorter piston rod, which resulted in a 20 percent increase in horsepower.† The tires were larger and the wheelbase longer; the radiator had a greater capacity to mitigate overheating; a running board had been added for easier entry and exit; and the paint job had been made more attractive, with, as the sales brochure described it, the Model B's "rich dark green" for the body and yellow running gear. (Many of these improvements did not emanate from the Ford team but came as a result of suggestions from the Dodges.) The company described the F as "the general all around car for the man who wants a powerful runabout or a comfortable and fast touring car for five people at a moderate investment and low cost of operating and maintaining, capable of taking all kinds of roads." The weight of the car had increased—as had the price, to $1,000 without tonneau.

With a lack of clear corporate strategy, Ford Motor was thrashing about. When, for example, the Model F went into production, it became awkward trying to sell the remaining Model Cs. Fortunately, demand for cars was so great in 1905 that buyers would often accept the earlier model rather than wait an indefinite period for a later one. But none of the three vehicles produced for the 1904–5 model year would survive to 1906. All served their purpose, however—the company's cash flow was sufficient to fund its operations and capital expansion,

* Interim letters, in this case D and E, were for prototypes that were never put into production.
† The diameter of the piston head is called the "bore," and the distance it travels—determined by the length of the rod—is the "stroke." Bore and stroke will determine engine displacement. The stroke-to-bore ratio is a major factor in determining both power output and how efficiently the engine functions.

as well as to pay the mounting legal expenses in the Selden suit, all without resorting to outside borrowing.

Avoiding Wall Street was extremely important to Ford because he saw financiers as parasites, enemies to business who fostered incompetence through a focus on short-term performance over long-term growth:

> Businessmen believed that you could do anything by "financing" it. If it did not go through on the first financing then the idea was to "refinance." The process of "refinancing" was simply the game of sending good money after bad. In the majority of cases, the need of refinancing arises from bad management, and the effect of refinancing is simply to pay the poor managers to keep up their bad management a little longer. It is merely a postponement of the day of judgment. This makeshift of refinancing is a device of speculative financiers. Their money is no good to them unless they can connect it up with a place where real work is being done, and that they cannot do unless, somehow, that place is poorly managed.[2]

Poor management was never an issue with Ford, especially on the factory floor. While he could be harsh, even cruel—many of the practical jokes for which he was famous bordered on the sadistic and were most often foisted on the most innocent and vulnerable—he also was hands-on and encouraging, led by example, and was every bit the team player. Ford never stood still. Inside the factory, he could turn up anywhere at any time, "the shop, the experimental department, the drafting room or the power plant; he came and went as he liked."[3] By all accounts, he was one of those rare individuals with true charisma, idolized by his workers, especially those with whom he was in direct contact. They eagerly embraced his insistence that there was no component that could not be improved, no process that could not be streamlined, and they worked themselves silly trying to prove it. Ford welcomed, even demanded, suggestions from his workers, and then took responsibility for implementing any resulting changes. He also took the credit, especially when an idea worked. He tended to blame others when one didn't, but few complained. Ford later said that these early years of building his company were the happiest of his life.

Eventually, of course, charisma fatigues, and Ford's management style would wear thin. Almost all of those who had the most to do with his early success, including Wills, Couzens, Cooper, and Malcomson—a group Keith Sward called "the Ford Alumni Association"—eventually left him under less than amicable circumstances. Ford never expressed regret nor accepted responsibility for a rift; he foisted blame in some cases, but in most he simply pretended the person had never existed.

In *My Life and Work,* for example, Harold Wills's contribution is omitted. In fact, there is no mention of him in the entire work, although he remained a key member of Ford's design team for more than a decade and Ford was best man at his wedding in 1914. Even Allan Nevins, certainly a sympathetic Ford biographer, admitted that "in the design of all the company models of the next dozen years, it is impossible to disentangle Ford's work from that of Wills."[4] But Wills, who also eventually became one of the world's foremost metallurgists, would not be shoved down the corporate ladder, so he was eventually shunted aside, one of the many associates crucial to Ford's success whom Ford would ultimately consider disloyal ingrates. Alexander Malcomson is also not mentioned in Ford's account—less surprising given the acrimony that would characterize the collapse of their partnership but still a significant oversight. Ford never alluded to the fact that at the outset both he and Wills drew salaries paid by Malcomson.* But the most stunning omission is of James Couzens, whose name appears not once and whose indispensable contributions to Ford's success are either ignored or attributed to Ford himself.

By 1904, it had become clear to both Ford and Couzens that Strelow's Mack Avenue plant was no longer adequate. Couzens had built a

* Technically, only Wills was being paid, at $125 per week, but he was splitting that with Ford.

strong network of dealers, many of whom complained that they had sold an entire allocation of automobiles before a single actual car arrived at their showroom.

As a result, Ford Motor became one of a number of auto firms between 1904 and 1906 to move in to expanded facilities. Cadillac's new plant was capable of producing 4,500 cars per year, all to Henry Leland's exacting standards, and Packard added 50,000 square feet of floor space. Olds pushed against the tide of auto manufacturers and parts makers locating their businesses in Detroit and moved back to Lansing, albeit to a factory twice the size of the one he left.

Ford contracted for a huge new three-story brick factory on Piquette Avenue in Detroit, each floor 22,500 square feet, in total ten times the floor space of its predecessor. Despite its size and modernity, the plant had a number of oddities, the most curious being that Henry Ford did not have a private office in the headquarters of the company that bore his name. He worked from a desk out on the floor in the pattern department, "where he usually spent the first hours of the morning before circulating through the plant."[5] Assembly of the automobiles—Ford still manufactured virtually nothing onsite—was done on the third floor rather than the first. Deliveries came in and finished cars went out by means of an elevator at the rear. Material was sometimes moved to the appropriate place on the floor by hay wagons, and "the assembly of automobiles was as yet a primitive operation. While the engines, frames, and bodies were assembled separately, with every effort to promote efficiency, they were brought together for final assembly simply by being carried to a designated spot and set on wooden horses."[6] Whereas both the Olds and Cadillac factories worked on an assembly line principle, Ford clearly had yet to grasp the efficiencies of that method of production and assembly.[†]

But perhaps the strangest feature of the new Ford plant was the placement of the other executive offices. Couzens and all the business

---

* A pattern was in essence a three-dimensional sketch, a model of a part or component. Patterns were particularly important at Ford's because Ford "never quite understood what a design looked like" without one.

† Most observers considered the Ford factory inferior to the Packard plant as well.

staff were with the machine shop and the electrical and shipping departments on the first floor, where Ford rarely visited. And Couzens almost never went to the second floor to the engineering and experimental sections, where Wills and an expanding staff of engineers, designers, and pattern makers worked directly with Ford. This distance, born of mutual antipathy, would have sunk most companies, but Ford and Couzens were unique: their moving in separate orbits was instead the making of the Ford Motor Company.

Couzens, at this stage of the company's growth, was considered "already one of the keenest, most experienced, and most ambitious businessmen in Detroit."[7] Although he and Ford could not stomach having offices on the same floor, Ford was savvy enough not to get in Couzens's way:

> The man was made of nails. [He] displayed an energy no less fierce and a passion for work no less intense than Ford's. He performed on a dozen fronts. He was the company's chief publicist, its foremost buyer, its super-salesman, its best-known missionary in the small town, and the canny keeper of the exchequer. His office was the nerve center through which all Ford dealers and shippers and suppliers had to clear. Over a period of thirteen years, the firm's sales force and office personnel were selected and groomed under his personal supervision.[8]

Even Charles Sorenson, who thought as much of Henry Ford as any man alive, acknowledged, "From 1903 to 1913 was the Couzens period. True, the company had Henry Ford's name, its product and production were his. There never would have been a Ford car without him. But the Ford Motor Company would not have made Ford cars long without James Couzens. He controlled expenditures, organized sales, and set the pattern for business operation. He drove Ford and the production side to produce cars to meet the public's demand."[9]

But perhaps the most important role Couzens played was among the least publicized—driving the ouster of Alexander Malcomson and the elevation of Henry Ford to majority shareholder.

The mutual antagonism generated by Malcomson's forcing Ford to build the Model B had not diminished. Malcomson insisted the company produce at least one model, which would be called the K, for the upscale market.

The K was, despite Ford's distaste, a fine automobile. It featured a vertical six-cylinder engine—the first Ford had built for a commercial vehicle—which could generate 40 horsepower and reach 50 miles per hour. The gas tank had been enlarged to 15 gallons, which gave the car a range of 250 miles. Tires were 34-inch on a 114-inch wheelbase. The carburetor and ignition had been improved and the axles were fitted with extra ball bearings.

To appeal to its market, the K was built with front and rear seats standard and offered an optional top and gas lamps. "Special attention" was given to the body "to make it of most pleasing design. It is of the Victoria type with swelled panels and graceful in every line, yet eminently distinct in design. The seats are large, roomy and handsomely upholstered with buffed leather, rolling well back over the top edges and tufted over coil springs and curled hair."

With all the improvements, however, the K did not sell to anyone's satisfaction except Malcomson's, and that was likely because Malcomson's standards were based in pride of authorship. But neither was the car a flop. In the end, it sold just enough to ensure that Ford and Malcomson would remain unyielding.

"Couzens saw that eventually either Ford or Malcomson would have to leave the company. If he himself wanted to stay, he had to choose sides."[10] Malcomson soon made the decision more pressing by insisting that Couzens resign his position at Ford and return to run the coal company so that Malcomson could manage the car business full-time. When Couzens told Malcomson that he would do no such thing, Malcomson demanded at a board meeting that Couzens be fired. He needed two of the other four directors—Ford, Gray, John Dodge, and his lawyer, John Anderson—to vote with him for the motion to pass. (Votes were individual, not proportionally based on stock holdings.) Only Anderson did, and Couzens was retained. A furious Malcomson was further marginalized when the board voted 4–1 to double Couzens's $4,000-per-year salary. Malcomson had lost far more than a test of wills at two company meetings. He had forgotten that Couzens was no longer his clerk, and he made an enemy of a man who was a good deal smarter, tougher, and more ruthless than he.

A scheme for forcing Malcomson out was hatched in late fall 1905, and it bears Couzens's stamp. If all went according to plan, Ford would finally succeed in gaining unquestioned control. And while they were at it, Ford and Couzens decided, they might as well use the opportunity to remove other dead wood—Malcomson's allies—from the investors' ranks.

In late December they set their project in motion. As reported in the trades, "The Ford Manufacturing Company has been organized in Detroit, its capital being $100,000 and its purpose being to build motors, parts and accessories to be used in Ford cars. Henry Ford is president of the concern: John F. Dodge, vice-president; C. H. Wills, secretary, and James Couzens, treasurer."[11]

On its face, the plan seemed to be sound business—the new company was under the control of Ford Motor, and the creation of a dedicated manufacturing arm would end some of the costly subcontracting and put more of the fabricating process under the direct control of Ford executives. But in a clever little wrinkle omitted from the published reports, the prices that Ford Manufacturing could charge Ford Motor were left open, meaning that if they were set high enough, all the profit from the sale of a car would flow to the subsidiary rather than the parent. This would be of no consequence if the shareholder lists of the two companies were identical, but of course the entire point was that they would not be. Malcomson, Gray, Albert Strelow (whose $5,000 had saved them all), and some other minor stockholders—Malcomson's personal friends—were not offered stock in Ford Manufacturing.[12]

Had he not been so overmatched, Malcomson could have launched an effective counterattack. He remained both treasurer and a principal stockholder of Ford Motor. But his speculator's heart got the better of him. Instead of building support inside the company he had founded, he announced that he would form another car company, Aerocar, to produce "the Car of Today, Tomorrow, and of Years to Come."

John Gray, who seemed a target of the cabal, was actually a supporter. He went along with being shut out of Ford Manufacturing because he was assured it was merely a short-term ploy to rid the company of his nephew, with whom even he had finally lost patience. "I have Mr. Ford's promise," he said, "that when they get things straightened out with Mr. Malcomson, the Ford Manufacturing Company is to be taken into the Ford Motor Company, just as if it had never existed."[13] The directors further turned up the heat on Malcomson by officially asking him to resign as treasurer and give up his seat on the board, citing as justification his intention to establish a competing car company. Malcomson refused amidst harsh words on both sides. Soon afterward, Ford Motor contracted to purchase ten thousand engines from Ford Manufacturing at a price to be determined. The subsidiary had even leased a factory on nearby Bellevue Avenue, ostensibly to produce the contracted material. (These engines would all be for the next rollout, the N, a low-priced model that Ford and the engineering team had been working on feverishly for months. Motors for the Model K would continue to be produced in the Dodge brothers' plant—although, with John Dodge having a prominent position in Ford Manufacturing, full consolidation of manufacturing and assembly was inevitable.)

In May 1906, having convinced himself that the Aerocar would be a brilliant success, Malcomson agreed to sell his 25 percent stake in Ford Motor for $175,000. On July 12, the transaction was finalized. With the proceeds, he built an 80,000-square-foot building to produce a five-passenger touring car, featuring four air-cooled cylinders that generated 24 horsepower, priced at $2,800. By 1908, he was offering three models priced from $1,500 to $2,200. No one bought them. Aerocar folded, and Malcomson left the car business forever.* The following year, department store owner Joseph L. Hudson bought the building and formed the Hudson Motor Car Company—headed by Roy Chapin—to build low-priced cars. Never an immense success, Hudson was sufficiently profitable to remain in business until 1954.

Neither Couzens nor Ford ever expressed misgivings about oust-

* Malcomson returned to the coal business, which remained successful. He died in the 1920s, a multimillionaire.

ing at a wildly deflated price "the real founder of the Ford Motor Company," the man who "had given both men their start." Ford, in fact, would gloat over his triumph in the coming years, never missing an opportunity to remind Malcomson of how much money he had lost. In time, as with many of Ford's dealings, the series of transactions was sanitized to protect him.* Charles Sorenson presented such a version:

> As Model N neared production stage, Malcomson became so troublesome that he alienated even the Dodge brothers. There were rumors that he was backing another motorcar company, whereupon Ford, Couzens, the Dodges, Wills, and two other Ford Motor Company stockholders organized the Ford Manufacturing Company, which would make parts for Model N, while the Dodges continued as suppliers for Model K. This move had three results: First, it brought the manufacture of motorcar parts under Ford control. Second, it enabled stockholders to take two profits, one from manufacture of parts and the other from sale of cars. Third, it forced Malcomson to sell Ford Motor Company stock.[14]

In fact, the first two were contrivances—no one had ever found fault with the Dodges' work, and stockholders would profit only selectively—and only the third was germane to the move. In addition, although Ford Manufacturing was contracted to produce those ten thousand motors for the soon-to-be-released Model N, Ford, Couzens, and the Dodges assumed that by the time the motors had actually been built, Ford Manufacturing might well no longer exist.

With Malcomson's departure and that of other minor stockhold-

---

* The most pathetic of the former investors was Strelow. He took the $25,000 he eventually received for his Ford stock and invested it in a gold mine that went bust. A story, perhaps apocryphal, made the rounds that some years later, Strelow was spotted in a line of common laborers trying to be hired on Ford's assembly line for the famous $5 a day.

ers, Henry Ford brought his holdings to 58.5 percent of Ford Motor Company. Couzens purchased Albert Strelow's shares and became the second-largest stockholder at 11 percent. When John Gray died in July 1906, his 10.5 percent passed to his estate—in which Alexander Malcomson was not a beneficiary. With Gray gone, Henry Ford became president of the company.

Malcomson's prejudice for larger cars had again worked to Ford's benefit. The Model N, which would turn out to be Ford's most innovative product and the effective prototype for the Model T, drew heavily on the engineering and design that Ford had been forced to undertake for the Model K. "Shortly after my arrival at Ford," Charles Sorenson noted, "designs which plainly were parts for a lighter car began to show up on the blackboard and drafting tables. Mr. Ford was applying to this car ideas he had worked out with Models B and K. He was seeking a successor to Model F which would have four instead of two cylinders and torque instead of chain drive, and yet could be made to sell under the $800 minimum for his earlier runabouts."

With that new model, Henry Ford, at age forty-three, would finally begin the ascent that would make him the richest man in America.

CHAPTER 18

THE FIRST SHOT OF
THE REVOLUTION

n January 1906, Ford Motor Company began a series of full-page ads that featured both the N and the K, one pictured under the other. For the former, the copy read, "This car—Model N—is the biggest revelation yet made in Automobile construction. A car of this type for less than $500.00 seemed an impossibility, but here it is. 4-cylinder—15 H.P. Direct Drive. Speed—40 miles. 78-inch Wheel Base. 700 pounds." For the K, which ran underneath and appeared to be a gussied-up N, the copy read, "6 cylinders—40 H.P. 40 to 50 miles per hour on high gear. Perfected magneto ignition—mechanical oiler, 114-inch wheel base, luxurious body for 5 passengers, weight 2,000 pounds. Price, $2,500.00." While certainly both cars were made to appear attractive, the N was presented as distinct and innovative, while the K was simply another luxury car in a virtually saturated market.

For example, also early in 1906, Packard phased out its own Model N and replaced it with the Packard 24. Priced at $4,000, it epitomized comfort, luxury, and the very best in automaking. "The motor has four vertical cylinders cast in pairs, with integral water-jackets and valve chambers," *Motor World* wrote.

It is made in France from stock the best adapted to cylinder construction, but the machine work is all done in the Packard factory. The bore is 4 inches, and stroke 5 inches, so that there is an increase in the piston area over the model "N" of more than 20 per cent, and represents an increase in motorpower of 35 to 40 per cent, with only 5 per cent increase in weight. The pistons are fitted with four rings. For ignition an Eiseman high-tension magneto is used, although a storage battery is retained for the purpose of starting the motor from the seat, and is always in reserve. The magneto is bolted to the front arm of the motor support, and is operated by chain from a small counter-shaft, which is geared to the left camshaft. The current is carried through a single high-tension coil on the dash to the commutator. In the same box with the magneto coil is a single coil, with vibrator, for the storage battery, magneto and "open." Individual switches connect with the stems of the spark plugs, so that a plug can be removed without disturbing the wires, or a fault in firing can be traced, by simply lifting one switch at a time.[1]

The Packard certainly cost a good deal more than the K, but it was also a good deal more car for the money. This is not to say that Ford was trying to sabotage his own product—he would certainly have been thrilled to sell every K he built. But it seems clear that the Model N was where he was placing his bets. To add to the sense of excitement, the early January Ford ads contained this postscript: "No further particulars will be given until these cars are shown for the first time at the Automobile Club of America's Show at the 69th Regiment Armory, New York, January 13th to 20th. Deliveries for Models N and K will not be made before March. 1906 will be a 'Ford Year.' Agents who have closed with us can congratulate themselves."[2]

But as had often been the case with Ford proclamations, Ford and Couzens were acting on a good bit of bluff, particularly for the N. To build a prototype to take to an auto show was one thing, but manufacturing ten thousand automobiles in a year—which is what they promised—was quite another. And they *needed* to build those ten thousand cars, for that was the cornerstone of their pricing. To defend their claims—which elicited serious skepticism, even disbelief, among automobile cognoscenti—Couzens took out a four-page ad in the January 1906 edition of *Cycle and Automobile Journal.* Under the heading "The Successful Ford," the first page of copy read:

> This is why we can build the Ford 4 cylinder Runabout for less than $500. We are making 40,000 cylinders, 10,000 engines, 40,000 wheels, 20,000 axles, 10,000 bodies, 10,000 of every part that goes into the car—think of it! Such quantities were never heard of before. For this car, we buy 40,000 spark plugs, 10,000 spark coils, 40,000 tires, all exactly alike. If we made a profit one-fifth as much on each car as is usually figured as a proper profit, we would make as large a gross profit as a manufacturer who builds two thousand cars. But who builds two thousand Runabouts? The first Runabout (Model C) we built cost $30,000, yet we sold duplicates of that model for $750. It is the quantity that counts.[3]

The ad went on to say that thousands were already in production, which was blatantly false, and that the Model N was a radical departure from previous Ford models, which was at least potentially true.

What was certainly true was that, despite the mythology that would settle around him only a few years later, Henry Ford at that point knew next to nothing about interchangeable parts, mass production, or even how to effectively set up a factory. He had squandered his chance to learn when he refused to even try to work with Henry Leland, and so, unless he could acquire those skills, and quickly, the Model N was doomed, no matter how good a car it was or how cheaply it was sold.

Although the car had to be "rushed through for the show"—it was completed only a few days beforehand—and had not been previously exhibited, "even to agents," Ford, as promised, brought a prototype Model N to exhibit at the Automobile Club of America's New York auto show that opened at 8:00 P.M. on Saturday, January 13, 1906, at the 69th Regiment Armory, at 68 Lexington Avenue. Opening at the very same time just steps away at Madison Square Garden was another automobile show, this one sponsored by ALAM. In a further attempt to choke off competition, the ALAM board had "suddenly and unexpectedly" made the decision in mid-1905 to no longer allow unlicensed manufacturers to exhibit at its annual auto show.[4] Shut out of their industry's most important trade show for the first time—the two sides had endured an uneasy coexistence at shows during the previous five years—the independents had been forced to scramble about, and the only appropriate venue they could find was the under-construction armory, which at that point was surrounded by scaffolding and crawling with masons, carpenters, and electrical workers. Like the Model N, the building in which the car would be exhibited was also "rushed through for the show." When the ACA show opened, the scaffolding was gone, but large sections of the cavernous building lacked paint and other finishing touches.

The dual—or dueling—auto shows were, to that point, the most significant public display of the rift among automakers. While many buyers of automobiles had been at least vaguely aware that their purchase either conformed or did not conform to the Selden patent—and that Henry Ford was the most visible and outspoken *refusé*—the legal disputes had played out largely out of the view of the general public. But with automobiles attaining a popularity that would have struck dumb those who had watched the Chicago auto race ten years before, the stakes both inside and outside ALAM had escalated, and the battle had become plain to see.

"The makers of all the machines in the Garden recognize the rights of the Selden patent as covering the principles of the internal combustion engine, which is the scientific term for the gasoline engine," *The New York Times* reported. "The armory exhibitors, on the other hand, are known popularly as the independents, as they have thus far refused to recognize the basic rights of the patent. This sharp legal division is really the reason for the two shows."[5]

Each side billed its show as the "sixth annual," dating from the first show in 1900. "Magnificent is the only word that aptly sums up the universal sentiment expressed last night by several thousand visitors to the two big automobile shows," the *Times* went on. "If any spirit of rivalry were apparent, if any public favoritism had been anticipated, there were no evidences of such conditions in either the Madison Square Garden or the Sixty-ninth Regiment Armory."

But the trade journals saw things differently, and according to them ALAM had a clear advantage:

> The Madison Square Garden show, held under the auspices of the Association of Licensed Automobile Manufacturers, having the benefit of an old show building and the management of show promoters of many years' experience, was as nearly complete as it is possible for a show to be on the opening day, and everything was cleaned up ready for the public. The Automobile Club of America's show in the 69th Regiment Armory, not half a block away from the Garden, was not in the same fortunate condition, owing mainly to the fact that the building was still in an unfinished condition when the exhibits were installed and much new work had to be completed, so that although every exhibit was in place much cleaning up had to be done after the public was admitted.[6]

The ALAM board had, in fact, spared no expense, and their show could not be matched in opulence. "In appearance and effective decorations the Madison Square Garden show undoubtedly excelled anything of the kind which has ever been held, and persons who have visited the large building many times during the past 12 or 15 years, declared that never before was it so well planned or so magnificently decorated." Thirty thousand electric lights had been mounted along

An automobile calendar for 1906, when cars became synonymous with glamour

the ceiling, potted evergreens lined corridors, and sculptures had been commissioned for the bases and tops of stairways. "The girders are hidden from end to end of the structure, and the ceiling has been transformed into a sea of blue, colored as an Italian sky, through which the dim gleam of hidden electric lights may be discerned, giving the effect of a clear night sky. Thousands of yards of cloth were used to gain this effect. . . . Dazzling to the eye, artistic and beautiful, the huge building had been transformed into a veritable fairy palace," gushed *Horseless Age*.[7] The armory decorations, on the other hand, were described as "very neat and tasty." If ALAM's goal was to project solidity, prosperity, and trust in its products—and that automobiles were big business—it certainly succeeded. "One hundred and twenty pleasure vehicles of forty-eight different makes represented the Garden Show, and, remarkable as it may seem, there was not a freak among them."[8]

But attendance at each show was, in fact, close to identical, with an estimated 95,000 attending the ALAM show and 85,000 visiting the armory. For all the expenditures and frills, it was the actual cars that people had come to see. Automobiles had become so much a part of the culture that the crowd "swarmed through the Garden, climbed into the various cars, played the gear and brake levers, tried steering wheels, peeked under bonnets and into the mysteries of the working parts ... asked prices, talked carburetor, spark coil, gears and transmissions like old time veterans ... It was a surprising revelation to hear young girls, and at times their younger brothers, talking automobiles and using the proper names for the various parts."[9] Reaction at the armory show was the same. And, as with any burgeoning technology, new products would attract particular attention, which left Ford with his revolutionary $500 runabout in a particularly favorable position.

Ford had brought a Model K—the lowest-priced six-cylinder car— and a Model F with him as well, but it was the Model N that drew the attention. And Ford's runabout fared well, in terms of both its "decidedly pleasing appearance" and its specifications—described as "better at every point than was generally expected."[10] When Ford left to return to Detroit, he had assurances that thousands of orders for his runabout were soon to follow.

But the prospect of a clamor for the Model N did not make matters easier for Ford and Couzens, who were frantically trying to get the Bellevue Avenue factory in shape to actually produce their engines. And Ford wasn't the only manufacturer who was trying to apply modern methods but had run into problems. "The demand for machine tools and automobile parts by competing companies was insatiable; and bottlenecks developed in half a dozen supply lines."[11]

The operation Ford and Couzens encountered on their return to Detroit was indeed archaic, much of it reflecting manufacturing techniques already abandoned by Packard, Cadillac, and especially Olds. Certainly compared to George Condict's battery-changing operation for the fleet of electric hansoms, Ford's factory looked primitive. An engine block under construction needed to be passed by hand from one station to another, a process that continued until the completed apparatus was toted to the assembly plant on Piquette Avenue by the ever-trusty horse-drawn hay wagon.

As a result, the prototype that had been exhibited in New York had a number of problems that had to be eliminated—poor casting on the engine block and failures in the crankshaft and cooling system, among others—particularly before the company began to turn out one hundred identical automobiles per day. (Ford had been given a reprieve, however: because the Model N had been exhibited but not driven, its flaws passed largely unnoticed.)

But Ford once more proved that he knew not only when he needed help but also who could provide it and how to best avail himself of their talents. Setting up the Bellevue Avenue factory required heavy equipment, and in shopping for it, Ford had met a machine tool salesman named Walter E. Flanders, who also owned a small factory that made crankshafts. Flanders had previously worked for the Singer Sewing Machine Company, a pioneer in mass production, and Ford recognized instantly that Flanders was a man he should badger for advice. (In doing so, Ford again set aside his prejudices. Exceeding even Spider Huff in his appetites, Flanders was a hard-drinking carouser who was noted also as a brawler and an epic womanizer, all of which Ford overlooked in pursuit of product.) Flanders persuaded Ford to hire Max Wollering, a young engineer who was then working for International Harvester, and to give Wollering a free hand in setting up the Bellevue Avenue floor operation.

Wollering started work in April 1906 and immediately streamlined the workflow. "We put up short conveyers to push it along to the next operation. It was not automatic. It had to be hand conveyed. When the man finished the milling operation, he'd take the block, put it on the slide, and push it along to the next station."[12]

Although the assembly line was still years away, with Flanders and Wollering, Ford finally began to add the refinements that could keep pace with Olds's and Cadillac's production methods. "We didn't group our machines by type at all," Wollering recalled. "They were pretty much grouped to accommodate the article they were working on. . . .

When I got there, they had the milling machine, which was very big, and the boring machine, which is large, in place. I left them stand and we built around them. We put the others in to make a kind of progressive arrangement."

Standardizing the product flow made improving the actual product much easier. For safety and stability, the weight of the car was brought up from 700 to 1,000 pounds and the dimensions were increased to carry the weight.[13] The crankshaft and cooling systems were improved, as was the casting of the engine block. By the time the Model N was ready to be examined by auto journalists, Ford agents, and potential buyers, it had been transformed and, at the proposed price, promised to be one of the most sought-after cars ever produced in the United States.

What received the greatest praise in the trades was Flanders's and Wollering's machining:

> The feature that strikes the experienced manufacturer most forcibly is the care and accuracy of the work. Parts are ground that makers of high priced machines consider well enough made when done on a lathe. Cylinders and pistons are first rough cut, then annealed to relieve the strains in the castings, after which, in the case of cylinders, they are reamed, an operation that insures a perfectly straight as well as a perfectly round cylinder. This method is now considered superior to grinding by most engineers. Pistons, after being annealed are given a finishing cut on another automatic machine, after which they are ground. The top is ground four-thousandths smaller than the bottom end, the section between the first and second rings, three-thousandths, and that between the second and the third, two-thousandths smaller than the main portion of the piston.[14]

When Ford saw what Wollering was capable of, he put him in charge of the Piquette Avenue factory as well. Within two months, the operation was turning out a steady stream of automobiles—although nowhere near one hundred per day—so that Ford agents could begin taking orders for the Model N. Still, the N was not ready for actual sale until after Malcomson sold his stock to Ford on July 12.[15]

As good as Wollering was, Couzens knew that Walter Flanders was better. But Ford was reluctant. "Couzens, Wills, and the Dodge brothers were behind this selection," Charles Sorenson wrote. "Ford . . . was aware of Flanders's ability, yet feared the man might take his place. There was a streak of jealousy here. Flanders, a forceful, boisterous man, was popular with the directors and got along well with men in the shop."[16]

But Ford never allowed personal feelings to keep him from talent, so, ultimately, he hired Flanders in August and made him head of production with complete control over manufacturing operations at both plants. Wollering and another talented young production man, Thomas S. Walborn, became his assistants. Flanders proved himself every bit as brilliant in his métier as were James Couzens and Harold Wills in theirs. Even more impressive was that Flanders often displayed his genius through the haze of massive hangovers:

> He took on the Ford job and in a few weeks completely revamped the plant's production methods. The whole interior of the factory was rearranged, new machinery installed, workers given new jobs. It was not assembly line production, which was to come later, but it was the most efficient production system that had been introduced in Detroit up to that time. In the final assembly, for instance, each workman had specific jobs to perform. Each group of assemblers had runners to keep material always on hand; and there were helpers who supplied small tools at the exact moment they were needed. There was no hit-or-miss assembly as there had been before. Everything was done systematically, and thus the job of putting Fords together was considerably speeded up.[17]

Charles F. Kettering, a noted inventor, engineer, and, for almost three decades, head of research at General Motors, was unstinting in his praise of Flanders's brilliance.

Flanders' specialty was simplification of work. He constantly shifted machines and equipment to minimize the
handling of materials. He made each machine more
adapted to a specific job by developing special jigs and fixtures to eliminate as nearly as possible the chance of human
error. Not only did he rearrange production machines, but
he used the principle of simultaneous machining operations wherever possible. He installed milling machines that
could mill two faces of a casting at the same time, made
other machines more automatic and set up scores of punch
presses. All of these had been and were being used in the
production of other things, but no one up to that time had
brought all these production methods and machines to
bear upon one model of an automobile.[18]

Sorenson summed it up: "In the nearly two years he was at Ford,
his rearrangement of machines headed us toward mass production.
Ford, a quiet, sensitive person, got a few gray hairs at this stage, but he
learned a great deal from Flanders, and so did I."*[19]

Flanders's operation also had substantial impact on the way money
moved through the company.

He found that the demand was in excess of capacity . . .
and . . . set up a production program for twelve months
ahead. This enabled the purchasing department to get better prices with fixed deliveries. Instead of our carrying in-
ventories, he got the foundries and other suppliers to do it.
Our stock keepers were told not to have on hand more
than a ten-day supply of anything to meet our production
requirements. Previously the funds locked up for this pur-

* In 1908, after he had created the production system that would eventually produce tens of millions of Model Ts, Walter Flanders would join the Ford Alumni
Association. He joined with an auto body manufacturer, Barney Everitt, and William Metzger, a salesman from Cadillac, to form the E-M-F Corporation. After
only two years, E-M-F was taken over by Studebaker.

pose had been very large. Now, thanks to Flanders, those funds were freed and much of the confusion of hand-to-mouth operation that Ford Motor Company had been working under was now ended. The results were a revelation to all of us.

Much of that money went into research, in particular for the next-generation Ford automobile, which in 1908 would be christened the Model T.

Literally one day before Alexander Malcomson left to build his "car of the future," *Horseless Age* published an evaluation of Ford Manufacturing:

> All parts, where it is at all possible, are finished on automatic machines, regardless of size. Each machine makes that part and nothing else; and since many of the machines are specially designed, they are fitted for nothing else. High-speed steel is used to its limit. A large corps of inspectors constantly follow the different operations in order to instantly detect any variation and rectify the error before it is made in a large number of pieces. For it will be readily seen that this system, which can only be applied where cars are made in very large quantities, cuts down the total cost of production enormously, and goes a long way toward putting the automobile in the same class with typewriters, sewing machines, guns and other interchangeable products.[20]

The piece then proceeded to praise the corporate vision that resulted in such a system, which went to the heart of Henry Ford's brilliance:

> In manufacturing any machine cheaply two distinct courses are open to the maker: Either he may use the cheapest possible material, make parts as small as he dares, finish as few

surfaces as possible, and by employing cheap workmen and making fits so loose that the parts can be thrown together from a distance, he will be able to produce an article which will be cheap in more senses than one. On the other hand, he may use a quality of material amply good for the purpose to which it is put, design his machine so that the parts are as few and simple as possible, make them of sufficient size for proper strength and wearing qualities, and by systematized methods of manufacture finish all necessary parts as well as they need be finished. It is this latter course that the Ford Motor Company are endeavoring to follow in the manufacture of their little car.

By autumn 1906, while Ford would fall short of his goal of ten thousand cars (he would produce only eight thousand) and not be able to hold to the $500 price (he would raise it to $600), he had the best-running factories, which were producing one of the lowest-priced, highest-quality automobiles to be found anywhere in the world. Thanks to his own indefatigable efforts—and those of Alexander Malcomson, James Couzens, Harold Wills, Walter Flanders, the Dodge brothers, and a host of others—he had successfully transitioned from one of the hundreds of small, hopeful start-ups to an industry power; from an operation that threw automobiles together to one that used the incipient techniques of mass production.

With the N, Ford also demonstrated how his insatiable drive for improvement, his refusal to allow either himself or his company to stand still, could bear unexpected fruit. The Ford Manufacturing Company had been a contrivance, a paper fiction created to squeeze out an unwanted associate. If Ford and Couzens wanted to gain closer control over building engines and transmissions, there were any number of simpler ways to do it. But once Ford Manufacturing was a reality, Ford got the most out of it. Starting from scratch, he went out and obtained the human and mechanical resources required to initiate the manufacturing techniques that he would later be credited with inventing.

CHAPTER 19

MR. SELDEN COMES TO NEW YORK

B y early 1906, while Ford and Couzens were scrambling to produce the Model N, Ralzemond Parker was contending with a patent suit that had taken on Dickensian heft. The defendants had completed their testimony, which ran to "2,400 typewritten pages and 140 exhibits." In February, *Horseless Age* noted that "although a decision was confidently expected last fall, very little has been heard recently of any progress in the proceedings. This remarkable case promises to develop into a record in patent litigation as regards the length of time during which the patent has been under dispute before the courts."[1] That statement proved prescient: a decision would not be forthcoming for three more years.

The main problem in reaching resolution was that patent suits were conducted as if they had actually been lifted from the pages of Charles Dickens's *Bleak House,* where the entirety of a huge estate was eaten up by legal fees, leaving nothing for the heirs. In American patent law in the early 1900s, a judge wasn't even assigned to the case until after massive amounts of material had been generated by each side, all totally outside the court system or rules of evidence. All that was required in the taking of a deposition, for example, was that it be done in the presence of a neutral third party. Therefore, if either the witness or the lawyer wanted to drag the proceedings on, either by asking irrelevant questions or by giving irrelevant answers, there was no way to speed the interrogation along. Exhibits submitted by each side might or might not be germane to the issue at hand. Many patent lawyers, either because of self-interest or because they thought volume would impress the trial judge, would submit massive briefs supported by staggering quantities of what passed for evidence. Lawyers for the other side, fearful that a streamlined submission would be interpreted as a lack of thorough preparation, would match or outdo their opponents. During this entire process, not surprisingly, each side would continuously announce its desire to move the case along and decry the excesses of its opponent in protracting the process.

Ordinarily, it was more in the plaintiffs' interest to push for a conclusion, since until a decision was rendered, no licensing fees would be forthcoming, and each month's delay worked against the patent's seventeen-year life. While victory in court did entitle the plaintiffs to royalties retroactive to the date the patent was issued, collecting back taxes is always a touch-and-go affair. Better to set up a mechanism to collect the fees as they were taken in. But here, ALAM was contending with what it saw as a growing weakness of both the patent and the infringement suits it had initiated on the basis of the patent. The obvious and quite serious holes in the plaintiffs' case had been relentlessly exploited by Ford's lawyers, and there was more than a little doubt about how the trial judge would view the evidence, especially in an industry that had advanced immensely in just the three years since the suit had been originally filed. And, of course, the Ford Motor Company was no longer merely a speck on the automotive landscape.

So, although the United States patent office had seen fit to grant George Selden his patent without requiring that his theoretical machine actually be built and tested, the ALAM lawyers no longer felt they enjoyed the same luxury. While the patent examiners had taken it on faith that the Selden road carriage was both workable and a radical departure from all that had come before, the trial judge, whoever it turned out to be, might actually want a bit of proof.* The plaintiffs feared they might need to demonstrate not only that Selden's plan had been an original concept in 1879, which might not prove to be all that difficult, but also that his design could be turned into a practical automobile—a far taller order.

The chief problem was the same as it had always been—George Selden had never really built anything. The only piece of the puzzle that had even tentatively been brought to life was the unfinished three-cylinder motor, which, except for being briefly employed to power a lathe in 1904, had spent its entire life in Selden's storeroom.

In 1902, before the first infringement action was taken, the Electric Vehicle Company management had anticipated the problem and assigned an engineer, Henry Cave, to build a Selden machine. "This was quite a contract," Hiram Percy Maxim noted later, "as the engine shown in Selden's patent drawings was a fearful and terrible affair."[2] The work was to be done in secret, with an open checkbook—and, significantly, the process would not involve Selden. In fact, it would take Cave, working exclusively on this project, a full four years to come up with something, although just how much it conformed to Selden's patent specifications would be one more drop of water in an ocean of disputes. "Had he not been the essence of patience, tenacity, and resourcefulness," Maxim observed, "he certainly would have failed and brought himself to the madhouse." Still, with all that resourcefulness, Cave's final product did not seem to be what George Selden had designed but rather "resembled a truck."[3] Actually, "cart" would be more accurate, for it had a body that appeared to be sheets of metal painted a uniform green, and it lacked even the barest amenities.

* Part of patent law at that time was the concept of a "pioneer" invention, which was one that represented such a radical departure from the previous state of the art that the inventor was entitled to licensing fees not just from those who used his specific invention but from anyone who employed even the general principles used by the pioneer inventor. Such a patent, if granted, would be immensely valuable, but the standards under which the courts applied the rule were extremely vague. Thus anything the Selden forces could do to establish that Selden's invention was truly groundbreaking would help tilt the case in their favor.

Although in theory no more sophisticated construction was required to demonstrate workability, as the case dragged on, there was simply no way to determine whether Cave's creation—later to be labeled Exhibit 157—would be sufficiently persuasive. So the decision was made to produce a Selden road carriage that appeared both to have been built from the patent specifications and to have been done so by Selden himself.

Even for this effort, however, *George* Selden was not involved. Instead, the project, the full cost of which was borne by ALAM, was assigned to be overseen by his sons, Henry and George junior, both in their early twenties, although neither would have a hand in the actual construction. Like Cave's creation, the 1877 Buggy, as it would come to be known—or Exhibit 89—was constructed in secret, this time at the Gundlach-Manhattan Optical Company factory in Rochester. The product, which, other than the resurrected motor and crankshaft, contained not one component that was built or even designed by anyone named Selden, at least appeared to be a primitive motorcar. And even the motor had been completely rebuilt in the Gundlach machine shop. The body, fashioned by a maker of fine sulkies and finished in black lacquer with a gold stripe trim, sat over red-orange springs, wheels, and metalwork. The word "Selden" was emblazoned on the sides at the front of the machine, and "1877" was painted prominently farther back, thus predating even the application by two years. "It is an exact copy of the drawings of my patent and I defy any cross-examination to show any substantial variation," George Selden announced.

Selden's challenge was sufficiently pugnacious to give pause, but the machine was not. The 1877 Buggy would not have stood up to even the most casual scrutiny. It might have superficially resembled the drawings in the patent application, but both it and Cave's machine had been built with vast departures from its specifications. The Rochester vehicle, for example, had a modern carburetor and oil pump, timed ignition rather than constant flame, and new cylinder heads and valves. In fact, the only component of the buggy that had not been updated was the cooling system, likely thought unnecessary by machinists working in the Rochester winter. Cave's machine represented even a greater departure. In addition to all the improvements in the 1877 Buggy, Cave had installed a water jacket to cool the engine, pneumatic tires, and gears to change speeds. This last enhancement allowed his machine to generate 15 horsepower, rather than the 2 horsepower that the Selden buggy achieved.

But even if all the alterations were made public—and they were not—it remained an open question whether or not they would invalidate Selden's claim. According to 1900's patent law, validation would depend upon whether or not the patent was granted pioneer status—which, of course, was the crux of the case. If it was, then the "substitutions" would be perfectly acceptable because it was expected that a pioneer concept would be improved on. If not, however, the substitutions would not be allowed because the patent would apply only to the specific design in the application.

While the evidentiary benefits of the Selden vehicles remained problematic, the ALAM lawyers were not interested only in demonstrating their virtues to the judge. By producing the machines, particularly the 1877 Buggy, which had been constructed in the inventor's hometown and—at least by implication—by the inventor himself, they were hoping to establish with the general public Selden's status as "the father of the automobile," the term Selden used to describe himself.

Oddly, the door to achieving that goal was open. That Selden had never before built the road carriage specified in his patent was, considering the notoriety of the case, not at all widely perceived. In several Sunday newspapers, the 1877 Buggy was described specifically as having been built in that year.[4] Even *Motor World*, in May 1906, termed the 1877 Buggy "Selden's original car," implying a link with the date conveniently emblazoned on the machine, although the editors should surely have been aware of its true origins.[5] As late as May 1907, *The New York Times* reported, "The original Selden car, it may be interesting to know, is stored in a garage in this city and has been exhibited in many automobile shows."[6] Although Ford's lawyers continually stressed both machines' recent construction, ALAM largely succeeded in keeping from the public that for three decades the Selden car had been little more than a phantom.

The Selden forces timed the appearance of the 1877 Buggy and Cave's machine to coincide with Selden's arrival in New York to give rebuttal testimony in early May 1906—"rebuttal" meaning he would be cross-examined by Ford's lawyers based on the deposition he had given on direct examination. Again, this interrogation would be held not in a courtroom but rather at his lawyers' offices in the presence of an unbiased observer. Ralzemond Parker was certain to feature any Selden misstep prominently when the case went to trial, and the plaintiff's lawyers were extremely concerned about what their proud and sometimes arrogant client might be prodded into blurting out.

They decided to try to turn weakness to strength, to create a mood of a triumphant entrance into New York City, and so announced with great fanfare that the inventor would personally demonstrate his automobile by driving it through Manhattan. When they got a closer look at Selden's "automobile," however, their plans changed. Both man and buggy were kept under wraps for the next two weeks. Selden was shuttled between his hotel and lawyers' offices, and the buggy was parked in a basement garage on West 56th Street. Since the plaintiffs had introduced the buggy as an exhibit, however, defense lawyers had the right to examine the machine. Finally, Selden's lawyers announced that both the man and his machine would be exhibited on the Manhattan streets, and they invited a gaggle of reporters to witness the event.

Despite their trepidation, Selden turned out to be an excellent ambassador. Age fifty-nine, thin and impeccably groomed, with military bearing and a trim mustache, he wore a tiepin fashioned after the vehicle that bore his name, with hubcaps and lamps of small diamonds and a body made of sapphires.[7] Before he left for New York City, he had granted a long interview to a reporter for the journal *Technical World,* who described him as having "a strong chin that clenched tightly when he spoke of the jeers he had endured, and quick eyes that gleamed like steel points when he spoke of his ultimate triumphs. He is intensely himself—defiantly himself. Once his heavy jaw sets, all the world cannot change him."[8]

The reporter had certainly witnessed a man transformed. After decades of obscurity, George Selden had become quite comfortable with his newfound aristocracy. Just how much of the more than $1 million in licensing fees had found its way to his personal coffers was never completely clear, but it was sufficient for him to engage in conspicuous acts of largesse. In October 1906, he visited Hadlyme, Connecticut, where his ancestors had been interred in a local cemetery that had been abandoned a century earlier. Arriving in a "touring car," Selden, "the inventor of the gasolene engine for automobiles," discovered that "an old gray horse" had been buried close to the graves of his forebears. Selden then declared that "he will buy the whole cemetery and own and run it himself." The purchase was to include surrounding property and the right-of-way to the graveyard. Lionized for his display of family loyalty, Selden, "before he bade his ancestors goodbye, had a picture taken of himself in an automobile and one of his sons driving a yoke of oxen as illustrative of the progress made since his father in an oxcart drove out of town to seek his fortune."[9]

On Saturday, May 19, that same ennobled George Selden appeared on 56th Street next to his automobile. Photographers eagerly snapped pictures of him at the wheel of his buggy, the shaft of which rose directly from the engine positioned under the seat, and Selden, with a small proud smile under those steel-point eyes, eagerly posed. Ralzemond Parker was furious. In the first place, the buggy had been pushed to the spot rather than driven—or even started—and in the second, the examination was supposed to be private. "We cannot imagine how [the reporters] found out that we were going to examine the car," he said, adding that if his opponent had somehow been the source, it would be an affront.[10]

"I see no good reason for it," ALAM's attorney replied when told of the protest, summoning up every bit as much righteousness as had his opponent. "I cannot believe the newspaper men interfered with the examination. We did not mean any affront. Naturally, the various automobile journals have taken a very great interest in this machine, and we thought it was a good opportunity to let them learn something about it."

What the Ford lawyers learned was that "in the engine shown us, the only parts that date back to 1877 are the castings for three pressure cylinders without heads, and for three air cylinders; also the piston for one cylinder of each type." Ford's representatives did all they could to discredit the machine while news photographers were shooting it from every angle, but the novelty overwhelmed their cavils. Selden himself said little, but, as it was no secret that Selden's two sons had "assisted" in the construction of the buggy, reporters turned their questions to them. Where the elder Selden could be haughty, the younger duo proved charming and deft. When a Ford attorney broke in to ask George junior, "What is there in existence in this vehicle that was in existence in 1879?" he replied, "As I was not in existence in 1879, I cannot truthfully answer that question." There was "resounding laughter."[11]

The only aspect of the buggy's presence that was germane, of course, was whether or not it would run. Both Selden and his sons, abetted by their attorneys and some friends from Rochester, assured questioners that it had gone as far as 30 miles at speeds approaching 4 miles per hour. They further claimed that the engine had run continuously for twenty-five minutes. "We could have sold some of the machines if we had been in the position to make them," George Selden insisted. These claims seemed corroborated by *Motor World,* which reported the "original car . . . on which he applied for a patent on May 8, 1879 . . . was run across the basement [of the garage] several times."* In fact, it was unclear whether the Selden buggy had run across the basement of the garage even once. The engine seemed to have started, but it developed less than 0.5 horsepower and, even with all the modern enhancements, may have barely moved before the test was ended. According to Parker, "It did not run on its own power 50 feet, but was pushed by five men."[12] From there, further demonstra-

---

* The journal was forced to admit that the buggy had been "pushed by hand to the street."

Henry Ford was persuaded to be photographed with Selden in the 1877 Buggy
© *Corbis*

tions were postponed and, after a series of motions filed by the ALAM lawyers, would not take place until the following year.

Both before and after the brief public exhibition of the 1877 Buggy, Selden was subjected to an intensive cross-examination by Ralzemond Parker, the interchange that the plaintiffs had most feared. Parker was an indefatigable interrogator and had achieved the reputation of being able to crack the veneer of even the most stolid witness and obtain admissions that could be used to great advantage at trial.

In George Selden, however, he met his match. The tale that Selden had told Leroy Scott of *Technical World*—of the lonely toiler pursuing a dream, of the visionary rejected by his family and jeered at by his neighbors—was brought forth over and over. When Parker asked about specifics of his invention, Selden replied with a tale of the difficulties in working on such a complex machine with limited funds. When Selden meandered, Parker cut him off and repeated the pointed question, only to have Selden return to his recitation of hardship and ultimate triumph. Selden was unswerving in referring to the automobile as "my invention" and all gasoline vehicles that had come subsequently as "exemplifications" of his patent.[13] Selden, of course, was every bit as versed in the intricacies of the pioneer concept as was Parker and thus knew precisely what to say to strengthen his case and what not to say to avoid prejudicing it. He "artfully refused to be ensnared by Parker's demands for details, and frequently rambled on at excessive length into a maze of irrelevancies."[14] Parker's frustrations grew as weeks of jousting dragged on, but he could not puncture Selden's composure. And, without a judge to compel the witness to be more responsive, Parker was helpless. Eventually he gave up and allowed Selden to leave the examination, the old man sporting nary a dent.

Although it was not required in order to validate the patent, the fact that Selden had never made any attempt to enter the business that his invention had spawned might also not be viewed favorably by a trial judge. So after he returned home from his battles in New York City, Selden and his boys, at the behest of his lawyers, made to at least appear to enter the automobile business.

"Although information regarding it is difficult to obtain," *Motor World* reported in October 1906, "enough is known to say that George B. Selden, world famed because of the now celebrated Selden patent, and his two sons, Henry and George B., are interested in a new automobile plant, which, if present plans do not go awry, shortly will blossom in Despatch, N.Y., which is close by Rochester." Selden and his sons vociferously denied that the venture was initiated as mere propaganda, but none of them had put up any money, nor was the elder Selden going to have any involvement beyond lending his name to the letterhead.* "Indeed, the Despatch factory will be in the nature of an offshoot or extension or sub-company of one of the present members of the Association of Licensed Automobile Manufacturers."[15]

---

* Selden's sons might have had some involvement in "an engineering capacity."

In December 1906, to again increase Selden's visibility as an actual participant in the manufacture of automobiles, "the Buffalo Gasolene Motor Co., Buffalo, N.Y., who, after negotiations with none other than George B. Selden himself, unexpectedly decided to engage in the manufacture of complete cars, has filed a formal application for permission to change its name to the Selden Motor Vehicle Co." Once again there was a caveat: "Mr. Selden's name, however, does not appear among those of the directors of the company named in the application."[16]

Trying the case in public was a two-sided affair, and Parker engaged in no small amount of absurd posturing of his own. At one point he attempted to foster the notion that ALAM had pulled back from its initial claims as to the breadth of the patent by asserting that the organization "has, for the past year or so, refrained from . . . advertising that the Selden patent 'covers all gasoline automobiles which are accepted as commercially practicable.'" Parker claimed that Selden himself had taken this view, as "a glance at [his] testimony . . . shows that this broad claim of the scope of that patent would appear to have been definitely abandoned, and that . . . it is limited to the special form of the Selden engine shown in the patent, and any equivalents of that form."[17] Parker went on to note that the proof was that ALAM had decided to limit the infringement actions to companies that used Selden's specific design . . . of which there were none.

This was nonsense, and ALAM's lawyers answered in kind. A letter "submitted by Messrs. Betts, Sheffield & Betts, counsel for the owners of the Selden patent" stated, "It is the intention of counsel for the complainant to argue the Selden patent case in the courts, not in the newspapers. . . . Therefore, the only comment we desire to make on Mr. Parker's statement is that it utterly and absolutely misstates the position of the Association of Licensed Automobile Manufacturers and their counsel and experts in the Selden patent litigation."

ALAM, in fact, had initiated an entire battery of new lawsuits, approximately twenty in all. More than seventy suits in total had been brought against manufacturers, dealers, and even purchasers of unlicensed automobiles when Parker released his statement. All the suits were dependent on the outcome of the case then being deposed, but the intention was surely to have the means in place to immediately obtain a sweeping array of judgments if Selden prevailed over Ford. Still, for ALAM's counsel to react with umbrage at "trial by press release," a tactic the organization had so gleefully employed six months before, demonstrates the banal name-calling to which the case had descended.

Henry Ford had his own take on the proceedings, and the language, at least vaguely, seems to be his own. "That the Association of Licensed Automobile Manufacturers has undertaken to sue some more manufacturers is a fitting climax to some of their other childlike acts during the past few months. Driven to desperation by the unexpected developments and the exposure of their weak structure, nothing else was to be expected but a move of this kind. When nothing substantial can be shown, the officers of the ALAM seem ever ready to start suit against some small dealer. It is a pitiable state of affairs."[18]

Ford's attorneys continued to press what they saw as their most significant advantage and demanded a demonstration of both the 1877 Buggy and Cave's machine, while ALAM lawyers continued to stall. Finally, in May 1907, the plaintiffs reluctantly agreed to produce both vehicles for tests on the streets of New York. Soon afterward, however, most likely after getting reports on the machines or perhaps checking them out for themselves, ALAM lawyers claimed that New York City law forbade the demonstrations and that the tests would need to be held elsewhere, preferably somewhere less amenable to prying eyes. They adjourned to a racetrack in Guttenberg, New Jersey—a place to which spectators were unlikely to trek, but where "a smooth and level surface offered optimum conditions."[19]

The tests were scheduled for Friday, June 14, which turned out to be gray and rainy. Both machines had been housed in a shed from which they could coast down a modest incline to the track. Cave's machine went first. Despite feverish attempts, the engine would not start until it was connected to the hose from a large air compressor, which was brought to the machine in a large cart pulled by two horses. But even that didn't work for long. Exhibit 159 coasted down the ramp, traveled for about eight feet, and promptly died. The engine was started with the compressor once more, but once more died. Five men pushed the cart a short distance before the Selden people, claiming inclement weather, decided to wait until the next day to continue the test.

The 1877 Buggy performed even less auspiciously. It repeatedly started, coughed, and died before the gears could be engaged. Parker was quick in pointing out to reporters that the machine would not run, "not even an inch," but over his objections, the test of that machine was also postponed.

The next day the tests were repeated, and, in keeping with the spirit of the proceedings, the two sides had vastly different versions of what transpired.

From the perspective of the Selden camp, the tests were a rousing success:

> The first test was made with the "Hartford" car, which is a duplicate of the original "1877" buggy, with the exception of slightly increased horsepower. The car was made at Hartford from plans and specifications, duplicates of which were filed at the Patent Office and on which Selden received a patent. It made a very remarkable showing, going around a mile track twice and returning to the stable in which it was kept for safe keeping. It attained a speed of over 8 miles per hour for 2 miles. In passing through the paddock, it was necessary to negotiate a grade of over 8½ per cent.[20]

Parker's version was different:

> There was much smiling among automobile dealers yesterday over the effort of what is known as the Selden group of manufacturers to make capital out of a trial of the Selden car at the Guttenberg track. The car built at Hartford two or three years ago ran two miles in 15 minutes, but the complainant's management refused to stop and restart it or do anything that a practical road carriage should do.

Mr. Parker says he never claimed the newly built cars could not run, but that they were not practical even with their new spark plugs, batteries, and other parts.[21]

Cave's machine actually did stop and start many times, but always involuntarily, due to "numerous mishaps to the engine."[22]

For the buggy, the Selden forces contributed this snippet:

The small 1877 original motor was then brought out and made a most creditable demonstration. It was run 8 or 9 times through the paddock and back to the stable. The showing made by the cars was remarkable when it is considered that the original motor had been inactive for nearly 30 years. That the car was practical beyond a doubt was proved by the demonstration. It is expected that the test will result in a manner highly agreeable to the owners of the Selden patent.[23]

Parker once again differed. About the vehicle that he had categorized as "built expressly as an exhibit in the litigation," he reported with obvious glee that it "took an hour to start, never got out of the yard to the track and took about five minutes to go 1,400 feet and then stopped. Mr. Selden refused to restart it, to back it up, or to turn it around. The counsel for Ford was much amused at what he termed a desperate but lame attempt to make capital out of the demonstration." An independent observer added that there was "labored cranking of the engine between brief journeys," and that "the oil in the crankcase boiled furiously."[24]

Two weeks later the 1877 Buggy was back in the garage on the West Side of Manhattan, where it gave a "fearful performance." With all three Seldens by then back in Rochester, mechanics worked on the car nonstop for two months, watched over by Pinkerton Agency detectives, some of whom were employed by each side, at which time it was brought above ground for its final test, on the streets of New York. (There seemed to be no legal impediment to its operation there after all.)

The buggy, "despite added improvements" and under remarkable security, gave an unremarkable performance. On September 6,

> at 10:02, a wire was connected from the batteries on the car to the coil, and after five minutes of cranking, at twenty-five turns every ten seconds, the motor started to run, with but few misses. The wires from the batteries were disconnected at 10:08, and the car was run from the room to the large storage room in the garage under its own power. . . . It was then pushed on an elevator and taken to Forty-ninth Street. On electric ignition it started on the first turn of the crank.[25]

Without the electric ignition, which had not been part of Selden's patent, the engine could not start. Even with electric ignition, the buggy could do no better than putter along for short distances before overheating, dying out, or suffering some other mishap. Repeat trials on September 12 and 16 were no more successful. "How long this litigation will last it is, of course, impossible to say, but what it is proving, except the general incapacity of Exhibit 89 to perform the tests witnesses said it made in Rochester and the lack of desire on the part of the complainants to end the suits, is more than uncertain."[26] The buggy had proved so difficult to start that *Horseless Age* could not resist attaching the moniker "Cranky Louis" to the buggy's operator, Louis Gibson, for "his frequent performances in that line."*

Whether or not the lackluster performance of both putative Selden machines would invalidate Selden's patent would be the decision of the trial judge, but as 1906 drew to a close, ALAM could not have looked back on it as a particularly good year. They were to find, however, that 1907 would be worse.

---

* Ford's team, in an attempt to demonstrate that the Lenoir motor could be made to operate an automobile, which would invalidate Selden's pioneer status, built a car that they also demonstrated on the streets of New York. The Ford-Lenoir, as it was called, employed a "non-compression motor" and performed a good deal better than the Selden buggy, but it was no more reflective of the original Lenoir design than was Selden's of his own.

CHAPTER 20

FORD MOTOR COMES OF AGE

L ess than three months after George Selden's quixotic appearance in New York, Ford announced the "consolidation of the present Ford Motor Company, the Ford Manufacturing Company, and other allied interests in one mammoth concern," and plans for a major expansion, so "the various plants now building the Ford car will all be under one roof." The Ford Manufacturing Company was indeed to be a paper fiction—Ford had kept his promise to John Gray—and the entire operation would be moved to what "promises [Detroit] the largest automobile factory in the world . . . of sufficient capacity to manufacture every part of the Ford cars from motors to tires."[1]

With the Model N, Ford was on the verge of a great breakthrough, and he decided, regardless of any legal complications, that he needed a manufacturing facility that would allow him to press his advantage. So Ford, John Dodge, and Couzens spent weeks scouring the Detroit area to find a location of sufficient size, at least one hundred acres, with access to both labor and railroads "sufficient to meet the needs of the company in the future."

They would eventually settle on a 60-acre site (which would later quadruple) in Highland Park, a small island of a city almost fully surrounded by Detroit.[2] The building would take three years to complete and would, as the article implied, make Ford Motor Company the largest automaker in the world, the final break from being a stubborn little David engaged in a noble battle with the ALAM Goliath.[*]

Motor Way, which had generally been sympathetic to Ford and the independents, was effusive about Ford Motor's prospects, albeit somewhat shaky on the facts.

> The success of this Detroit concern has been phenomenal and the advent of the sensational $500 Ford four-cylinder runabout has added impetus to it. About one thousand of these cars have been delivered to date and they are now coming through at the rate of thirty-five per day. Inside of sixty days, runabouts will be turned out at a rate heretofore unprecedented, over one hundred cars per day. Ten thousand of this model are now under way and another ten thousand more will follow immediately.

In fact, the ten thousand number was vastly inflated and it would be years before Ford could meet the hundred-car-per-day quota. But even with an output of thirty-five, he had become the industry leader. The journal had bought into other company propaganda: "Ford believes he has so perfected and simplified the design of this runabout it will be unnecessary to make any changes for several years." (He would change the design the following year.) "It has been frequently asserted by competitors that the car could not be manufactured at the price, and that after a few hundred were delivered and the quality of the car been demonstrated, the price would be raised. This report has

---

* The architect would be Albert Kahn, a pioneer in the use of reinforced concrete. Kahn, although he would design many buildings for Henry Ford and become known as "Ford's architect," also would design corporate headquarters for both Packard and General Motors. Kahn's father had trained as a rabbi, and after Ford's anti-Semitism had publicly escalated, he refused to ever again set foot in the buildings he had designed.

been emphatically denied." (The price was raised to $600 almost immediately.) But the most important statement in the article was true: "It is claimed by the Ford company that by reducing the manufacturing of automobiles to the same terms as are applied to the making of sewing machines, typewriters and other machines in immense quantities, a fair profit can be made at the price and give better quality than can be incorporated in a car by more crude methods."

And finally, *Motor Way* noted that the man who would become famous for his loathing of the patent system was not above exploiting it when it offered an advantage. "Many features of the Ford cars are broadly covered by patents in all countries of the world, and some of them are so comprehensive as to constitute basic claims. Without infringing on these patents it is impossible to attain the degree of simplicity which makes the Ford prices possible." This was also overstatement, but the tooling developed by Walter Flanders, much of which had been patented under the Ford Motor umbrella, gave the company, at least for a time, a sizable competitive edge.

With all their success, however, Ford and Couzens never lost sight of the corporate image: if you were marketing yourself to the common man as an underdog, it was important to continue to be seen as an underdog. In fact, the split between the independents and ALAM had evolved into one based on price. "Virtually all of the expensive automobiles made by American manufacturers [were] licensed under the Selden patent. . . . In any given year between 1903 and 1911, the ALAM never had more than four makes selling for less than $1,000." The independents, on the other hand, generally produced the less expensive models. "By 1909, the independents offered twenty-six models costing $1,000 or less."[3] ALAM, therefore, was coming more and more to be identified with the rich, "not interested in producing a poor man's automobile." Of the independents, because of their vocal and public opposition to the oligarchs, Ford and to a lesser extent Rambler were the most prominent—a position that had served Ford remarkably well. "In all of the great industrial conflicts over patent rights in American history, nothing parallels Ford's shrewd instinct for marshaling popular feeling to his side."[4]

The split in product cost was not coincidence. ALAM members, who had thought themselves secure in the fortress of the Selden patent, had far less incentive to innovate than independents, who were operating in a more uncertain environment. Since virtually all the ALAM members had catered to the wealthy, they simply continued to do so. In fact, if ALAM won its infringement suit, its members would be in the position, through high fees and restriction of licenses, to force the public to pay whatever it chose for a product marketed to whichever segments of society it wished. But lethargy had its costs—in its decision to litigate rather than innovate, ALAM was strengthening rather than inhibiting its opponents.

"Probably nothing so well advertised the Ford car and the Ford Motor Company as did this suit," Ford wrote in *My Life and Work*. "It appeared that we were the underdog and we had the public's sympathy. . . . Prosecuting that suit was probably one of the most shortsighted acts that any group of American businessmen has ever combined to commit."[5] Couzens added, "The Selden suit was probably better advertising than anything we could put out."[6]

Part of the company's strategy to foster the heroic everyman role had taken shape the year before, in the wake of ALAM's decision to exclude nonlicensees from the auto show. To demonstrate solidarity in the struggle against injustice, Ford and Couzens, possibly at the instigation of John Gray, had decided to form a trade group comprising firms that would not knuckle under to the ALAM bullies. At a secret meeting at the Ford plant, a group of prominent independents—not including Thomas Jeffery, who still refused to join any organization—formed the American Motor Car Manufacturers Association (AMCMA). Although the group promised to use its combined influence in the marketplace to outmaneuver ALAM, members were specifically exempt from contributing either money or resources to aid Ford in contesting the infringement suit. Many of the smaller firms would never have joined an organization that thrust them into an ongoing and open-ended legal battle, and Couzens and Ford were perfectly content to be seen as standing alone against the juggernaut. By the end of 1906, of course, the Ford Motor Company had become something of a juggernaut itself, willing to allow its smaller, more fragile members to be pulled along in the wake.

But there was also value in being seen within the industry as the leader of a movement. At a members' lunch in New York in early December 1906, preceding the second ACA (non-ALAM) auto show, Couzens, who had been appointed chairman of the AMCMA management committee, addressed the troops:

> We are followers of that great American doctrine that ultimately brings the best results in an industry of any sort. We see before us many examples of unsuccessful combinations and we who own or control our plants are easy in mind for the outlook for future business. Although we are competitors in business, there are certain mutual interests which can be best cared for by a central association and that was the main reason for the formation of this association and counts largely for its increased strength the past few years. . . . In my opinion, every manufacturer of motorcars who is an exhibitor at the present show should be included in the ranks of the American Association. There is not one of you who likes to be in the position of a man who wants to secure benefits without shouldering his part of the work.[7]

The Model N, while not reaching the dizzying production or sales numbers that Ford spokesmen had been throwing about, accounted for almost all of the more than fivefold increase from the company's previous year's sales, to 8,423 cars, placing the Ford Company for the first time in the number one position in the industry. Ford's sales were more than double Cadillac's and three times Rambler's. But to naysayers, Ford was still aiming at a segment of the market that most industry professionals were certain would be stagnant at best, while higher-priced, more luxurious automobiles, by then often costing $5,000 or more, would garner the greatest profit in an era of unbridled prosperity.

Woman learning to drive; by this time, the automobile had become integral to American life

But as 1907 progressed, growth began to slow—until, in October, the economy collapsed. In what would become known as the Panic of 1907, a failed attempt to corner copper in a fragile, highly leveraged stock market precipitated a cascade of business and bank failures. Before the crisis ended, there would be an 11 percent decline in gross national product, industrial production would drop by 16 percent, and unemployment would almost double. The nation was saved only when that noted man of the people J. P. Morgan, with the support and acquiescence of President Theodore Roosevelt—although the two men loathed each other—stepped in and single-handedly pumped liquidity into the system. As a result, to replace Morgan before the next catastrophe, Congress initiated the Federal Reserve System to help smooth out economic swings.

Although the nation suffered greatly, the effects were not felt evenly. The impact was most acute on stockholders, at that time predominantly upper-income individuals and families. And in a nation that was still largely agrarian, people who grew their own food, sewed their own clothes, and canned their own preserves were better equipped to weather the storm. Consequently, the market crisis was felt dispropor-

The economy had gone as flat as this Buick's tire

tionately by city dwellers and the wealthy, precisely the markets that ALAM members were targeting for their expensive cars.

But Ford was perfectly placed. Tales of the automobile continued to be splashed across the front pages of American newspapers and, as with other examples of new technology, a financial crisis did little to depress demand.[8] Thus, in marketing a car that received accolades for performance and reliability, all at a remarkably low price, the company actually *increased* production, to more than fourteen thousand cars, for the 1907–8 model year. (In this success, Ford was not alone—REO, Rambler, and a newcomer in the lower-priced car market, Buick, also saw their production numbers rise. However, Cadillac and virtually every other high-end carmaker were forced to cut back.)

As orders rolled in for the Model N—and its spiffed-up and slightly more expensive successors, the Models R and S—Ford Motor expanded its workforce both on the production side and in sales and marketing. The wisdom of seeking out a larger facility became manifest as the Piquette Avenue plant strained at the seams only three years after it had been constructed. As the company grew, tasks became more specialized, with Ford and Couzens of one mind about continuing to find the best people for each job. Again demonstrating that he was happy to employ people who were not at all like him, Ford hired a former convict as his sales manager and a flamboyant circus promoter to be the company's first head of advertising. Both would be pivotal in the company's growth.

The ex-con was Norval Hawkins, who had been imprisoned after embezzling $8,000 from a previous employer, Standard Oil. Hawkins, a self-proclaimed "good liver" who made no apologies for his crime, was a man so well liked and of such enduring charm that a crowd of well-wishers met him at the prison gates on his release, then helped him establish a successful accounting firm. Hawkins was the perfect salesman, exhibiting "extraordinary talent" for his job. An "astute Detroit attorney" later described Hawkins as "the greatest salesman that the world ever knew."[*][9]

But Hawkins was no huckster. He knew as much about salesmen as he did about selling, and he deftly set car dealers competing with one another by posting and then manipulating both results and quotas. Hawkins also had a good deal to say about production, since the company would need to turn out enough cars to meet dealer orders. He made certain that the best-performing dealers got the quickest and most reliable deliveries, and that underperforming dealers knew it. He both cemented the Ford name in public awareness and gave an increasingly far-flung enterprise a sense of community by having the company publish a weekly newspaper, *Ford Times,* which packaged corporate propaganda in homey prose.

His most significant contribution was in expanding, organizing, and standardizing the sales force, although he wasn't the first to do so

---

[*] In 1920, Hawkins would publish "Certain Success," whose opening was:

There are particular characteristics one can have, and particular things one can do, that will make *failure* in life *certain.* Why, then, should not the possession of particular opposite characteristics, and the doing of particular opposite things, result as *certainly* in *success,* which is the antithesis of failure? That is a logical, common-sense question. The purpose of this book and its companion volume, "The Selling Process," is to answer it convincingly for you. Success *can* be made certain; not, however, by the mere *possession* of particular characteristics, nor by just *doing* particular things. *Your* success in life can be *assured;* but only if you supplement your qualifications and make everything you do most effective *by using continually, whatever your vocation, the art of salesmanship.*

and likely had borrowed the innovations from a competitor. He introduced contracts with dealers that "gave the company substantial control over distribution without the financial and organizational burdens of ownership. Contracts established the resale prices of cars and parts, responsibility for service, and the number of cars and parts that dealers were required to take and the prices they would have to pay."[10] Thus, when the Model T was rolled out, the company had a structured national network of dealers ready to sell them.

The advertising man was E. LeRoy Pelletier, a showman who knew how to catch someone's eye. He was described as a

> little fellow [with] a great head; he is fairly charged with nervous energy; is a brilliant, plausible, rapid-fire conversationalist and a clever writer, and is hospitable, ingratiating and likable to a degree and resourceful far, far beyond the average. In the course of a varied career, he has had experience in the Klondike and as an advance agent for a circus, which partly may be accountable for the fact that in the art of "putting them over" he has few peers. Even the great Barnum himself would have found him a valuable assistant. For he can almost make himself believe there are moonbeams in cucumbers—and induce others to share his near-beliefs.[11]

Pelletier created perhaps the most notable of all of Ford Motor's advertisements and certainly its most enduring slogan. In 1908, he commissioned a giant billboard set on the roof of the Detroit Opera House in, of all places, Cadillac Square, which featured a huge Model N with turning wheels and burning headlamps. One of the car's passengers was a woman wearing a long scarf that draped behind her and fluttered in the wind. Beneath the automobile, in flashing lights of different colors, were the words "Watch the Fords Go By."

Although there are no reports of friction between him and Ford, Pelletier eventually left the company to become Flanders's advertising man at E-M-F.

With the Model N, Ford, by then forty-four years old, had finally hit his stride, not simply in the production of automobiles but also in the development of the corporate structure that within a decade would be the most sophisticated in America. Although Ford was aware of the work of certain "experts" in organizational dynamics, especially Frederick Winslow Taylor, the Ford Motor Company evolved in the same manner as did the Ford automobile—through tinkering and a constant process of trial and error undertaken by a group of people who were, to a striking degree, superb at their jobs.* That many were either discarded or left disgruntled—in almost every case after they had served their purpose—adds to Ford's natural genius for business, rather than detracts from it.

But no matter the potential of the automobile, there remained the issue of finding places to drive it. Although telephones, typewriters, electric lights, gas stoves, and indoor plumbing were appearing in increasing numbers in American homes and cities, road paving was a skill that, despite decades of Albert Pope's Good Roads movement, remained primitive. In 1904, more than 2 million miles of American roads were dirt, compared to only 150,000 miles deemed to be "improved," and of these, two-thirds were gravel. Most of the better roads, of course, were in and around the large metropolitan areas. While most of the automobiles built in that decade were capable of negotiating the rocky, rutted, sometimes dusty, sometimes quagmire-like trails, bouncing around or through obstacles limited speed and made breakdowns more likely. That demand for automobiles still

* Taylor was America's foremost authority on "scientific management," and much is made of Ford being told of his punctilious industrial time-and-motion studies and then being inspired to create the production system that would result in the assembly line. But Ford had been made aware of Taylor's work before the Piquette Avenue plant was built, and until Max Wollering and Walter Flanders joined his company, that operation was, as has been described, a scattershot affair. Ironically, Taylor's most devoted follower among the automakers was Henry Joy at Packard, who opened a fully "Taylorized" plant in 1913, just about the time Ford's assembly line was reaching fruition.

grew as it did was an indication of just how vast the market might be if the public could somehow be convinced that automobile travel was "convenient."

Willie Vanderbilt provided the seeds of the solution.

Despite the great success of the Vanderbilt Cup and the tens of thousands of dollars of revenue Nassau County took in from the race, the hue and cry over the closing of taxpayer property for an automobile race did not evaporate. After a spectator who had wandered onto the course was struck and killed in the 1906 race, bureaucratic resistance to Willie's extravaganza stiffened further. Despite his wealth and influence, receiving further race permits seemed unlikely. So, with typical flair, Willie K. decided that if public roads would not be made available for his race, he'd simply build a road of his own.

He put together a corporation to construct the nation's first road that would be built exclusively for automobile traffic. It would be flat, constructed of reinforced concrete, with over- and underpasses to keep traffic moving, and it would be free of police, pedestrians, and horses. Willie named it, appropriately, Motor Parkway.

In an address at the Automobile Club of America's banquet, Willie K. laid out his vision: "It has been the dream of every motorist to own a perfect car and to have a road without speed limit." He then described a fifty-foot-wide road on a one-hundred-foot-wide right-of-way, tarred and oiled to be bump- and dust-free, fenced its entire length, with access through tollgates placed every 5 miles. The road being private, there would be "no interference from the authorities." But his ultimate objective was more grand. "If we can prove to the public it is a paying investment, we will not only have the Long Island Motor Parkway, but roads of a similar character extending to Philadelphia, Albany, Boston, and many other smaller towns."[12]

It took him only a few months to put together a group of "directors and incorporators" that was as impressive as any in America. On December 3, 1906, when Long Island Motor Parkway, Inc., was born, the roster boasted not only a Vanderbilt but also a Whitney, a Belmont, an Astor, a Schiff, a Barney, a Bourne, and a Heckscher. Oddly, only one automaker had joined a group that would create the blueprint for a highway system that would revolutionize America—Henry Ford.

It was Willie K.'s initial intention to have the road completed in time for the 1907 Vanderbilt Cup, but once again reach far exceeded grasp. Buying a right-of-way more than 50 miles long turned out to be a good deal more difficult than he thought. In addition, construction of a road so advanced from the prevailing technology would be both costly and fraught with error. The 1907 race was therefore canceled, with a new target set in the following year. The official groundbreaking was not until June 1908, but after a major effort, on October 10, 1907, a 9-mile section of the road was officially opened. *Automobile* magazine called it "an epoch in motor-driven land transportation." Two weeks later, that same stretch accounted for 9 miles of the 23-mile course for that year's Vanderbilt Cup race.

Eventually, Motor Parkway ran for 43 miles, from the New York City line to Ronkonkoma.*

---

* Motor Parkway still exists, stretching from Ronkonkoma to Dix Hills in Suffolk County, and can be accessed directly at Exit 53 of the Long Island Expressway.

CHAPTER 21

AROUND THE WORLD IN 169 DAYS

The increase in auto sales after the Panic of 1907, when just about every other consumer item was losing ground, occurred in good part due to a constant stream of news spotlighting the glamour and desirability of an exotic technical marvel that, thanks to Henry Ford and friends, had become possible for many average people to own. Much of that news was generated within the nation's borders, where racers such as Barney Oldfield had become idols. But the most arresting and compelling headlines were generated from the other side of the globe, where an American driver in an American automobile seemed poised to perform a feat that many had considered impossible.

In the spring of 1907, when George Selden was preparing at last to demonstrate the automobile he claimed to be the first of its kind, the French newspaper *Le Matin* announced sponsorship of a race to Paris from Peking, China, a distance of more than 6,000 miles. The course would take the participants through territory that was as exotic to Westerners as the surface of the moon: through the Gobi Desert; around Lake Baikal (so deep that no one had ever reached the bottom); through Kansk, Omsk, and Tomsk; to Moscow, St. Petersburg, and Berlin; and finally, down the Champs-Élysées. The course was so alien that estimates of the race's duration varied by months. One of the entrants, Prince Scipio Borghese, journeyed to China in advance of the event and walked with a pole the precise width of his automobile, a 40-horsepower Itala, to ensure that it would fit through a series of narrow rocky passes.

Le Matin received inquiries from forty potential competitors, but that number was winnowed to a mere five when the race began on June 10. The spirit of pioneering adventure was established almost immediately. On the third day, Prince Borghese's car

> was buried over the axles in a morass, and held up by immense roots of trees, which had to be cut away with axes, whilst two days after, it had to be drawn through about 18 miles of deep sand by coolies and mules. Near Urga the car stuck in a morass and fell on to its side. With the aid of Mongolians using beams as levers, and oxen, the car was pulled backwards out of the swamp. On the next day the vehicle again sank in thick mud to the axles, and gradually sank lower until rescued by Mongolian shepherds.[1]

Another of the competitors, a swashbuckling Frenchman named Charles Godard, driving a 15-horsepower Dutch Spyker, "drove through the Gobi Desert without a sufficient supply of gasoline. For two days he had to lie beneath his car while the sun was burning fiercely." Finally, "camel riders brought him the gasoline." Godard, who was riding with a *Le Matin* correspondent, sold all his spare parts for cash to finance the journey, then, when that ran out, borrowed money from virtually everyone he encountered, assuring them that the newspaper had agreed to pay all his expenses. Unfortunately for the luckless Godard, that turned out not to be the case, and he was eventually sentenced to eighteen months in prison for swindling the Dutch consulate in Peking. (The charges were later dropped.)[2]

Progress of the race was front-page news in Europe and was regularly featured in trade magazines. Even though there was no American presence in the race, neither car nor driver, it also turned out to be extremely popular in American newspapers. In an article titled "Daredevil Motorists Defy Death in Mad Dash from Peking to Paris," syndicated across the United States, a "special correspondent" reported, "Grave dangers confront the intrepid motorists, who are wildly speeding from Peking to Paris in the most notable automobile race ever undertaken. The course covers 6,200 miles and traverses the pathless wastes of northern Asia."[3]

The article was a mixture of high adventure and exotic travelogue.

> Of the five entries who left Peking, only one has dropped out, [Auguste] Pons, who became lost in the Gobi desert and had to hire camels to get his car back to Nankin, himself almost dead with fatigue. In the Gobi desert the Italian car's petrol tank began to leak and by the time the fault was discovered, the motorists found themselves stranded, with no motive power left. They were not provisioned for a long isolated stay, and they could not get forward. The sun beat on them throughout a long day. Their water gave out. A caravan of camels suddenly made its appearance. The automobilists tried to secure relief from the nomads, but the latter refused to halt and callously passed by.

The party searched for four hours before stumbling on a Mongol village where aid was given.

> Everywhere they went the motorists had to overcome fear on the part of the natives before they could be induced to render any help. In the woods near Krasnolarak, a company of bandits, heavily armed, appeared, and the tourists began feeling for their guns, expecting a fight, but needlessly. The bandits caught one good look at the vehicle, moving by itself, and became panic stricken. They hurled themselves into the shrub, threw down their arms, and

Daredevil Motorists Defy Death
In Mad Dash From Peking to Paris

THE "LIVING GOD" OF OURGA TURNS MOTOR ENTHUSIAST

provisions. The Italians were rescued just as they had abandoned hope and had laid down near their car to die.

Everywhere they went the motorists had to overcome fear on the part of the natives before they could be induced to render any help. In the woods near Krasnolarak, a company of bandits, heavily armed, appeared, and the tourists began feeling for their guns, expecting a fight, but needlessly. The bandits caught 1 good look at the vehicle, moving by itself, and became panic stricken. They buried themselves in the shrub, threw down their arms and made signs that they surrendered to the mysterious spirit that propelled the horseless cart.

Daredevil motorists meet the living God

made signs that they surrendered to the mysterious spirit that propelled the horseless cart.

Tales of colorful foreign dignitaries were popular as well.

At Urga, the Chinese governor asked permission to ride in the automobile. Dressed in the greatest pomp, the celestial got into the car, somewhat nervously, but, gaining courage, he asked that the car be speeded up. The chauffeur moved the levers to five miles an hour, and the party flew along, leaving far in the rear, in wild disorder, a great cavalcade that had hoped to keep up with the pace of the automobile. The governor returned to his palace shaken and pale, but

conscious that he had enormously increased his importance in the eyes of his subordinates.

The adventure continued for weeks until the race ended on August
10, two months to the day from when it began, when Prince Borghese
drove into Paris, "escorted by a squadron of cavalry, and followed by
hundreds of automobiles," and cheered by hundreds of thousands
from every economic and social stratum.[4] He had completed the journey in one day less than Horatio Jackson's trip across the United States
only four years earlier. The prince was given a celebratory banquet
attended by thirty thousand guests. It was ten days before the next
finisher, a De Dion–Bouton, appeared in Paris.

At the victory banquet in Paris, Prince Borghese expressed the desire to motor across America, a sentiment that was duly reported in
the press. The editors at *The New York Times* decided to take the prince
up on his idea. In late November 1907, they announced sponsorship,
with *Le Matin,* of a race from New York to Paris—going west. The
plan was to make almost the entire course land-bound. The cars would
be shipped from Seattle to Valdez, Alaska, would traverse the (hope-
fully) frozen Bering Strait, and would then head across Siberia to Moscow. (Boats would, of course, be available if ice on the Bering Strait
was not.) And, the *Times* was pleased to note, interest was "immeasur-
ably increased when it became known that an American car had entered the race."[5] The *Times* also observed that "a year or two ago [this
undertaking] would have been termed the wildest dream of the automobile imagination."

The course was a daunting 20,000 miles, which, in addition to long
stretches in the desert, would require the entrants to climb mountains,
several over 10,000 feet, and "drop down the sides of mountain ranges
on passes and roads that are well-nigh impassable. The drivers will
have to go through rivers which in many cases will completely cover
the wheels and the flooring of the car, and the motor will have to do
its work at a temperature of 100 degrees as well as 50 below zero."[6]

The New York Times was the most widely read newspaper in the
United States, and it threw its full editorial might into publicizing the

event. Just four days after the article announcing the race, the newspaper ran a full-page feature filled with harrowing tales of automobilists who had braved just some of the terrain the race would cover. European newspapers, fresh off the Peking-Paris bonanza, needed little incentive to hail this new test of human and mechanical endurance.

At 11:00 A.M. on February 12, 1908, Mayor George Brinton McClellan Jr. fired a gun, and six automobiles departed Times Square, heading north on Broadway for Albany. Three of the cars had been shipped from France: a De Dion–Bouton; a Sizaire-Naudin, one of whose drivers was Auguste Pons, who had almost died in the Gobi Desert; and a Motobloc, whose team included the intrepid Charles Godard. A German Protos and an Italian Züst were also entered, although Prince Borghese had decided against participating. Representing the United States was an automobile built by the E. R. Thomas Motor Company, an ALAM member. The car, a standard 1907 model that had already proved itself in endurance contests, was known as the Flyer.

For the journey, the Thomas machine, more than 4,000 pounds of it, had mounted "skid planks" atop its mud guards—boards 20 feet long that ran the full length of the car. A winch had been installed at the front. Supplies included two shovels, two picks, two axes, two lanterns, three searchlights, two extra gas tanks with a capacity of 125 gallons, a 10-gallon reservoir of oil, extra springs, and myriad other spare parts. The Flyer was also equipped "with a top similar to those used on the old prairie schooner," complete with ribs over the chassis, so that the automobile could double as a tent at night. "As an extra precaution" the drivers carried 500 feet of rope, a rifle, and revolvers.[7] Lacking in this array were a windshield and a heater. The other automobiles were of similar size and similarly equipped, although the proportions varied depending on whether the drivers thought the desert, the Arctic, or the American West would present the greatest challenge. The Protos, for example, custom-made by a team of six hundred workers on the direct orders of Kaiser Wilhelm II, was made extra wide to allow the driver—a military officer—to sleep bundled up on the floor.

Each car had a crew of two or three, one or two drivers and a mechanician. The Flyer carried one driver, the dashing Montagu Roberts, and George Schuster, a mechanic at the Thomas factory in Buffalo who had been summoned only three days before to, he thought, perform a final tune-up. He brought only a few changes of clothing since he believed he would be returning to Buffalo in a day or two.

With Mayor McClellan's starting gun, bands played, the flags of the four entering nations flew, and fifty thousand cheering people crowded into the square to see the racers off. The racers would pass a quarter million spectators lined up for miles as they left the city.

The feeling of the endurance test to come was captured on that very first day. *The New York Times* had assigned a young reporter, T. Walter Williams, to ride along with the Flyer, and his page-one lead on February 13 was "Autos Fight Snow Drifts." North of the city, it seemed, much of the snow that had descended on the East Coast from a series of blizzards in the previous weeks had yet to be cleared from the roads, and the shovels that the participants carried had to be put to good use. In addition, many of the local children decided to amuse themselves by pelting the shovelers with snowballs. By day's end, only three, the Flyer, the Züst, and the De Dion, escorted by a man holding a lantern, had reached Hudson, New York, 116 miles north, and the other three had made substantially less progress. Two days later, one of the drivers of the German vehicle declared on finally reaching Albany, "Siberia will be a picnic after this." He would find that he had underestimated Siberia.

The *Times* ran page-one updates nearly every day, but it would be another forty days before the newspaper could announce that the Thomas Flyer, still in the lead, had reached San Francisco. By then, only four cars remained, as the Sizaire-Naudin and the luckless Auguste Pons were forced to drop out only nine days after the start, still short of Albany, when a broken casting was found to be unrepairable without a part shipped from France. By that time the Flyer, still in the lead, had already passed Buffalo. At Omaha two weeks later, the Motobloc was also forced to give up the chase due to numerous break-downs, although Godard did escape in this instance without any criminal charges lodged against him. The *Times* had a casualty as well. At Chicago, Walter Williams had debarked and refused to continue even if it cost him his job. "Insanity" was the term he used to describe the proceedings.

For a good part of the journey, especially in the West, there were still no roads on which an automobile could travel. Like Jackson in 1903, the automobiles bumped along railroad tracks, sometimes for hundreds of miles. Even then, not all the contestants ran under equal conditions. The Thomas was sometimes granted right-of-way on a stretch of track while the foreign contestants were denied the same privilege. In Indiana, large volunteer crews showed up to help dig the Flyer out of deeper snowdrifts than were encountered in New York, while the foreign crews were forced to get by with limited hospitality from the locals. On still another occasion, the Flyer was allowed to use a tunnel cut through a mountain, while the Italians were required to navigate a much longer route around.[8]

For each of the four survivors, the trip across the United States, the first ever in winter, was dismal. Cars broke down regularly or were disabled in unforgiving terrain. Drivers were frequently injured in crashes or making repairs. The entire trip in the West was a series of ruts, chuckholes, knee-deep mud, and shoulder-high snow. In Wyoming, temperatures rarely rose above zero. More than once, drivers discovered that thieves had relieved them of personal possessions or spare parts. Even celebrations were not always to be savored, such as when arriving automobiles were pelted with oranges in Los Angeles. And except for the final jaunt across Europe, the United States leg was considered the least challenging on the course.

That became clear as the Alaska run commenced. On March 28, the Flyer left by steamer for Seattle, where another vessel would trans-port the car to Valdez, a deepwater port on the southern coast, for what George MacAdam, the reporter that the *Times* had sent to re-place Williams, termed "the most hazardous part of the whole 20,000 mile journey." Insanity or no, MacAdam would ride in the Thomas for the remainder of the race. And MacAdam was not the only replacement on the Flyer. Roberts quit in frigid Wyoming, and neither of the two replacement drivers E. R. Thomas engaged would go farther than San Francisco. So George Schuster doubled up, becoming both driver and mechanic for what promised to be the most grueling automobile ride ever attempted. Eventually he would be joined by another mechanic, George Miller, so that the Flyer would cross Asia with a crew of three Georges.

Tens of thousands of cheering San Franciscans had lined the streets when the American automobile arrived and tens of thousands saluted them as they left. But Alaska was an unexplored wasteland. The attempt to cross the vast expanse "is regarded as foredoomed to failure, but Schuster said the same predictions were made . . . after Indiana blizzards, Iowa mud, and trackless Wyoming, so he was not prepared to accept what anyone said of an automobile's possibilities until he had tested them himself."[9] So remote was much of the route mapped out by the organizers that sending dispatches by telegraph would be impossible and the only means of communication would be by carrier pigeon.

On April 6, Schuster, MacAdam, and the Flyer arrived in Valdez. They had traveled 4,836 miles, less than one-quarter of the planned total, in fifty-four days. The Züst had arrived in San Francisco, traveling 4,090 miles, but was forced to wait for a vessel to carry it north. The De Dion had just entered southern California, 3,586 miles, where it stopped for repairs. The Protos, also stopped for repairs, had not made it across Utah, a mere 2,616 miles from the start.

The Flyer's lead over the Züst might have been only 800 miles, but because of sailing time, that translated into an advantage of almost two weeks, an enormous edge in the Alaskan spring. "If the freezing weather continues on the trail, it might be possible for the Thomas car to go where the others could not follow a fortnight later." But if the thaw had already set in, "it might necessitate stopping in the interior, out of reach of assistance that could readily reach the other cars coming later."[10]

Theories of the relative advantage or disadvantage of the Alaska trails turned out to be moot. Four days later, with the De Dion by then in San Francisco with the Züst, and the Protos still mired in Utah, Schuster concluded an inspection of the first leg of the mail trail to Fairbanks and declared it impassable. Not only was the trail too narrow for an automobile, something no one had thought to measure, but the "unprecedented" early spring thaw meant that the "crust of snow" that was supposed to support two- and three-ton automobiles had melted into a sea of mud.

The Thomas had no choice but to return to Seattle and from there sail to Vladivostok. When the Flyer arrived in Washington State on April 17, Schuster discovered that the De Dion and the Züst had departed three days earlier, not for Alaska but for Yokohama, whence they would motor across Honshu and then sail to Vladivostok for the beginning of the run across Asia and Europe. E. R. Thomas telegraphed to formally ask for a time allowance, since his car, which could not depart until April 21 because of visa complications with Russia, had wasted more than three weeks in a fruitless journey north. The Protos had yet to leave Utah, but the head of the German team decided that his automobile should leave with the Flyer, which meant driving to Idaho and then packing the automobile on a railroad flatbed. As it turned out, the Protos did not depart until the following day, but it procured direct passage to Vladivostok—the Germans were the only crew able to locate the Russian legate before entering their territory—meaning that the car that was last and had driven only 2,966 miles would arrive five days before the lead car, which had driven 6,036 miles.

During the passage across the Pacific, the committee refereeing the contest, made up entirely of Frenchmen, assessed a fifteen-day penalty to the De Dion, the Protos, and the Züst to account for the extra time the Thomas had taken on the detour to Alaska, and the Germans an additional fifteen days for shipping their car by rail from Pocatello, Idaho, to Seattle. They also required the other three entrants to await the Flyer's arrival, so that they would all leave Vladivostok on the 10,000-mile race to Paris together.

This was too much for the ever-excitable Albert de Dion, who was convinced he had been betrayed by his own countrymen. He promptly withdrew on the grounds that the remainder of the race was so similar to the Peking-Paris run—which he had lost—that it "has no longer any attractions for his firm." The Züst was also said to be withdrawn at Vladivostok, a rumor that was quickly scotched from Milan by R. M. Vollmoeller, chairman of the Italian firm. What was more, a Züst would be entered in another cross–United States race, this one from New York to San Francisco and back, planned for the following summer. (Such was the passion the New York–to–Paris race had incited that no fewer than twenty automakers from the United States and Europe—though not Ford—immediately announced their intention to enter.)

The racers left Vladivostok on May 24, and it became immediately apparent that whatever hardships had been encountered in the race across America would be dwarfed in Siberia. Spring thaw was in full flower, and only two days out the *Times* correspondent, traveling in the Thomas, wrote, "We have traversed an endless stretch of mud, save where the pools were so liquid that they no longer may bear the name of mud. The trans-Siberian post road, of which we talked so glibly while on route across the Pacific, has been untouched since the Trans-Siberian Railroad line has been opened, and its condition is simply execrable." In order to allow horses to pass, "huge boulders and great logs" were thrown in the road and submerged just below the effluent surface. "Each time the wheels strike one of these sunken obstructions, it is hurled in the air, and we have all we can do to prevent ourselves from being thrown into the ditch. The fearful racking the machine gets is worse than anything that America affords by a thousandfold." Bridges were rotted or washed away and the auto had to ford "stream after stream," on each occasion requiring the crew to either lead the car across the mud bottom, often over their boot tops, or push from the rear. The crew ate hard-boiled eggs and canned meat for days on end, and the mud was so deep and persistent that for some stretches, progress for a day was measured in feet rather than miles. "We will push on with all dispatch to reach Irkutsk," the correspondent wrote glumly, "but Irkutsk is still 1,884 miles away. It is more than 5,000 miles to Moscow."[11]

Over the next weeks, among other mishaps, the Thomas crew broke through a rotted bridge, stopped inches short of the edge of a 200-foot precipice, encountered wolves and bandits, scaled mountains, pushed the Flyer through mud and water, ate terrible food, baked and froze, and spent day after day being tossed about on bone-jarring stretches of nonexistent road. But every hardship in the automobile made for more compelling headlines at home. Americans awaited news of the Flyer's progress with the same breathless anticipation devoted to cliffhanger serials.

Finally, on July 29, the Flyer and its crew reached Paris, driving through a series of cheering crowds yelling *"Vive la voiture américaine"* that began 25 miles outside the city limits. American flags flew in the streets of the French capital, photographs of which would run prominently in American newspapers. The Protos had arrived four days earlier, but every one of the thousands who turned out to greet the Flyer—including the crew of the German machine—knew the Thomas was the winner. The journey had taken 169 days. The Züst would not pull into Paris until the end of September.

Motor Age captured the spirit of the race—and its legacy—in a long article written just as the Flyer was to make its grand entry down the Champs-Élysées:

> From the sunlight and gayety [sic] of Times Square, through the arctic wilds of the Empire state, over the rutty roads of Ohio and into the unprecedented blizzard-ridden Indiana, thence on through the mud of Iowa, the alkali of Nebraska and Wyoming, the spring floods in the Wasatch range of the Rockies, the awful silence of the Utah deserts, the parched plateau of the Goldfield district, the menacing grandeur of the treacherous Death Valley and up through the dust of California, through San Luis Obispo and the triumphant entry into San Francisco, the passage to Seattle and the lonely but demonstrative trip of the Thomas car into the snow-bound and rocky trails of Alaska—a futile sticking to the original route that contemplated motoring north of the arctic circle where no wheeled vehicle ever

had gone in the memory of white man, Indian or Eskimo—the runaway confederacy of the foreign cars across the Pacific Ocean to the Orient; the pluckiness of the Thomas crew in hastening to Japan, crossing the big island and arriving in Vladivostok in time to make it an even race with the Protos and Züst, and then the most marvelous narrative of motoring the world has ever known—the story of crossing Siberia, the Ural mountains, flying through Russia and the German empire and the grand climax of the run through France and into Paris ... the New York-Paris racing machines have created a series of chapters in motoring that not only are novel, new and thrilling, but they have breathing through them all the slogan, "the world needs more good highways."*[12]

The New York Times was even more glowing, although, as a sponsor, it could be forgiven a bit of self-congratulatory hyperbole. "As a sporting event," it declared, "the New York to Paris event takes precedence over any contest ever organized in the world. There is scarcely a part of this entire distance that lacks its dramatic interest, while reviewing the whole journey in its entirety, it seems incredible."[13]

The victory was billed as a national triumph, and on their return George Schuster and mechanic George Miller were feted as American heroes, with newspapers across the nation reporting in detail on the incredible odds overcome to complete a journey of more than 15,000 miles in a machine that just a decade earlier could barely complete a run 1 percent of that. E. R. Thomas told reporters that "the victory of the American flag was more important to him than the victory of the Thomas car."[14]

And the Flyer was certainly as much a celebrity as its drivers, described almost as a hero of battle. When it was unloaded in New York,

---

* Those highways were begun almost immediately, including, in 1912, the Lincoln Highway, America's first transcontinental road (paved with asphalt), which began in Times Square and terminated in San Francisco.

Schuster and the Flyer on page one

as the last cover dropped away and it stood revealed, it told its own story of the hardships it had withstood and overcome. It was battered and worn from front to rear, but its inner mechanism was uninjured, as it soon showed. The skids that it bore on either side when it started out from Times Square on Lincoln's Birthday had disappeared. The treads of its tires were torn and snagged, and its hood was dented and bent. . . . Parts of the body had been cut away as souvenirs, while the whole surface was covered by a countless number of autographs gathered in every part of the world which it circled. The blue body was so covered with mud that it looked gray from a distance, but the mud and grime exactly fitted it.[15]

With the victory of the Flyer, the automobile had passed its final test, dispelling any doubts of both its efficacy and its desirability. True, the price for a car such as the Flyer was prohibitive for the majority of Americans. But the automobile was no longer looked on as an affectation of the rich. The automobile was heroic, unconquerable, pioneering—so very American. There were few in the United States in that summer of 1908 who did not feel an urge, despite whatever economic hardships they might be enduring, to own an automobile of their own. For few objects in the history of this nation was there so much pent-up demand.*

Five weeks later, on September 27, 1908, the first Model T rolled out of the Piquette Avenue factory.

* Victory and acclaim did not help E. R. Thomas. The race had cost him many thousands of dollars—one hundred thousand, he told the press—and his company went bankrupt in 1912.

CHAPTER 22

▰*FORD'S PHENOMENON*

The Russian revolutionary Leon Trotsky is purported to have said, "Power was lying in the streets, waiting for someone to pick it up." In the case of the automobile, what was waiting in the streets to be picked up in the fall of 1908 was vast wealth. That the notion of a car for the masses had so little permeated the awareness of most automakers, particularly ALAM automakers, at a time when automobiles could not have been more prominent in the public consciousness; when contests between automobilists, either around the world or at home, were drawing tens of thousands of onlookers; when automobile shows reported record attendance; when every major newspaper virtually every day had some tale of the glamour or appeal of the automobile, now seems unfathomable.

It certainly was unfathomable to Henry Ford. So, while most of his competitors vied to make a more *prestigious* automobile, a more *luxurious* automobile, a more *unique* automobile, Henry Ford set about making an automobile that was plain, dull, and precisely the same as every other, right down to the color of the paint. But his car would also be supremely functional, simple to operate, and built not to impress but to get its passengers reliably from one place to another, even over channels of mud or rock-strewn paths. And, he was convinced, it would sell in the millions.

To build his creation, Ford contributed few if any specific design elements but instead provided a steady hand and an unshakable vision. He had hired talented people to do what he could not and had not been too proud or too headstrong to refuse to let them exploit their talents. Nor had he been too loyal to discard them when their usefulness had run its course. Ford shamelessly trawled for ideas from competitors and thought nothing of expropriating any process that would improve either the product or the means to manufacture it. While the Model T would have many features that were genuinely innovative, virtually every detail of its construction had its genesis outside the Ford team. Realizing that European engineering was generally superior to American, for example, Ford ordered foreign-built cars to be shipped across the Atlantic, specifically so that they could be dismantled, studied, and, if an advantage was found, copied.[1]

Sometimes Europe came to him. After a race in Palm Beach, Florida, in 1905, Ford claimed to have picked up a small piece of metal from a valve stem of a wrecked French car and noticed it was lighter than he expected. The metal seemed to be used throughout the car, including the engine block. He brought the piece with him to Detroit, assigned a team to analyze it, and imported a metallurgist from Britain to help. The group eventually discovered it was a vanadium steel alloy, which was not only lighter than ordinary steel but also almost three times stronger. To successfully produce vanadium steel, however, a blast furnace was required to run 300 degrees hotter than most American steel producers could manage. So Ford financed a steel mill in Canton, Ohio, that was willing to run its furnace at the requisite temperature. As a result, the Model T became the only American automobile to employ an essential component that was superior to anything else on the market.*

* The valve-on-the-track story might well have been apocryphal. Vanadium steel had also been written up in European engineering journals, and more than one account has it being brought to Ford's attention by one of his staff, probably Har-

Europeans also were more advanced in carburetion technology and gearbox construction, so Ford borrowed liberally from those designs as well. While in almost every case Ford engineers improved on what they had borrowed, each improvement was given a name to denote its Ford origins. The vanadium steel alloy, for example, was advertised as "Ford Heat-Treated Steel." And the "Ford Planetary Transmission" that he and his engineers proudly claimed as their own invention, while excellently wrought, had been borrowed from Panhard and others, who had received their inspiration from William Murdoch's design, developed in the days of James Watt.[2]

Ford later sought to perpetuate the notion that the development of his automobiles had followed a straight and rigorous path—in other words, that he had always known what he was doing. In his description of the Model T's evolution, for example, he wrote, "The big thing is the product, and any hurry in getting into fabrication before designs are completed is just so much waste time. I spent twelve years before I had a Model T—which is what is known today as the Ford car—that suited me. We did not attempt to go into real production until we had a real product."[3] This, of course, is transparently untrue, as the very fact that he got to the Model T attests. But what Ford did do was continue to tinker with even his most successful models, like the N, until he had produced a quality product that precisely intersected the point of greatest consumer demand—and then he was smart enough to stick with it.

His description of the company's process of innovation was misleading as well. "We are constantly experimenting with new ideas. If you travel the roads in the neighborhood of Dearborn you can find all

old Wills. (When Ford suggested its use, Charles Sorenson noted, "We had already read about vanadium steel.") But these journals were available to everyone, and only Ford chose to employ the alloy in his cars. Why other American carmakers did not seek an improvement so readily available is uncertain. But, with the point of view that luxury trumped utility, that bigger was better, and that focusing on high unit profit margins was better business than seeking to make money on volume, perhaps Ford's competitors also assumed that heaviness connoted quality and lightness the lack of it. Similar thinking in the 1970s, the association of "made in Japan" with light and flimsy, doomed the Big Three automakers—including Ford—to failure in their competition with Toyota, Honda, and Datsun.

sorts of models of Ford cars. They are experimental cars—they are not new models. I do not believe in letting any good idea get by me, but I will not quickly decide whether an idea is good or bad. If an idea seems good or seems even to have possibilities, I believe in doing whatever is necessary to test out the idea from every angle."[4] While Ford is implying that the "good ideas" are homegrown, he was also not letting anyone else's get by him. But that he would try anything, never sitting still in the drive to improve his product was, at least at that point in his career, true.

This is not to imply that Henry Ford simply stumbled on the Model T while thrashing about hoping to find a car that would sell. He and his team of engineers worked on the design for more than two years. And while he didn't draw up any blueprints, the vision and the parameters within which his designers worked were his. Not all of those ideas turned out to be practical, but many of those that did work changed car manufacturing for a generation. The result was precisely what Ford had sought—a car that could be used by ordinary people in cities and, even more significantly, on farms. (One of his chief designers, testifying before Congress years later, stated unequivocally that the Model T was "a farm car.")

Charles Sorenson worked on the machine from the beginning, in early 1907.

> Henry Ford dropped in at the pattern department of the Piquette Avenue plant to see me. "Come with me, Charlie," he said, "I want to show you something." I followed him to the third floor and its north end, which was not fully occupied for assembly work. He looked about and said, "Charlie, I'd like to have a room finished off right here in this space. Put up a wall with a door big enough to run a car in and out. Get a good lock for the door, and when you're ready, we'll have Joe Galamb [a key Ford engineer] come up in here. We're going to start a completely new job."[5]

When the twelve-by-fifteen room was ready, Ford suddenly announced that he was strictly limiting access. One of the employees *not* allowed entry was Harold Wills, which Charles Sorenson admitted was "for some reason I can't account for." But Ford did "tie Wills in on the vanadium steel development, which without question furnished the real impetus for abandoning the sensational success of the Model N for the evolution of the Model T."*6

In that room, ideas were formulated, discussed, accepted, or rejected; drawings were rendered and models were built; components were tested, improved, then tested again. By spring 1908, Ford and his team had produced their prototype. Whatever missteps he had made, whatever partners and associates he had betrayed, whatever ideas he had borrowed from colleagues and competitors, and whatever credit he had taken for work done by others, with the Model T Henry Ford had produced a machine that would become a phenomenon the likes of which the world had never seen.

Ford began advertising his new vehicle in March 1908, a full six months before it was shipped to his dealers. He saturated newspapers, magazines, and trade journals, making certain a constant stream of articles was placed about his revolutionary new product. "In the Ford Model T is offered the biggest value ever announced in automobiles" was a typical claim. "A car guaranteed by the biggest Automobile Maker in the world . . . a guarantee that means something. Designed by HENRY FORD, who never designed a failure."

The reviews matched the ads. On September 24, *Motor Age* ran a four-page article dedicated to the $850 machine's roll-out, in which it noted that the car possessed "features heretofore untried in motor-car engineering, all of which are introduced with the aim of building a light-weight machine, capable of irregular road conditions, and possessing reliability features equal to the demands of motorists." It then detailed, complete with cutaway diagrams, every feature of the engine, transmission, cooling and lubrication systems, chassis, and driver and

---

* These decisions buttress the notion that Wills was the source of the vanadium steel idea and that, while Ford might have been cooling to Wills as a colleague, he felt he needed him until the metallurgy had been finalized. Ford had brought in an English metallurgist, J. Kent Smith, to establish production parameters for the alloy, and Wills became his liaison at the company, spending a good deal of the following year with Smith in Canton, at the blast furnace Ford had acquired to produce the metal.

passenger layout. The second paragraph of the article gave a sense of just how revolutionary a machine the Model T would be:

> In the car, which is a 20-horsepower machine with 100-inch wheelbase and weighing 1,200 pounds, a few of the cardinal innovations are: The four cylinders with the top of the crankcase are formed in one casting; there is a separate one-piece water-jacketed head casting for all four cylinders; ignition current is furnished by a low-tension generator incorporated in the flywheel of the motor; the flywheel of the motor becomes the lubricator in that it is enclosed, operates in an oiled bath, and distributes the oil through a lead to the motor crankcase; the improved planetary transmission has some of the planetary gears carried on the flywheel; the car has but two springs—a transverse semi-elliptic in front and a similar one in the rear; the lower half of the crankcase is continued to the rear, forming a housing for the flywheel as well as constituting the lower half of the transmission case, and a protection for the universal joint at the rear of the transmission, thereby eliminates the necessity of the mud apron. Last but not least must be mentioned the left-hand control, in which the steering wheel, control levers, and pedals are on the left side, a design particularly suited for American road conditions, where vehicles, traveling in opposite directions pass on the right.[7]

Along with the new was the best of the old. "Hand in hand with these innovations, go the unit, motor and transmission construction, now employed on Ford cars for 4 years; the three-point suspension of this; the peculiar triangular Ford drive; and the employment of Vanadium steel in axles, springs, motor shafts, transmission parts, real axle driving parts, frame brackets, and all parts of the car."[8] With unintended synergy, the same issue of *Motor World* contained an article on new techniques employed in building wide, smooth roads for state highway systems.

Ford Model T, 1908

The Model T was an immediate success. In its first model year, Ford sold 10,607 of the car that would come to be called the "flivver" or "Tin Lizzie." Ford knew, or so he claimed later, that he had found his bonanza. "In 1909, I announced one morning, without any previous warning, that in the future we were going to build only one model, that the model was going to be Model T, and that the chassis would be exactly the same for all cars." His reasoning was simple. "It is strange how, just as soon as an article becomes successful, somebody starts to think that it would be more successful if only it were different. There is a tendency to keep monkeying with styles and to spoil a good thing by changing it."[9]

Despite the acclaim, however, the Model T was hardly the perfect car. There was no means of accessing the motor or lubricating system for repairs from underneath, so if anything did go wrong that could not be repaired from the top, the car had to be essentially rebuilt. The crank starter became notorious for explosive backfires that took many a hand, arm, or shoulder with it. The Ford suspension was bone-rattling, and although a buyer could choose a paint color—the initial rollout was red, but there were blue and gray Model Ts as well—the first run had no tops, windshields, or headlights.*

In fact, despite all the accolades, while the Model T was undeniably a major step forward in mass-consumption automaking, in 1908 and 1909 it was not the most advanced low-priced model available. That honor went to a $900 runabout manufactured by a man who was every bit the match for Henry Ford in vision, dynamism, and nerve, a diminutive comet described as "an organizing genius, a reckless speculator, a super-salesman, a glib promoter, [and] the one man, not excluding Henry Ford, who really saw the future of the automobile."[10] He would create a consortium that would ultimately eclipse Ford Motor and, in doing so, would persuade Henry Ford to agree to sell his entire share of Ford Motor stock for what would have been a ridiculously low price. And he did it twice. His name was William Crapo Durant, but everyone referred to him as "Billy."

Durant was born in Boston in December 1861, about a year and a half before Ford. His maternal grandfather, Henry Crapo, had made a fortune in whaling but cashed out when he decided the New Bedford boom was coming to an end. Grandfather Crapo relocated to Michigan, where, after making even more money in lumber, he acquired a mansion in Flint, from which he launched a successful campaign for governor just before Billy's third birthday. Durant was fortunate that his grandfather was so successful, because his father, of whom no solid record remains, appears to have been a no-account drifter, alcoholic, and failed land speculator.

Durant, like Ford, left school to get an early start in business, in this case in his grandfather's lumberyard. But unlike Ford, Durant exhibited no mechanical aptitude. Billy Durant was pure business, mostly

---

* The famous line "You can have any color you want as long as it's black," which may or may not be attributable to Ford, wasn't uttered until 1913, when the assembly line was running at full tilt and varying the paint colors would slow down production.

sales. Walter Chrysler later observed that Durant "could coax a bird right down out of a tree." As a teenager he sold everything from cigars to real estate to bicycles; still not yet twenty-one, he was appointed to manage the Flint Water Works.

At twenty-four, Durant was ready to go out on his own. A Flint carriage maker had patented a two-wheeled cart that was supposedly so precisely balanced that it could replicate a four-wheeler. After the inventor was sufficiently cooperative to allow his shop to burn to the ground, Durant bought up the patent for $50, then borrowed $2,000 and, with another salesman as a partner, opened his own carriage firm. Durant realized early in the game that you didn't have to make something yourself to make money from it. He got a local carriage maker to produce two-wheeled buggies at $8 apiece, and then the two young salesmen used their considerable talents to foist their product, marked up by more than 50 percent, on the public. Soon they were building a variety of carriages to cater to different markets. Fifteen years later, Durant was one of the leading manufacturers of horse-drawn carriages in the United States, producing more than fifty thousand a year, and had made himself the first of the many fortunes that would come and go for the remainder of his life. Eventually, he acquired a factory, but only for assembly. Manufacture of each of the components, "down to the whip socket," was subcontracted.

Durant disliked automobiles, not simply because they threatened his business but because he thought them loud, ugly, and foul-smelling. But for Durant, aesthetics could never stand up to opportunity. In 1904, he bought up controlling interest in the Buick Motor Company. The firm's founder, David Buick, had moved from plumbing fixtures to gasoline engine design but, after five discouraging years and a series of unhappy investors, had become disgusted with the business. That was when Billy Durant showed up. Buick might have been a grumbling malcontent, but he could design a quite serviceable car.

Buick had manufactured only sixteen automobiles in 1904, but Durant immediately proclaimed his ambition to increase that number into the hundreds of thousands. For most people, outrageous public utterances tend to be an impediment to their business. But for some—

Billy Durant

none more than Billy Durant—such pronouncements somehow pro-
voke serious consideration as to whether they just might be true.
(That Durant never drew a salary or submitted an expense report did
not hurt his credibility.) Before he had built one additional machine,
Durant entered Buick in the New York Auto Show—and then returned to Flint with orders for 1,108 cars. He reorganized the factory,
hired engineers and managers to run it, and whirled constantly through
the plant making sure his product was properly constructed. All the
cars were delivered.

David Buick left the company that bore his name in 1906, his legacy being a solid, well-designed automobile.* Two years after that, in
the same year that the Model T rolled out, Buick, with 8,500 cars, not
Ford, was the leading American automobile manufacturer. During
this period, Durant invented the dedicated dealership system, an idea
that was eventually copied by his competitors, including Norval
Hawkins at Ford.

* Buick could not settle into anything and lost all his money. At one point, Durant
gave him $100,000.

Durant was a peerless salesman, with astounding energy—associates sometimes wondered when he slept, if at all—which often obscured, both during his life and afterward, a sophistication for structure, organization, and flow that would fifty years hence become the staples of many business school curricula. He saw in 1908—as did Ford—a market for automobiles poised to explode, but he also perceived a layering of that market that Ford chose to ignore. "Durant's remedy for this situation was combination—put together a big organization, with a variety of models and its own parts factories, so that it would not only have the resources to meet the growing demand for automobiles but, by offering several kinds of car, would have some insurance against shifts in public preference."[11] The notion was brilliant: a company with divisions targeting different segments of the market, some based on low margin/high volume, some the opposite, and some in between. Firms were popping up by the hundreds and going under almost as fast. But public fascination meant that some of those companies were bound to survive and thrive. By spreading both risk and potential, Durant increased the odds that his divisions would be among them.

To provide the cash flow to bring his vision to reality, Durant intended to use Buick's latest rollout, an automobile at least the equal of and probably superior to Ford's: the Model 10.

Durant marketed the 10 as a "gentleman's light four-cylinder roadster" and saturated newspapers with ads. It had a four-cylinder engine, like Ford's Model T, but delivered a superior 22.5 horsepower. Unlike Ford cars, Buick had perfected a system of overhead valves that delivered better performance than the traditional side valve system and was also easier to access for repairs. The Model 10 initially came only in white; it had such a peppy ride that, helped along by Durant's sloganeering, it was soon referred to as the "White Streak." Durant also employed a planetary transmission with two forward speeds and one reverse, but unlike Ford's machine, which had only two pedals, the 10 had a pedal for each of the three gears. Vanadium steel notwithstanding, the Model 10 had a superior housing for the rear differential— cast iron instead of stamped steel—and better arrangements to circulate the oil and water.

The 1908 Model 10 was $50 more expensive than the first Model T, but it included brass trim, acetylene headlamps, side- and taillights, and a horn. It was 200 pounds heavier, but the suspension was far more advanced, making the ride more comfortable. (Although the 10 was crank-started as well, it was engineered to avoid the infamous Ford backfires.)

Buick was an ALAM member, so Durant chose the automobile show at Madison Square Garden in November 1907 to exhibit the Model 10 for the first time. While Durant's runabout was by far the lowest-priced four-cylinder machine, it did not attract that much attention amidst the ALAM-favored luxury automobiles selling for as much as $7,000. But Durant was unfazed. He knew precisely what to emphasize to get his new car noticed by consumers: speed and performance.

Durant took direct aim at the Model T. "The Fastest and Most Powerful $1,000 Runabout Sold on the American Market," read the early ads. "Can Climb a Street Hill Faster Than Any Two, Four, or Six Cylinder Car. This Car Has Recorded 61 Miles Per Hour." The Model 10 engine was fashioned with an equal bore and stroke, unusual but highly efficient, so Durant entered his new runabout in a series of races, where it would be driven by some of the nation's top drivers, including Louis Chevrolet.* The 10 did quite well, often against competition that was larger, heavier, and, at least in theory, more powerful. When he won, Durant made sure the public knew it. But Billy Durant knew how to gain advantage even if his entry lost. A later ad for the Model 10 read:

> Won First Place Among American Cars AND Second Place in International Light Car Road Race. AFTER LEADING THE ENTIRE FIRST HALF of what proved to be the most exciting and most stubbornly fought speed battle in automobile racing history, the Buick Model 10's gasoline

---

* The others were Bob Burman, Louis Chevrolet's brother Arthur, and Louis Strang. The trio would win more than five hundred races in the next three years, driving the Models 10, 16, 17, and D.

Buick roadster waits for horse-drawn wagon to pass on narrow country road

tank came loose and because of stops totaling over twenty minutes from this trouble, the Buick lost the 196-mile Savannah race by six minutes. Hilliard in his $3,300 Lancia won and all credit is due him. Burman in his $1,000 Buick gave him the fight of his life and brought his car in with such a lead over the remaining contestants that there was no question concerning the standard which the Buick has set in low-priced automobile construction. The Buick used a regular stock chassis except that for the sake of securing less clearance, the frame and machinery were under hung. Our regular motor, transmission and axle parts were used. During the entire race, the hood over the engine was not raised.

With the Model 10's success, Durant moved forward. He had set his sights on some of the most successful carmakers then in operation, and no one was more successful than Ford Motor. Henry Ford, with an automobile poised to tap into a vast market and a court case that he insisted was no more than a nuisance, seemed an unhittable target. But Durant sensed vulnerability and went right for it.

With every car Ford sold, Durant knew, his potential indemnity to Selden increased. By the time the Model T was released, it was more than $1 million. In addition, if Ford lost, he could be liable for interest and legal fees, which could add hundreds of thousands to the bill. But the future held more risk than the past. If Selden won, he would be free to negotiate a new licensing agreement that could strip Ford of virtually all of his profits until 1912 or even put him out of business. Durant decided that Henry Ford might just be willing to free himself from all that inconvenience.

And so, to pull the conglomerate together, Durant initially approached three other carmakers. Ford was one, REO—Ransom Olds's firm—was another, and Maxwell-Briscoe was the third. Benjamin Briscoe was the most enthusiastic, and Olds agreed to go along as well.

Then so did Henry Ford.

The specifics of the tale remain vague. Neither Ford, Couzens, nor Durant ever provided details.* The only account was by Benjamin Briscoe, which had him playing a key and likely inflated part in the negotiations. What is clear is that for the acquisition, the Ford Motor Company would be valued at $3 million. Whether Ford, Couzens, or Durant initially proposed this figure is not known, but in any case it was wildly low. If Ford's assertion that the Model T was poised to change the face of American transportation was correct, it was not inconceivable that Ford Motor could have earned that much in one year, as it ultimately did. Ford never indicated why he would have been

---

* As with a subsequent attempt by Durant to acquire Ford Motor, sympathetic Ford biographers have used the lack of detail to justify their extreme skepticism that Henry Ford would have seriously considered bailing out when he was so close to success. But the overwhelming evidence, from a number of sources both inside and outside the Ford family, is that he did. Herbert Satterlee, for example, who was Pierpont Morgan's son-in-law as well as Benjamin Briscoe's lawyer, stated unequivocally, "Ford and Olds were planning on getting out of the business." George Perkins, a Morgan partner, was so enthusiastic about merging the three automakers that he had even come up with a name for the new firm—The International.

willing to sell out at such a price—never, in fact, acknowledged that the offer had been made, although others, including James Couzens, did. What was more, Ford himself would not have gotten $3 million, but only 58.5 percent of that payment, representing his share at the time of Ford Motor Company stock.

But the deal collapsed.

Durant's notion was to put together his consortium by granting stock in the new company to the owners of the carmakers he absorbed. While he likely could have raised a good deal of cash—there were any number of financiers he could have persuaded—Durant did not want to be burdened by debt. Rather, he wanted to give everyone who threw in with him a stake in the company's future, in effect making the owners of the acquired companies partners rather than sellers. Olds and Briscoe agreed. But Henry Ford did not want partners. He was, in fact, intending to divest himself of the ones he already had. So he demanded that the $3 million be paid in cash.

Again, accounts differ on what happened next. Briscoe insisted that when Ford demanded cash, Olds did as well, the same $3 million, and that $6 million was more than even Billy Durant could raise. It seems unlikely, however, that if Ransom Olds was serious about joining up with Durant and the others—and with far lower sales, he certainly had more incentive to do so than Ford—that he would have valued his company at the same level. In addition, Durant seemed to have been able to raise the sum he needed, or almost as much, as he soon proved.

With the collapse of the first deal, sometime in the summer of 1908, Durant immediately sought another. Briscoe would not come back so soon, so Durant went it alone. On September 16, 1908, eleven days before the first Model T shipped, the General Motors Company was incorporated in New Jersey, capitalized at $2,000. Within two years, that figure had increased to more than $60 million as Durant brought ten carmakers, two truck manufacturers, and thirteen parts fabricators into the fold. Some of the names would remain familiar for a century, including Buick, Cadillac, and Oldsmobile, while many, such as Elmore, Marquette, Ranier, and Welch, would eventually wither away. The acquisitions included Champion Ignition Company, where Albert Champion had invented a high-performance, porcelain-coated spark plug, and eventually Fisher Body, which remains a division of General Motors.[12]

"Nobody at the time knew what would work best," Durant said later, "what types of motors, gears, axles, magnetos, wheels, springs, radiators, would become permanent or practical and useable. Everybody in the business was experimenting. We sought to control basic patents. We scrapped what wasn't considered practical. But the essential and tried product of the several companies was kept and developed."[13]

This time Durant was almost entirely successful in persuading his new partners to take stock in lieu of cash. "I bought that company in 1908 for $2,500,000," Durant said of the Olds Motor Works. "We paid $18,500 in cash, which was the amount of the Olds company's current liabilities. The balance was paid in the stock of the newly formed General Motors Company."[14] But Henry Leland at Cadillac balked. Like Henry Ford, he wanted cash on the barrelhead. Cadillac was integral to Durant's plan, so he acquiesced, paying Leland $4.4 million, which he raised in a matter of weeks from Michigan bankers only months after he theoretically could not come up with Henry Ford's $3 million.

Durant's General Motors, of course, turned out to be every bit the brilliant idea that its founder claimed it would be. Just not for Durant. Ambition and a lack of moderation—also two of his greatest strengths—did him in.

"General Motors was a conglomeration of companies acquired because they were available rather than because they fitted into any coherent pattern. Only Buick and Cadillac were money-makers. Oldsmobile had a great name but not much else, Oakland was a promising newcomer, and the others have to be classified as odds and ends, some of them sheer gambles on Durant's part."[15] By moving too fast and not sufficiently thinking through the company's expansion, Durant had sacrificed cash flow to ambition. By 1910, General Motors seemed poised to go under. The company was saved by a consortium of bankers, who exacted both high interest and draconian concessions, one of which was that Billy Durant withdraw from running the business.* (He would, however, retain his stock.) Durant agreed and left the company he put together with vision, energy, and, mostly, nerve.

He would be back.

---

* The Model 10 lasted only as long as Durant. It represented almost half of the 8,820 cars Buick sold in 1908, doubled to 8,100 in 1909, and then rose to 11,000 in 1910. With Durant's departure, the new management team discontinued the Model 10 and instead focused on higher-priced cars. Sales plunged, dropping by more than half in just one year, and Buick went from being the second-largest automaker to fifth.

CHAPTER 23

FALSE END OF
A LONG TRAIL

n spring 1909, after six years of depositions, demonstrations, and delays; after reams and reams of paper, much of it extraneous; and after an advertising war that had cost each side hundreds of thousands of dollars, the patent infringement suit against Henry Ford by the Electric Vehicle Company seemed ready for trial. In the interim, Ford had grown from an obscure, quixotic independent, the vulnerable fledgling whose resources could be overwhelmed by legal fees, to the largest automobile manufacturer in America. At that point, in fact, Henry Ford was far more powerful than any of the parties who were suing him. Even if he lost, ALAM (through the Electric Vehicle shell) could no longer feel confident about running him out of business, but the millions of dollars the cabal stood to collect in royalties, penalties, and interest were of course as appealing as ever.

But in order to have a call on those millions, ALAM had a steep grade to ascend. There was little doubt among most of the knowledgeable observers following the case that Selden's assertions were at best flimsy. It did not seem possible that the Selden, which its putative inventor had so unfortunately chosen to exhibit, could be the control-

ling example of automobile technology. Although the trade magazines had, in most cases, contorted themselves to remain neutral,
there was a stream of hints that the suit had devolved to anticlimax,
with Ford's victory ensured. Any remaining doubt should have been
dispelled when the case was assigned to Judge Charles Merrill Hough,
who had been appointed to the federal bench just three years before
by fellow Republican Theodore Roosevelt, whose war on monopoly
and oligopoly was at the apex of his domestic agenda.*

Then Ford lost.

Hough, fifty-one, had graduated from Dartmouth in 1879, then returned to his native Philadelphia, where he taught school and read law,
gaining admission to the bar in 1883. Soon afterward he moved to
New York to practice, and despite poor eyesight, he also served in the
state naval militia. He became an authority on admiralty law, but he
had almost no experience with patents. Hough was never considered
to have a brilliant legal mind, nor was he especially active politically,
but he was appointed because of a reputation for being thorough,
serious, and fair.

Those traits were tested soon after his appointment when, in April
1908, he was assigned to preside over the trial of the "Ice King,"
Charles W. Morse, who had been one of the prime movers in the attempt to corner the copper market that had precipitated the Panic of
1907. Morse was one of the most flamboyant and notorious of the
speculators who had run rampant through the financial system.†

Morse had experience cornering markets—in 1900, he had done so
with ice, at the time derived mostly from river water and stored underground. Once he had control, he proceeded to squeeze families and
businesses that had no other means of refrigeration. "The sixty-

---

* Ralzemond Parker was alone in thinking Hough a dangerous choice. He preferred George C. Holt, another of the judges on the federal bench, but judges
were chosen randomly, so Parker had no recourse.
† What follows is merely a hint of Morse's vast dealings. He was among the most
brazen and joyously dishonest financiers in American history.

million-dollar Ice Trust, known as the American Ice Company, which has succeeded in securing what is practically an absolute monopoly of the ice business in New York City, has just increased the cost of ice to consumers 100 per cent, and threatens further advance in prices," wrote *The New York Times* in 1900. "This 100 per cent tax upon a commodity that is a necessity to all the people of this city has aroused the bitterest feeling in the community."[1] Morse's ruthlessness did not impact his position in polite society. In 1901, his boxmate at the opera was William K. Vanderbilt Sr., Willie K.'s father, and Willie K. himself often spent evenings listening to tenors and sopranos with Morse as his companion.

Although Morse continued to make lurid headlines—his marriage to an Atlanta socialite was annulled in 1904 when it was discovered she had not bothered to properly divorce her first husband—he also continued to thrive. By 1906, among his other holdings, Morse served on the boards of more than fifty banks and was majority owner of eighty-one steamships. But late in 1907, soon after the copper scandal, the National Bank of North America, in which Morse held controlling interest, collapsed. Morse was arrested the following February as he stepped off the gangplank of a luxury ocean liner returning from Europe. He was charged with illegal manipulation, selling essentially worthless American Ice stock to the bank for hundreds of thousands of dollars, as well as obtaining overdrafts of more than $200,000 "at the height of the panic," immediately before he was forced to liquidate his interest. The bank's president, Alfred Curtis, widely seen as a dupe, was charged as well.

In April, Judge Hough was assigned the case. It was a delicate situation—Morse still had quite a few influential friends, and many of his stock market gambits were not all that uncommon. He amassed a legal team that consisted of, among other luminaries, a former United States congressman. Morse assumed that a newly seated judge with no real reputation might be reluctant to take too aggressive a stance against such an array.

But Hough set his tone early on when he denied virtually all of Morse's pretrial motions. When the trial finally began in October, prosecuted by assistant United States attorney and future secretary of war Henry Stimson, Hough infuriated Morse's lawyers—who took his actions as a "reflection on themselves"—when he broke a twenty-five-year precedent and sequestered the jury. He also ordered Secret Service agents to guard key witnesses.

Once the proceedings began, Morse tried to portray himself as an innocent victim of unscrupulous characters, which elicited public guffaws. Curtis testified that Morse "dominated" the bank and that he, Curtis, had warned him often, sometimes in writing, that the institution was threatened with insolvency. When Morse saw the tide moving against him, he unsuccessfully feigned illness in an attempt to postpone the proceedings. The case went to the jury in early November and both men were found guilty the next day, although the jury recommended mercy for Curtis, whom they regarded as a "weak tool." Morse took the verdict stoically, but Curtis wept. They were then returned to a cell they shared in the Tombs.

Two days later, Hough sentenced Morse to fifteen years imprisonment at the Atlanta Penitentiary and denied bail pending appeal. When Morse was removed, "the crowd, which filled every inch of the room . . . jeered."[*] Curtis received five years, but Hough suspended the sentence, to the cheers of the spectators. The case received nationwide attention and vaulted Hough into prominence. Within months, he was assigned the Selden-Ford patent case.

But while fame could disguise Hough's shortcomings, it could not eradicate them. He was thorough but not profound, energetic but not insightful, even-handed but extremely impressionable. "His was not a

---

* Morse got the last laugh, however. After exhausting his appeals, Morse finally went to Atlanta in 1910, but two years later he contracted a mysterious illness that a team of army doctors agreed would soon kill him. He was pardoned by President William Howard Taft and sailed to Germany for treatment. He recovered miraculously, however, and later revealed he had been drinking soap suds and a chemical brew to precipitate his symptoms. Again a free man, Morse returned to New York and the shipping business, which he conducted no more scrupulously than before. He was ultimately indicted for mail fraud and war profiteering, among other charges, but never spent another day in prison. He died peacefully in 1933, at age seventy-seven, in Bath, Maine, the town in which he was born.

reflective mind. . . . He had a firm command of the rules and principles of patent law, but he knew nothing of automotive history and
mechanical engineering. . . . Like most judges who sat in patent cases,
he had less than a passing acquaintance with the background and
terms of the art."³ While Hough was certain to plow through the
mountains of evidence that were presented to him, he would be challenged to grasp the nuances of a technology that he had never before
seen.

But in this, Hough cannot be judged too harshly. It is the essence
of patent infringement suits, especially those involving new technologies, that the presiding judge will likely know less about the intricacies
of the case than either of the parties. Both plaintiff and defendant will
be well versed, of course, and each side will choose lawyers with sufficient experience in patent law to be aware that learning as much as
they can about the technical aspects of the patented device is part of
their job. And they have their clients to learn from. Judges do not. In
most judicial proceedings, knowledge of the law is sufficient to render
a proper decision. In patent suits, however, it is generally not the law
that is in dispute, or even the actions of the participants, but some
arcane and often impenetrable technical definition.

In pioneer cases, pressure on the judge was exacerbated. He was
required to unravel not only the specifications of the device at issue
but also whether or not similar and more advanced devices fell under
the same umbrella. Hough would therefore be required to, in effect,
create a definition of a hydrocarbon-powered internal combustion
engine and then determine whether or not Selden's version controlled
Ford's.

For all the thousands of pages of testimony and exhibits, then, the
case was really about only three basic questions. First: Did George
Selden's patent describe a practical theory? In other words, could a
workable automobile be built from the specifications in his patent?
There was no requirement that this be a *good* automobile, only that one
could be built. Second: Was Selden's patent deserving of pioneer status, which meant that it described a great and original leap forward in
the art of automaking? Third: Had Ford extrapolated from the prin-

ciples enunciated in the Selden patent, or had he employed an unrelated technology?

Hough gave an early sense of what Ford's lawyers in particular were up against when, during the opening remarks, he suggested with surprising candor, "Someone will have to explain to me what the liquid hydrocarbon gas engine is." Further, he tacitly warned the lawyers to keep to the larger issues, as "during the hearing it became increasingly evident that precision of argument irritated him."[4]

The judge seemed to accept early on that Selden's machine had, in fact, run, which would establish practicality—and that it *was* Selden's machine. Although he did ask the plaintiffs at one point whether the patent was simply a "prophecy," overall Hough also seemed to accept their contention that "there was no state of the art prior to Selden."

That left the third question. From the start, both sides chose to reduce this to a question of engine type. In other words, was Selden's engine, based on the Brayton constant-pressure cycle, distinct from the engines used in virtually every modern automobile, which were based on Otto's four-stroke compression principle? In this, Ford's lawyers, relying on technical arguments, could not seem to make headway. When they attempted to demonstrate that the Otto model was different and, in being different, did not fall under Selden's patent, Hough did not seem to comprehend the distinction. To him, compression was compression and, as long as they were of the liquid hydrocarbon type, other petty distinctions were "beside the issue."[5]

Closing arguments were given on June 4. Frederick Fish, lead counsel for Electric Vehicle (who would later represent the Wright brothers in their infringement suit against Glenn Curtiss), presented an argument "marked with a charm rare in presentations of patent lawyers."[6] He focused principally on the question of pioneer status and was simple and straightforward, stressing the revolutionary nature of Selden's design—he compared the inventor to a poet—and asserting that every gasoline automobile manufactured since had been built atop Selden's foundation. He particularly attacked the defense's allegation that Selden had never built an actual machine. "It was not the work for a mechanic. Bell was not a mechanic. Edison was not a mechanic. They approached their problems not from the point of view of the mechanic at all, and neither did Selden."[7]

Ford's team stressed that Selden's design had never resulted in a workable automobile, that he had based it on an obsolete technology—Brayton constant compression—and that he was simply a man who had manipulated the patent system in order to profit from the work of genuine inventors, of which Henry Ford was one.

Judge Hough had given his word to both parties that he would read the entire record, and to that end he ordered all necessary paperwork, crates of it, to be shipped to his summer home in Rhode Island. The task would take three months.

Frustrated with their inability to get their ideas across during the trial, Ralzemond Parker and Ford's other attorneys, with the exception of the recently hired W. Benton Crisp (who would later represent Glenn Curtiss against the Wrights), had drowned their argument in detail with an immense brief of more than thirteen hundred pages. This was a thorough approach, to be sure, but hardly reader friendly—and why Parker and his colleagues would believe that Judge Hough, who had shown such a reluctance to delve into minutiae during the trial, would now be willing to wade through this impenetrable mass is uncertain. Frederick Fish and his fellow counsel did in writing what Fish had done orally and presented a relatively short, cogent, and direct argument—less than one-sixth the length of that of the defendants—focusing principally on justifying pioneer status of the patent.

Ford's attorneys were no more successful in written argument than they had been in the courtroom. On September 15, 1909, Judge Hough agreed that before George Selden filed for his patent, "there was no industry, the art existed only in talk and hope, and no vehicles even faintly fulfilling the requirements outlined had ever been built."[8] Hough did not indicate whether he gave any credence at all to Ford's arguments, but at the very least he used Fish's brief as his base. He fully accepted the argument that, regardless of current technology, Selden's formulation was groundbreaking and deserved pioneer status, rejecting the notion that Ford's automobiles were new technologies. He did not agree that there were fundamental differences between

Selden's machine, particularly the engine, and the automobiles that had subsequently been built.

Before getting into the case itself, however, the judge spent a good deal of time "protesting against the methods of taking and printing testimony in Equity, current in this circuit (and probably others), excused if not justified by the rules of the Supreme Court, especially to be found in patent causes and flagrantly exemplified in this litigation." Hough detailed what he termed a "horrible example" of the practice of taking testimony outside the rules of judicial procedure. "The records in these cases, as printed, bound and submitted, comprise thirty-six large octavo volumes of which more than one-half contain only repeated matter, i.e., identical depositions with changed captions, and exhibits offered in more than one case.* In reading the testimony of one side in one set of cases, there were counted over a hundred printed pages recording squabbles . . . concerning adjournments—and after arriving at this number it seemed unnecessary to count further."

Hough's plea for change did not fall on deaf ears. In November 1912, the Supreme Court would reform the manner in which "cases in equity" were heard. Describing the process as "too cumbersome, too slow, and too expensive," the Court limited depositions, required testimony to be taken in court, and restricted many of the stalling tactics in which attorneys regularly indulged to extend proceedings—and increase their fees.[9]

When Hough got to the issue itself, he began by noting, "Selden does not pretend to have invented any new machine or combination of matter in the same sense that Whitney invented the cotton gin or Howe the sewing machine," but that "he selected, adapted, modified, coordinated, and organized the enumerated parts (including the usual mechanical adjuncts of each part) into a harmonious whole capable of results never before achieved," and that "after thirty years, no gasoline motor car has been produced that does not depend for success on a selection and organization of parts, identical with or equivalent to that made by him in 1879."

* The actions against Panhard as well as some others had been combined in one case, but Ford's suit was by far the most important.

Hough cited Coxe's decision in the demurrer and traced the development of internal combustion engines, following almost verbatim the plaintiffs' outline. He accepted Frederick Fish's contention that differences between the Otto engine and the Brayton were merely semantic. All that mattered, Hough insisted, was that Selden "devised and used an arrangement of Brayton's engine never before attempted, one that Brayton himself never suggested, made or patented, and without which the road vehicle was an impossibility. This mental concept constituted invention, if capable of reduction to operation, and if an operative example (not all operative examples) thereof was shown by the patentee." When Hough wrote a bit later, "If I have correctly apprehended it, there was clearly room for a pioneer patent, and it must now be held that on its face and in view of the art, Selden's is such a patent," Ford's fate was sealed.

Hough did have a final comment as to the oddity of the case before him. "No litigation closely resembling these cases has been shown to the court, and no instance is known to me of an idea being buried in the patent office until the world caught up to and passed it, and then embodied in a patent only useful for tribute." And while "Selden has contributed very little to motor-car advancement . . . the patent speaks from the date of issue, and unless Selden did something unlawful during his sixteen years' wrangle with Examiners . . . he is within the law, and his rights are the same as those of the promptest applicant." Indeed, Selden had broken no law, had gone afoul of no statute. "Patents are granted for inventions, the inventor may use his discovery, or he may not, but no one else can use it for seventeen years. That seventeen years begins whenever the United States so decrees by its patent grant. That the applicant for patent rights acquiesces in delay, or even desires delay, is immaterial to the Courts so long as the statute law is not violated. On these principles, complainants are entitled to a decree."

And so no gasoline automobile could be sold in the United States without infringing the Selden patent. The patent was due to expire in 1912, but the total uncollected royalties from date of issue would total about $5 million, the largest chunk from the booming sales of the Ford Motor Company. In addition, as the losing party, Ford was now liable for additional fees and penalties if the Selden forces chose to pursue them.

There was little criticism of the decision in the trade magazines. Most, as they had done in the run-up to the trial, strained for neutrality while stressing the importance of the decision. *Motor World,* for example, merely stated that "in an opinion as pointed, pungent and comprehensive as it is long," Judge Hough "sustains the validity of the Selden patent, broadly construing its first claim as covering all gasolene automobiles."[10]

Horseless Age was the exception. It had always been kind to ALAM and seemed positively gleeful at the trial's result:

> It was the very prevalent view in the industry that [the patent] would not successfully withstand a test. In fact, this belief was so strong in recent years that the possibility of being compelled to pay royalties under the patent would have been laughed to scorn by many unlicensed manufacturers. Now, however, the patent has stood the test. One of the best known judges of the United States Circuit Court, widely experienced in patent litigation, has declared it to be valid and legal, and to cover all forms of gasoline automobiles.[11]

There were other expressions of joy at the verdict. In the same issue of *Motor Way* and *Automobile Trade Journal* that ran the complete text of Judge Hough's decision, the Selden Motor Vehicle Company ran a triumphant full-page ad. A banner halfway down the page proclaimed, "The Selden Car. Made by the Father of Them All." The text sounded as if it had been written by Selden himself, and perhaps it was. Whoever was the author, there is very little ad copy, then or now, that was anything like it. (If nothing else, this may be the only advertisement in history to contain a verbatim legal opinion.)

> The "Know-It-Alls" said derisively, "That patent is no good," but Judge Hough, of the United States Circuit

Court, says: "This Statement of complainants' position seems to show that the subject matter of these suits is the modern gasoline automobile. If I have correctly apprehended it, there was clearly room for a pioneer patent, and it must now be held that on its face and in view of the art, Selden's is such a patent. If these defendants infringe, it is because complainants own a patent so fundamental and far-reaching, as to cover every modern car, driven by any form of petroleum vapor, and as yet commercially successful. It is so found, and decrees will pass accordingly."

Don't let the "Wiseacres" fool you any longer. The "Selden Patent" is not air, it is *substance,* and its validity is recognized by the United States Patent Office and the Courts. Now, listen! If Mr. Geo. B. Selden was the original *inventor* of the automobile—of a vehicle propelled by a gasoline engine, under power produced by hydro-carbon internal combustion—as these highest authorities broadly admit, can any rational man believe the Selden car of today would be permitted by Mr. Selden to be anything but the best in material and in correct and careful mechanical construction? Such a supposition is absurd. This is not stated at all as a defensive argument, but as a simple fact which may not have occurred to some minds. The makers of the SELDEN car have nothing to apologize for. The car has a splendid record and speaks for itself, and the many hundreds of owners throughout the country are praising it in a chorus which reaches from coast to coast. Ask any Selden owner and he will confirm this statement. The Selden car has not figured conspicuously in spectacular "races" and similar "contests," it is true. We have never cared much to risk life and limb for the transitory glory of a race track "win." But the Selden car, built for comfortable riding and thorough service, has done innumerable "stunts," and amazing ones, in the way of hill climbing and long and difficult tours, which have not been heralded by paid press agents, and many owners of cars made by the "wise-acres" have been too dizzy and dust-blinded to identify the Selden car when it passed them on the road![12]

But George Selden's crowing was premature. Within three years, both his fame and his automobile would be gone.

CHAPTER 24

IT'S NEVER OVER . . .

n the wake of Judge Hough's ruling, nonlicensed manufacturers fell
over like so many dominoes. Within weeks, more than thirty of the
independents had been accepted into the ALAM ranks as paying
members. Billy Durant, whose General Motors had been refusing to
pay licensing fees, settled with the organization and paid $1 million,
although some portion of this would come back to him as fees for the
carmakers in his group—including Buick—that had held ALAM licenses.

Not surprisingly, ALAM members were exultant, filling the newspapers and trade magazines with a series of pronouncements praising
justice and the American legal system. The most ironic of these came
from Alexander Winton, who had more or less set events in motion
when, after the most vitriolic denunciations of his current allies, he
had accepted $40,000 to switch sides almost a decade before. "Every
automobile manufacturer was warned years ago not to infringe on the
Selden patent," Winton exclaimed. "The patent has withstood the as-
sault of the ablest legal talent on this continent; it emerges from the
court triumphant, and nothing now remains but to exact from the

trespassers a share of that income which they have enjoyed for years without legal right and in utter defiance of the American law which rewards inventive genius with letters patent."[1] For Winton, this was the first time in many tries that he ended a contest ahead of Henry Ford.

Although Winton's remarks in particular must have infuriated him, Ford remained stolid, at least in public, categorizing the defeat as only a temporary setback. A boxed insert in *Motor Way* magazine, on the same page where Hough's decision was explained, read, "Selden suit decision has no effect on Ford policy. We will fight to a finish. Henry Ford." He sent the same terse vow to newspapers and the other trades.

"I simply knew we were right," Ford wrote later in *My Life and Work,* and portrayed his determination to see the matter through to the Supreme Court if necessary as always having been set in stone. He did admit that he had been apprehensive that "many buyers would be frightened away from buying because of the threats of court action against individual owners."[2] ALAM had previously sued a number of car buyers, albeit with mixed results, and some members of the association stated publicly that they would do so again. But ultimately, Ford insisted, such tactics would be moot. He told anyone who would listen that Hough's decision was "neither final nor conclusive" and that he would both "continue to produce motor cars to the limit of his capacity, [and] resist all overtures and threats from the Selden camp."[3]

Privately, however, Ford was apparently a good deal less confident. Horace Rackham, hardly a detractor, noted that Ford was gloomy, "in a very serious frame of mind."[4] Even with the Model T now an established success—he had sold seventeen thousand cars in 1909 and would double that figure in 1910—he seemed ready to get out. According to Couzens, "he constantly talked about retiring and becoming a farmer"—a telling comment given how much Ford hated farming.[5]

In the months before the case was decided, Couzens had approached Billy Durant on Ford's behalf and told him, "Mr. Ford is very much concerned about the Selden patent suit and its outcome.

The prospects of winning or losing the case are equal. To lose means payment of a very large sum of money. He is not a member of the license agreement and, on general principles, has opposed the right of any man to control this patent situation. General Motors, with its several companies holding licenses, would probably be able to make a very satisfactory adjustment with Selden if it owned the Ford Company."[6] Durant was unwilling to make a commitment to Ford until after the ruling, but just weeks after Hough's decision came down, he met with Couzens in a New York hotel to discuss the sale. Ford, who was staying at the same hotel, did not attend because, as Couzens put it, he was "sick in body and mind" and had entrusted Couzens with the negotiations.[7]

Hough's ruling notwithstanding, both sides knew it would cost Durant a good deal more to acquire Ford Motor than the figure agreed on the previous year. Couzens wanted to remain involved, but Ford intended to cash out. The number Durant and Couzens came to was $8 million, of which $2 million would go to Couzens in stock. Ford would receive $2 million at the time of sale and the remaining $4 million, with interest at 5 percent, within three years.[*] Ford would continue to draw a prorated share of the profits until he was paid in full. The remaining Ford shareholders would, like Couzens, receive stock. When Couzens went to Ford's room to recount the terms, he reported that Ford called out from the bathroom, "Tell him he can have it, if it's all cash. And I'll throw in my lumbago."[8] Ford was so anxious to sell, however, that he eventually agreed to the initial arrangement of cash and notes.

The deal progressed far enough for Durant to receive a written option, for which he paid $75,000, and to visit the Ford plant in secret to check inventory. On October 26, the board of General Motors ratified the agreement. Durant, his local lines of credit having no further leeway, was off to New York to secure financing.

His first stop was 23 Wall Street for a meeting at J. P. Morgan and Company. Durant later recalled the meeting. "Loan me $8,000,000

---

[*] The price, although more than double the previous offer, would prove to be quite a bargain since a consortium of bankers would soon value the company at more than $30 million, although much of that would be based on future sales.

legal tender," he proposed to a group of assembled partners and investors, "and for security I'll assign to you until repaid the whole of General Motors, and the Ford Motor Company, and will give my personal note." Durant said that George Perkins, the Morgan partner who had been most disappointed at the collapse of the previous scheme, gave him an hour to present his case.

> I explained to the Morgan partners that the age of the horse and buggy was over. That a new era in transportation, communication, and rapid travel between cities was coming. We explained the necessity for steel companies to enlarge their plants to be able to take care of the orders that would flood their present capacities; that the cotton growers in the south would have to double and treble their crops to supply the demand for textile material for automobiles; that good roads someday would cross the nation from ocean to ocean and from Michigan to Florida. I was then backing a young man in Michigan, who we called "Good Roads" Earle. The first good road we personally paid for. It was called the Buick Road, and was a gravel constructed route that went through Grand Blanc, to Atlas, and Clarkston, on to Detroit. That was the beginning of the Michigan Highway Department. We pointed out that a new prosperity would follow in America that would affect the entire continent, with the certain success of the motor industry. At that time we had our eyes on such men as Charles Kettering, Alfred Sloan, Walter Marr, Albert Champion, Charles S. Mott, A. B. C. Hardy, William Little, Robert Burman, and the Chevrolet Brothers, among others ... men of vision whose soundness of judgment and mechanical engineering genius would assure the eventual success of the new automotive industry.[9]

Durant claimed that the financiers listened for two hours, but other than Diamond Match Company president Edward Stettinius and Morgan himself, no one at the table felt that Durant was anything more than a salesman. (That refusal would ultimately cost the Morgan partners billions of dollars. Stettinius, unbeknownst to his skeptical colleagues, eventually bought a large block of General Motors stock on his own and made a small fortune.)

He next tried National City Bank, this time to attempt to secure a $2 million loan to cover the first payment to Ford. Frank Vanderlip, the bank's president, was enthusiastic about the deal, so approval seemed a formality. It wasn't. The bank's credit committee turned Durant and Vanderlip down on the grounds that Durant had placed far too high a value on Ford Motor Company. With that, Billy Durant lost his last chance to buy Ford's company.[*]

And so, against both his will and his better judgment, Henry Ford was back in the car business.

In this instance as well, most biographers have insisted that Ford, with Model T sales promising to soar, could not have been serious about selling his company. But Henry Ford was not a man to frivolously solicit an offer from a competitor. Ford was not a man to do *anything* frivolously. The option Durant obtained was real and, once more, there are too many disparate sources to conclude anything but that Ford was all too willing to be bought out.

And in some ways, Ford's exit would have made sense. For someone who was instrumental in ushering in modernity, Ford's essence remained in the world he was rendering obsolete. He was a man of

---

[*] Within a year after the bank syndicate ousted him from the management of General Motors in 1910, Durant had started a new consortium, teaming up with Louis Chevrolet, who had moved from racing to design. Chevrolet enjoyed solid success, which allowed Durant to use the profits to quietly buy General Motors stock. By 1915, although he had fallen out with Chevrolet, Durant, in a brilliant ploy, gained control of the company under the noses of the bankers who had thrown him out. But Durant simply could not restrain himself. On the verge of turning General Motors into a genuine challenger to Ford, he once again expanded too quickly and with the same result. In 1921, he left the company for good. He began his own car company, which went bust in the crash. In 1936, Durant declared bankruptcy and, until his death in 1947—the same year as Ford's—lived on a $10,000-a-year pension granted to him by friends, supplemented by whatever he could earn doing odd jobs. But whatever his failings, Durant was remembered with affection and admiration by almost everyone who had known him.

great sentiment and craved an innocent, almost frontier life, where recreation consisted of such simple pursuits as fishing and folk dancing, mostly jigs and polkas. And, of course, there were his beloved birds. After he'd made his fortune, he initiated annual camping trips with his closest friends, Thomas Edison, John Burroughs, and Harvey Firestone—they called themselves the vagabonds—although the quartet came to be accompanied by cooks, servants, photographers, and often other celebrated Americans, including a president or two. Yet for all of this, Ford had just spent the better part of a decade focused obsessively on work, most days seeing nothing but the inside of a factory or workshop. Under these circumstances, it is not difficult to imagine him grateful for the chance to leave that brutish existence—and as a rich man to boot.

In any event, after the deal with Durant fell through, Ford's spine stiffened. At this point, he had little to lose. The bulk of his indemnity was for cars already sold. It was true that future sales until the Selden patent expired three years hence promised to be robust, but pursuing the case on appeal would not cost him one additional cent in licensing fees. Had he accepted the judgment, he would have had to pay those anyway. His only risk was in legal fees, which, exorbitant as they may have been, would be only a small percentage of the reward he stood to gain if he won.

Ford supplemented his legal team with top patent lawyers from both New York and Chicago, as Ralzemond Parker gradually removed himself from the case. Ford always claimed he had affection for Parker, but Parker was old and tired, he had lost a case that everyone Ford spoke with—including Parker himself—had thought eminently winnable, and Ford had not demonstrated any tolerance for failure. The new legal team, with holdover W. Benton Crisp, was comprised exclusively of men with buttoned-up polish, which seemed appropriate for the appellate phase of the case.

If Ford had any doubts that he would fight on alone, they were dispelled early in 1910. In February, the American Motor Car Manufacturers Association, the trade organization that Couzens had put together to face off against ALAM, was dissolved. Officially, the reason was that the group's five-year charter had expired, but the real reason was that all but thirteen of its forty-three members had already signed on with ALAM, and of those remaining, a majority wanted to jump ship as well. By the end of March, ALAM boasted more than eighty members, each of which advertised under the banner of the Selden organization.

On April 2, Thomas Jeffery died of a heart attack while on vacation with his wife in Pompeii, Italy. *Automobile Topics* wrote, "Mr. Jeffery's death removes a man who has been one of the great manufacturers in the automobile field, and few men in the business were wider known in this country or abroad. He was the second man in the United States to take up the manufacture of automobiles, and he was among the first to see the great possibilities of the automobile as a commercial product."[10] Indeed, with the passing of the brilliant and idiosyncratic Jeffery, the one man with sufficient gravitas in the industry to join Ford as an effective ally in his appeal—assuming Jeffery would ever have joined with anyone—was gone.

Ford was hailed as a hero in his hometown—"Ford, the Fighter," the *Detroit Free Press* dubbed him in an editorial—but in the industry at large, many shied away. To them, at least for the time being, he was only "Ford the loser." ALAM pressed its advantage by returning to the same sort of threatening publicity campaign it had launched when the suit was first joined.

As he had in 1903, Ford offered to post a bond to protect his customers—and this time he had the money. ALAM responded with ads warning anyone thinking of purchasing an unlicensed automobile of legal liability. (Although at that point, with the case yet to be appealed, there was none.) ALAM also targeted "individuals listed as prospective customers" and sent them an "explanatory booklet, bearing on its cover the title, 'What is the Selden Patent on Gasolene Automobiles?'" On the cover, in a display box, and as a chapter heading on the last page of the booklet in capital letters was the statement, "No bond is required when you buy a car licensed under Selden patent." The text also asserted that "licensed dealers decline to take unlicensed cars in trade," and that "it should be borne in mind that such a bond does not permit the owner of a car to use his machine if an injunction is issued and that an unlicensed car may be difficult to dispose of."[11]

Eventually Ford responded by taking out full-page ads in the trade magazines and newspapers under the heading "This Advertisement is Published for the Protection of the Automobile Public." In it, Ford laid out his guarantee:

> If there are any prospective automobile buyers who are at all intimidated by the claims made by our adversaries, we will give them, in addition to the protection of the Ford Motor Company with its some $6,000,000.00 of assets, an individual bond backed by a Company of more than $6,000,000.00 more of assets, so that each and every individual owner of a Ford car will be protected until at least $12,000,000.00 of assets have been wiped out by those who desire to control and monopolize this wonderful industry. The bond is yours for the asking, so do not allow yourself to be sold inferior cars at extravagant prices because of any statement made by this "Divine" body.[12]

During this give-and-take, in addition to selling automobiles and preparing a complex legal appeal, Ford Motor was engaged in gradually shifting the company's operations to the Highland Park plant, which had opened at the beginning of 1910. Manufacturing was moved first, operation by operation, but the plant was also to serve as a proving ground for many of the techniques that would eventually result in the Ford assembly line. With Flanders gone, most of the work was done by Wills and Sorenson, but always in accordance with the principles in which Flanders had schooled them. Sorenson wrote later, "The entire plant had to be functioning before the Ford mass production and assembly system could be completely worked out into one great synchronized operation from one end of the place to the other. . . . We set up lay-out boards on which we worked out the production lines and placement of machines to scale. Numbered brass plates were attached to all machines in the Piquette plant with corresponding tags on the layout boards so that every machine would be set up in its assigned place when the move to Highland Park was made."[13]

When the mock-up seemed finalized, the construction manager drew up detailed floor layouts, which were then given to Albert Kahn, the architect, to be rendered into building plans. The process was exacting and laborious, requiring constant revision, and then, as operations moved from Piquette Avenue to Highland Park, testing and retesting without impeding the flow of production of Model Ts for which orders had already been accepted.

Ford himself had little input in the process. "Henry Ford had no ideas on mass production. He wanted to build a lot of autos. He was determined but, like everyone else at that time, he didn't know how. In later years he was glorified as the originator of the mass production idea. Far from it; he just grew into it, like the rest of us." Referring to the conveyer system that was later installed to move parts from one station to another, Sorenson added, "Years later, in *My Life and Work,* a book which was written for him, Mr. Ford said that the conveyer-assembly idea occurred to him after watching the reverse process in packing houses, where hogs and steers were triced up by hind legs on an overhead conveyer and disassembled. This is a rationalization long after the event. Mr. Ford had nothing to do with originating, planning, and carrying out the assembly line. He encouraged the work, his vision to try unorthodox methods was an example to us; and in that there is glory enough for all."[14] The fiction persists, however. On the website of the Henry Ford Museum, under "Did You Know?" is the entry, "The idea for using a moving assembly line for car production came from the meat-packing industry."

It is testament to the Ford team's ability and commitment, and to the quality of their product, that in a year of utter turmoil, they continued to sell cars, and a lot of them—more than thirty-two thousand. Billy Durant's Buick kept pace, with sales of more than thirty thousand cars, most of them Model 10s, but this was to be Durant's last year as Ford's chief competitor.*

At that point, of course, every one of those thirty-two thousand cars increased Ford's indebtedness to his adversaries. Ford therefore, for clarity if nothing else, wanted his appeal heard as soon as possible. Because of a series of procedural delays, however, it could not be scheduled until November 1910. ALAM had expanded the range of lawsuits to include almost every remaining serious independent as well as a number of prestigious foreign firms, such as Mercedes, and importers of foreign automobiles, such as Fiat. But each of these new actions would depend on the ruling of the appellate court in the Ford and Panhard suits.

The case would be heard by a three-judge panel of the Second Circuit Court of Appeals. Appellate cases are, in theory, not retrials but instead restricted to questions of procedure or judicial error in the original action. In this case, however, because of the nature of the ruling, the court, in the process of evaluating Judge Hough's decision, would also be passing on the merits of the Selden patent.

The judges' backgrounds would not have been a source of optimism for Ford's lawyers. The senior member, Emile H. Lacombe, had been a protégé of William Whitney when Whitney served as New York's corporation counsel, and he had helped in dismantling Boss Tweed's political machine. Another of the three, Henry G. Ward, had been a law firm associate of Judge Hough, and, like Hough, had specialized in admiralty law. Only the youngest and most recently appointed member of the court, Walter C. Noyes, was of independent

---

* Possibly spurred by Durant's success in promoting Buick through racing, Ford had finally gotten back into the sport. In 1909, he entered two Model Ts in a New York–to–Seattle race, staged to commemorate the Alaska-Yukon-Pacific Exposition. Thirty-five entrants were expected, but only six left the starting line on June 1 at 3:00 P.M.—directly under the window of the courtroom in which the infringement trial was taking place. The other four entries were the sort of large, heavy machines that had won the other long-distance races, but twenty-three days after the start, it was a Model T that arrived first at the finish line. Although the Ford car was eventually disqualified because the drivers had changed an axle in Idaho, the publicity was priceless, establishing that the light, small Model T could withstand the rigors of a drive across the United States.

background, and although he was the best-versed in patent law, he had only been on the federal bench for three years.

The hearing was on the court's calendar for only three days, a restriction that worked, perhaps unwittingly, to Ford's advantage. Crisp and his associates filed a more pointed, succinct, and comprehensible brief than had Parker in the original trial. Ford's lawyers focused on Selden's sixteen-year delay in receiving his patent, not debating whether the process was allowed under the law—it was—but rather emphasizing it as proof that Selden himself had been aware that he would be unable to construct a working machine from his specifications. But it was Frederic Coudert, the lawyer for Panhard, "who made the most effective appearance for the defense," whose "oral argument, reinforced by a superb brief, challenged the basic assumption of the trial court that the Selden patent, as viewed against the state of the art in 1879, marked the borderline between success and failure."[15]

In his most devastating attack, Coudert showed the court that the newest edition of the definitive work on gasoline engines—written by the plaintiff's key expert witness, an English engineer named Dugald Clerk, whom the ALAM lawyers had billed as the world's foremost authority on the technology—had mentioned Selden not at all and that, further, Clerk had written that no one had developed the Brayton motor to any greater degree than had the inventor. This was a direct refutation of Clerk's own testimony at the trial, when he had credited Selden with successfully adapting the Brayton motor for use in a road carriage. "Will this Court prefer the theories of Clerk, the retained witness, to those of Clerk, the disinterested scientist, composing the 'classic' on gas engines?" Coudert asked the judges.[16]

The appellate judges, unlike Hough, asked pointed and informed questions throughout the hearing, and after listening to closing arguments, including another bravura performance by Frederick Fish, they retired to consider the evidence. Given the mass of exhibits, a decision was not expected until spring. Instead, it was rendered in less than six weeks.

With this a case of great import, likely to go to the Supreme Court, it was significant that the two senior members of the tribunal deferred to Judge Noyes, the most expert in patent law, to write the opinion. Their confidence in him seemed not misplaced. The opinion Noyes wrote was praised as being "deft in its reasoning . . . [demonstrating] an understanding of automotive history, and a firm grasp of technical considerations, such as Hough had lacked."[17] It was also a complete reversal of Hough's decision, leaving no room for ALAM lawyers to find subjective language on which to take the case further. Nor did Noyes's opinion—tight, comprehensive, and meticulously thorough— seem to create any potential opening to claim judicial error.

After an exhaustive review of both the history of hydrocarbon engines and the technical specifications of the various types, in the most salient paragraph of the opinion Noyes wrote:

> It is our opinion . . . that in [Selden's] road locomotive combination embracing as its engine element an engine of the constant pressure type, the substitution in place of such engine of an engine of the constant volume type destroys the unity of the combination, because the two engines do not perform the same functions in substantially the same way. Granting the patent as broad a range of equivalents as its interpretation will permit, and giving due consideration to the degree of invention involved, still we are not able to hold that the Otto improved engine is the equivalent of the Selden engine or that the defendants infringe by employing it as an element of their motor vehicle combination.[18]

Noyes concluded with a statement directed at the more than ample royalties Selden had already received, although money was not likely to mitigate the sting to the old man's pride:

> While the conclusion of non-infringement which we have reached leaves the patentee empty handed . . . it cannot be regarded as depriving him through any technicality of the just reward for his labors. He undoubtedly appreciated the possibilities of the motor vehicle at a time when his ideas

were regarded as chimerical. Had he been able to see far enough he might have taken out a patent as far reaching as [Judge Hough] held this one was. But like many another inventor, while he had a conception of the object to be accomplished, he went in the wrong direction. The Brayton engine was the leading engine at the time and his attention was naturally drawn to its supposed advantages. He chose that type. In the light of events, we can see that had he appreciated the superiority of the Otto engine and adapted that type for his combination, his patent would cover the modern automobile. He did not do so. He made the wrong choice and we cannot, by placing any forced construction upon the patent or by straining the doctrine of equivalents, make another choice for him at the expense of these defendants who neither legally nor morally owe him anything.

Significantly, the court did not question the practicality of Selden's machine or whether it would have qualified for pioneer status had anyone chosen to build Brayton powered automobiles, nor did the judges address his delays in the patent process. If the Selden 1877 Buggy had been powered by an Otto, therefore, his patent might have been upheld. On this narrow basis only, Hough's decree was reversed, with court costs accruing to the original plaintiffs.

The appellate court's ruling has been almost universally extolled by historians and Ford biographers as a redress of a perversion of justice. Judge Hough has been dismissed as a man hopelessly befuddled by the intricacies of both the technology and the law, while Judge Noyes and his colleagues have been praised for sage and sound legal judgment.

The only problem with this interpretation is that Judge Hough's ruling, not the appellate decision, conformed to the law then on the books. Ford should have lost.

The essence of the pioneer concept was that a patent holder advanced a technology in such a fashion as to create an entirely new perspective and set of potential applications; to, in effect, forge a new trail into a previously impenetrable forest. Selden had done that by applying an internal combustion engine of the "liquid hydrocarbon compression type" to road locomotion. It was a great breakthrough and no American had previously thought to do it. Whether the engine that powered such a conveyance was an Otto or a Brayton was surely secondary.

This is not to say that Selden "deserved" such a broad patent, or that except during the roughly fifteen-year period that the pioneer concept was accepted jurisprudence, one would have been granted.* But Judge Hough was correct in his view that as the law was then interpreted, the model on which the engine was based was incidental to Selden's construct.

After the judgment was rendered, ALAM released a statement that said, "As the courts have disagreed on the merits of the Selden patent on gasoline automobiles, it was announced yesterday that the Columbia Motor Car Company and George B. Selden are arranging to apply for a writ of certiorari, with a view of having the case go to the United States Supreme Court for final decision."† Within days, however, they reconsidered and announced that no further appeals would be undertaken.

Benton Crisp also issued a statement:

> There is one thing about the decision . . . that is certain:
> The Ford Motor Company has never infringed the Selden
> patent. That fact is plain. It is also interesting to note that
> the court finds that Mr. Ford is one of the pioneer manu-
> facturers of automobiles in this country; that he gained
> nothing from the Selden patent when it actually came out

---

* Pioneer patents technically remain part of patent law. While some legal scholars contend that some form of pioneer status has been granted in contemporary patent litigation, inventions on a par with the automobile or the airplane have long since been denied the sort of controlling breadth that Selden sought.

† Columbia Motor Car was the successor to Electric Vehicle, which had been dissolved.

of the Patent Office, and that he owes nothing to the patent or to Mr. Selden either legally or morally.

After years of tiptoeing uncomfortably along the fence, the trade magazines now hailed the decision as if it had been handed down by Solomon. *Motor World,* for example, proclaimed, "Selden Routed," and praised the "learned judges" for deciding that "while the patent did not lack invention or utility, it was not such as to entitle Selden to rank as an inventor." Ford was equally acclaimed for "at no time showing symptoms of wavering" despite "the formidable interest arrayed against him."[19]

Once again, however, the most entertaining reaction was from the editors of *Horseless Age,* who, under the banner headline "Selden Decision Reversed by Court of Appeals," demonstrated that they could reverse course every bit as well. After commending ALAM for its "wise" decision not to pursue the matter to the Supreme Court, the editors wrote:

> The outcome of the litigation will certainly prove to the advantage of the industry as a whole, and Henry Ford and the Ford Motor Company, who carried the burden of the defense, deserve the unqualified commendation of the industry for having had the courage of their convictions and for keeping on fighting dauntlessly against great odds. The abandonment of the patent will save the industry considerable sums, but above all it will remove barriers in the trade which have been most obnoxious, to say the least.[20]

The best characterization of the Ford-Selden battle, however, came from Charles Sorenson. "The Ford fight against the Selden patent is a milestone in the history of the automobile industry. I believe it is one of the greatest things Mr. Ford did not only for Ford Motor Company, but for everybody in the automaking business. All of us around him took only minor parts in this long-drawn-out case. He carried full responsibility for success or failure on his own shoulders with little or no encouragement from members of his board. He rarely had a pleasant moment inside or outside his organization as long as this uncertainty lasted. Yet the affair did as much to inspire him as anything that had occurred up to that time. He knew that he could battle with the best there was in the country and not be stopped."[21]

So, as a result of his principles, his self-confidence, or simply his stubbornness—and with a healthy dollop of good luck thrown in— Henry Ford, who was by this time selling tens of thousands of Model Ts each year, with revenues in the millions and millions of dollars, could keep every penny.

EPILOGUE

On December 1, 1913, at the Highland Park plant, the Ford Motor Company initiated production on a fully functional, eighty-four-station assembly line, and the era of mass production had officially begun. Henry Ford was—and still is—almost universally credited as the inventor of the system that would transform both manufacturing and consumption, and he would later be asked to write the *Encyclopedia Britannica* article on the subject. (Harking back to his early days, Ford subcontracted the task out to Samuel Crowther.)* In the next model year, 1914, Model T production topped 300,000, almost double the previous year's and greater than all other American automobile manufacturers combined. By 1921, the Ford Motor Company, by then in an even larger plant in River Rouge, would produce almost 1.25 million automobiles.

Just weeks after initiating mass production, the Ford Motor Company instituted a policy of paying each of its workers $5 per day for

---

* The three-page entry could not be less Fordesque, with phrases like "It was out of social strife thus engendered that the idea began to emerge that possibly the difficulty lay in the neglect of scientific manufacturing principles."

eight hours of work. The wage was higher and the hours fewer than for almost any other factory in the United States; so generous, in fact, that many Ford workers were able to purchase Ford automobiles, which Ford later claimed had been his intention.

Like the assembly line, the $5 day has become synonymous with Henry Ford, but the origin of the idea remains as indistinct as most of the Ford legacy. Ford always maintained that he thought of it, and Sorenson backed him up, recalling a meeting at which Ford, seemingly out of nowhere, announced his intentions:

> The plan was worked out in his office one Sunday morning, January 4, 1914. Until this writing, all existing accounts of what went on that morning are, at the nearest, second or third hand. . . . It has been said that the idea originated with Mr. Couzens, but he knew nothing about it until Mr. Ford told him. Myth also surrounds the participants at that Sunday morning meeting. Couzens, Wills, and Hawkins were said to have been there. They were not. The only ones present were Mr. Ford, Ed Martin, Lee, and I. The events of that day are still very clear in my mind, which is understandable, for this was a milestone in industrial and economic history. I am the only man alive who took part in that meeting; and since none of the others ever set down their accounts, mine is the only first-hand recollection.[1]

Sorenson further claimed that Ford decided that Couzens should announce the plan and that Couzens agreed because it would help him in his plan to be elected governor of Michigan.

But Couzens insisted that there had been a good deal of discussion before Ford's ad hoc announcement and that the spur for the $5 day had been layoffs at the Ford plant in the winter of 1913. "I sat in my office on the second floor of the Ford building and every time I looked out the window, I saw a sea of faces looking up. There were men shivering in the cold with their coat collars turned up." His first notion was to suggest a pension plan, which he discussed in December with the muckraker Ida Tarbell, but he decided that a more immediate program was needed. He then thought, as he recalled, "Why shouldn't the Ford Motor Company take a decided lead in paying the highest wages to its workers, thus enabling them to enjoy better living conditions?" He claimed to have talked it over with Ford as Christmas 1913 approached, but Ford refused. After a good deal of wrangling, however, Ford agreed to have the idea introduced at a directors' meeting just after the New Year. Couzens lobbied for support among the other directors and found that Horace Rackham was also in favor of the wage increase. A meeting was held on January 5, 1914, and the company minutes bear out that Horace Rackham made the motion, supported by Couzens, and that "after considerable discussion," with no other directors present, Ford went along.[2]

To whichever of the chicken-or-egg interpretations one subscribes, the $5 day gave Ford perhaps his greatest boost of positive publicity and helped establish him as a champion of the workingman at the same time as he was building the workingman's car. Less public was that, no matter how much they were paid, workers on the Ford assembly line often burned out quickly from the pressure of endless repetition of a single task and were replaced like so many oxen in a team.[*] This clash of wage and workplace would not come to a head for decades, until the rise of the union movement, when Ford's image among workers would become quite different.

At the same time that Model T sales were soaring, Ford was shedding longtime associates. He never took the initiative in breaking off a relationship—he didn't have to. He had become so autocratic, so difficult to work with, so unwilling to share credit, that those most responsible for his success left on their own.

The first to go were John and Horace Dodge. In July 1913, the Dodges, despite having eight years remaining on their long-term contract, gave Ford one-year notice of their intention to end the affiliation. John Dodge resigned as a director, but both brothers retained their Ford stock. By late 1914, the Dodges were producing their own

---

[*] Eventually, "Fordism" would be parodied to devastating effect in Charlie Chaplin's 1936 film *Modern Times*.

automobiles, in which, unlike Ford, "they did not intensify work and drive their employees to their physical and mental limits."[3] Ford was loath to finance his competitors and so tried to squeeze them by suspending special dividends, which had been as much as $10 million per year. He announced that he intended to use the money for an additional, enormous expansion of the company at a new plant at River Rouge, which would include a smelting facility to fabricate his own steel. Ford Motor was sitting on more than $60 million in cash at the time, so on November 2, 1916, the day after the Dodges had attended Edsel Ford's wedding, they served papers on Henry "for a decree requiring Ford Motor Company to distribute to stockholders at least 75% of the accumulated cash surplus, and to distribute in the future all of its earnings 'except such as may be reasonably required for emergency purposes.'"[4] The Dodges also wanted Ford enjoined from building the smelting plant. The Dodges initially won on both points, although Ford won a reversal of the smelting plant ruling on appeal. In 1918, Ford was ordered to distribute approximately $19 million in dividends, the court ruling that "a business corporation is organized and carried on primarily for the profit of the stockholders." The Dodges, who held 10 percent of the stock, received a like share of the distribution. Ford, ironically, was forced to pay 60 percent of that sum to himself, more than sufficient to finance River Rouge.

Dodge immediately vaulted into the top five bestselling automobiles and the Dodges continued to produce them until 1920, when both men died of Spanish flu, Horace's illness compounded by cirrhosis. Five years later, with the company continuing to maintain a prominent position among the also-rans behind Ford, their widows sold out to an investment company for almost $150 million.

In 1915, it was James Couzens's turn. He and Ford had come to openly despise each other, and with Ford insisting on making the decisions, Couzens's role had become largely one of caretaker. On October 12, saying he had "had enough of [Ford's] goddamn persecution,"[5] Couzens quit. After an angry meeting, Couzens wrote out in longhand a letter of resignation, which Ford returned, dropping it back on Couzens's desk. According to a co-worker, at that point Couzens stood up, "put on his hat, and walked out of the office. He went downtown and notified a newspaper friend." To Ford's intense irritation, Couzens's resignation, like the Dodges', did not affect Couzens's stock holdings. Even more annoying was that Couzens did not resign his seat on the board of directors.

Couzens never became Michigan's governor, but in 1919 he was elected mayor of Detroit. As mayor, ironically, he was noted for installing a system of mass transit—street railways—to ease Detroit's growing traffic problem. He left the mayoralty in 1922 for an appointment to complete a term in the United States Senate. He then won two terms in his own right and served until his death in October 1936. After he left Ford, Couzens became noted for his philanthropic work, giving millions of dollars to various efforts to help the disadvantaged, particularly children.

By 1919, with Couzens and the Dodges gone, John Gray's heirs passive stockholders, and Horace Rackham and John Anderson no longer involved in running the company, Ford decided to buy them all out. He wanted to be the sole owner of his company, and after spending more than $350 million, he was. Anderson, who had cajoled $5,000 from his father to buy Ford stock, sold his shares to Ford for $12.5 million, as did his fellow Malcomson lawyer Horace Rackham. The Dodge brothers parlayed their $10,000 contribution in materials, labor, and some cash into $25 million, although neither would live to enjoy their riches. John Gray's heirs were paid $26.25 million for their shares. The biggest winner, of course, was James Couzens, who received $29,308,857.90. His sister Rosetta, who had invested $100, was paid $262,036.67.

Also in 1919, Ford's penultimate link to his original design team was cut when Harold Wills, tired of being increasingly marginalized, resigned as well.[6] Ford gave him a severance package of more than $1 million, a tiny fraction of what Wills's participation had been worth to the Ford brand. Wills also began his own automobile company, Wills Sainte Clair, which remained in business only six years. Although his product was well built, sturdy, and reliable, Wills, who had been so brilliant in design, showed a total lack of competence in production.

Only the ultraloyal Spider Huff remained. Huff, who was made head of the electrical laboratory, was with Ford until his death in 1933.

The Model T remained in production until 1927 and was one of the most successful consumer products in history. It eventually became available in a variety of styles and was adapted to everything from trucks to delivery wagons to ambulances, with total production of 15 million vehicles from 1909 until its demise.

The Model T did not simply alter the manner in which cars were engineered and manufactured. By introducing an automobile whose success was dependent on volume, Ford modernized marketing, sales, production, and worker compensation. It is quite possible that never before in human history did a single product so transform the business model for industry. And changes in the business model bred changes in the society that adopted it.

As a result, Henry Ford had enough money to buy anything he wanted, finance anything he wanted, and fund any idea he wanted, brilliant or crackpot. He did all of that and more. He began to see himself as the man who could solve the world's problems and tell other people how to live.

In 1915, for example, Ford, a self-styled pacifist—sentiments he would not extend to union members in the years to come—decided that he could end the war in Europe by Christmas. He financed a "Peace Ship," in which he sailed across the Atlantic with a ragtag group of peace activists—more-prominent Americans such as Thomas Edison, William Jennings Bryan, and Jane Addams declined to go—certain that his very presence in such a venture would create the moral push to get the warring parties to the negotiating table. The venture failed miserably, with squabbling among the participants, and the press dubbed the ocean liner on which they sailed the "Ship of Fools."

Ford returned home ill and dispirited, but by 1918 he had recovered enough to run for the Senate. His opponent, Truman Newberry, was also rich—although not in Ford's league—and had made his money largely as a financier. Ford, who disdained public speaking, proved a poor politician, while Newberry was a quite effective one. He harped on the deferment Ford had obtained for Edsel during World War I, accusing Ford of protecting his son while others did the dying. Although his profligate spending and dubious oversight of contributions would later cause him to be indicted, Newberry won by 8,000 votes out of nearly 450,000 cast. In 1921, Newberry was convicted of campaign fraud, the prosecution's case buttressed by dirt raked up by detectives Ford had hired, but the conviction was later overturned 5–4 by the Supreme Court. Newberry resigned his seat anyway and to Ford's even greater irritation, was replaced by another nemesis, James Couzens.

Ford's often bizarre and single-minded behavior has filled volumes. It ranged from the infantile (his insistence on the existence of an international Jewish conspiracy) to the bizarre (his doomed plan to build a jungle city in Brazil, Fordlandia, that would bring civilization to the natives and rubber to the United States) to the brilliant (his creation of the eighty-acre Henry Ford Museum, with its preservation of a dazzling array of buildings and artifacts of American history). What links all of these together is Ford's conviction—which he was not shy in enunciating—that he had the answers to fundamental questions of human existence and if the world would follow his formula, strife and misery would disappear. In these plans, he was almost never successful.

The most tragic example of Ford's dictatorial paternalism was with his own son, Edsel. Edsel shared his father's intelligence, his determination, and, to a great degree, his business sense, but little else. Where Henry was rough-edged, Edsel was smooth; where Henry was, at his core, an angry and bitter misanthrope, Edsel was affable, gregarious, and compassionate; where Henry would eschew alcohol as a substance that bred weakness of character, Edsel enjoyed a sociable cocktail; where Henry ruled primarily by fear, particularly after the Model T's ascension, Edsel inspired affection and loyalty; where Henry married "the believer," who would follow him anywhere, Edsel married an equal and treated her as such.

Henry hated it. And he hated it even more when Edsel demonstrated impressive business acumen despite going about things far differently than his father insisted. Edsel was, in fact, a perfect second-generation manager—he was thoughtful, he planned carefully, and he always considered the future as much as the present.

Henry dealt with Edsel's independence as he did whenever he was defied—he attacked until he had broken his adversary's spirit. But he could not break Edsel's. Edsel continued in the company, and even bought a home on the other side of Detroit from his parents' Dearborn home, in Grosse Pointe, an area Henry saw as filled with the country club set he loathed. By 1938, with Henry instructing his enforcer, Harry Bennett, to break the back of the autoworkers' union by any means necessary—meaning violently—and Edsel determined to enact a more enlightened labor policy, Charles Sorenson wrote that relations between the two "were stretched to the breaking point."[7]

The clash of wills became so debilitating for Edsel that his health broke down, and in January 1942 he was hospitalized with an acute case of stomach ulcers that his doctors told him had been caused by stress. They instructed him to get away from the company for a while, but with World War II on, Edsel did not. Henry, himself nearing the end of his life, never let up. He insisted that Edsel drink milk from the farm that Ford had set up, but the milk was not pasteurized, and Edsel was hospitalized again in November with undulant fever. Soon afterward he was diagnosed with stomach cancer. Edsel Ford died on May 26, 1943. He was forty-nine years old. Sorenson called the relationship "Henry Ford's biggest failure."

Henry Ford lived another four years and died at home at age eighty-three.

George Selden's life went a good deal differently.

According to George Selden Jr., his father eventually took in $360,000 in royalties from his patent, which would translate to approximately $10 million in 2010 dollars, but that figure, like all Selden family claims, is quite possibly inflated. The fate of their automobile, however, is a good deal more clear. The Selden Motor Vehicle Company would produce only three models, each costing at least $2,500, none of which sold especially well. Production never exceeded one thousand cars a year.

In 1912, Selden's sons decided to exploit what promised to be a fertile market and move into truck manufacture.* The company spun off a dedicated subsidiary and, to help sales, instituted an installment plan for buyers, a practice new to the industry and one that *Motor World* described as "generally considered an undesirable practice."[8] As the Selden automobile withered into extinction, the truck division thrived. With the coming of World War I, Selden trucks saw robust sales—Russia ordered one thousand in the fall of 1914—and in 1916, the truck division absorbed the parent company. In the years after the war, the Selden Model B Liberty truck became a common sight on the city streets. In 1930, in the wake of the stock market crash, Selden Trucks was sold to the Bethlehem Truck Company.

George Selden Sr. died in 1922, all but forgotten in the decade since he had merited national headlines. In the same year that Henry Ford would publish his triumphant autobiography, Selden's death on January 17 rated only a short obituary at the bottom of page fourteen of *The New York Times*. The article called Selden an "auto pioneer" and noted that the courts had upheld his patent but ruled his engine was of the wrong type. The final line read, "Notwithstanding the gibes of others, he persevered."[9]

Of Henry Ford's notion of creating a single model and sticking to it, Jonathan Norton Leonard wrote:

> Ford's single idea was a good one. Whether or not he thought of it first himself is unimportant, for it was Ford who stuck to it through thick and thin. He would build a cheap car for the large public. Every other consideration was out. Not a penny would he spend on appearance, on

---

* *The New York Times*, in December 1911, had run an article whose headline read, "Trades Interested in Motor Vehicles." The article listed a number of businesses, most prominently breweries, where a well-made truck would be welcome to replace horse-drawn carts.

sport or fashion appeal, on comfort or more than necessary speed. The cars would be alike. They would "get you
there and get you back"—nothing more. They would be an
expression of Ford's own personality: bare, utilitarian, per-
verse. They might have their own peculiar weaknesses, but
they would not cater to the weaknesses of others. Without
exception they would be painted black when they left the
factory—a symbol of their standardization in other re-
spects. Every Ford on the roads of America would look
like every other. Only the drivers would vary.[10]

Ford's two greatest triumphs, the Model T and the assembly line,
therefore, were both based on the forced acceptance of an immutable
group standard, the first among consumers and the second among
workers. And this from a man who despised communism for its suppression of personal initiative. His success was totally dependent on
the adoption of principles for which he felt the deepest contempt—
and which never, under any circumstances, would he attribute to himself. But only from the total repression of personal choice would it be
possible to construct the empire that he trumpeted as a triumph of
American individualism.

That Ford considered himself the inventor of processes he adapted,
borrowed, or appropriated from others is without question. And he
never acknowledged that the immense success of the Model T was
due as much to being at the right place at the right time as to creating
a piece of brilliant engineering. But Henry Ford, like other marketing
geniuses before and since, seemed to know instinctively that being in
the right place at the right time meant being in the right place *all* the
time. Unlike so many of his fellows, who chased the market by trying
to divine its pulse from moment to moment, Ford—the Model K
experiment notwithstanding—stayed where he knew he should be,
and eventually the market came to him. He did not so much create
demand as anticipate it.

On the one hand, there is little significance in whether or not Henry

Ford was an inventor, an innovator, or just a shrewd and talented businessman. Whatever role he did or did not play in Ford Motor's ascension, the company became a colossus, one of the most successful and profitable ventures in human history, and Ford was at the helm for the entire ride.

But from another viewpoint, where Ford fits on innovation's continuum becomes a good deal more salient. The great fortunes, after all, are almost never amassed by pure inventors, but rather by the men and women who recognize how to sell the inventions that others have created. Such sales, when successful, will then engender further—and usually faster—second-, third-, and fourth-generation innovation. Men such as Henry Ford—and Isaac Rice—therefore can be categorized as *accelerators,* catalysts in creating commercial applications from pure science, and thereby creating the consumer demand that prompts the research that keeps the process vibrant.

The degree to which the profit motive is required to propel creativity—or whether it crystallizes or corrupts the process—can be debated, but what is not in doubt is that men such as Henry Ford will always be patrolling the fringes, eager to convert ideas to cash. And it is that alchemy, more often than not, that defines the process we call innovation.

NOTES

Abbreviations are as follows:

HA—Horseless Age
MA—Motor Age
MW—Motor Way
MWo—Motor World
NYT—New York Times
SciAm—Scientific American

PROLOGUE: A DAY IN COURT
1. Sorenson, *My Forty Years with Ford*, 1.

CHAPTER 1: POWER IN A TUBE
1. *Automobile*, October 1899, 27.
2. Bryant, "The Silent Otto," 186.

CHAPTER 2: THE MAN WHO WOULD BE KING
1. Frances Murray, "Henry Rogers Selden," New York State Unified Court System, nycourts.gov/history/legal-history-new-york/luminaries-court-appeals/selden-henry.html.
2. Greenleaf, *Monopoly on Wheels*, 7.
3. *Technical World*, September 1906, 2. This revelation was part of a long interview Selden gave reporter Leroy Scott at a pivotal point in the trial.

4. Selden's son later claimed that his father's interest in horseless carriages was spurred by his Army mount, who was so willful that he almost killed Selden by trying to run him into a tree, but this seems less likely than the version in Selden's deposition, which also might be spurious.

5. *SciAm,* May 13, 1876, 1.

6. As applied to gas turbines, the Brayton engine has a compressor, a burner, and an expansion turbine. Ambient air is compressed and passed through a heat exchanger for preheating. The preheated charge goes to a combustor, where fuel is ignited, and the hot compressed air then flows to an expander, where the thermal energy is converted to shaft work. The hot exhaust gases from the expander are sent to the heat exchanger, where they are cooled and then discharged.

CHAPTER 3: MADE IN GERMANY . . .

1. Bryant, "The Origin of the Four-Stroke Cycle," 189.

2. Ibid., 192.

3. *Engineering,* December 1900, 357. *Engineering* engaged Daimler to write a narrative of the development of his motors, but Daimler died before it could be completed. Paul Daimler, using his father's notes, completed the account. Slanted toward Daimler's contributions, to be sure (and away from Maybach's), this article is nonetheless by far the best record of the development of the Daimler-Maybach engine ever published in English.

4. Ibid., 359–60.

CHAPTER 4: . . . PERFECTED IN FRANCE

1. Jarrott, *Ten Years of Motors and Motor Racing,* 6.

2. Ibid., 14.

3. *Automobile,* October 1899, 22.

CHAPTER 5: AN UNEASY ROMANCE WITH THE HORSE

1. Notorc, "Does Mourning Become the Electric? 1: The Rise of the Electric Automobile," *Postscripts* (blog), December 28, 2006, notorc.blogspot.com/2006/12/does-mourning-become-electric-1-rise-of.html.

2. Greenleaf, *Monopoly on Wheels,* 59.

3. Musselman, *Get a Horse!,* 29.

4. "A Memorial to Congress on the Subject of a Road Department," February 1893.

5. Greenleaf, *Monopoly on Wheels,* 59.

6. Maxim, *Horseless Carriage Days,* 47.

7. Ibid., 88.

CHAPTER 6: EARLY AMERICANS

1. Garrett, "Illinois Commentary," 178.

2. Ibid., 176.

3. Duryea, *America's First Automobile,* 5. Charles died in 1938, taking credit for the design and virtually all of the components of the Duryea automobile. In 1942, Frank broke decades of silence and wrote this book to "set the record straight."

4. Quoted in Garrett, "Illinois Commentary," 177.

5. Garrett, "Illinois Commentary," 180.

6. Ibid.

7. Ibid.

8. Musselman, *Get a Horse!*, 40.

9. The magazine's name was changed to *The Automobile* in 1909 and *Automobile Industries* in 1917, as it remains today.

10. *HA,* October 1895, 7.

11. Ibid., 17.

12. Other companies were at this point building gasoline automobiles, key among them Haynes-Apperson (Elwood Haynes being the inventor of stainless steel). While some initiated improvements to automaking, none would play a significant role when the industry began in earnest.

13. *HA,* October 1895.

14. "Charles B. King," Automotive Hall of Fame, automotivehalloffame.org/inductee/charles-king/751.

15. An excellent first-person biographical sketch of King appears in King's own *Personal Side Lights of America's First Automobile Race.*

CHAPTER 7: THE SELF-CREATED MAN

1. Rae, ed., *Henry Ford,* 4.

2. Wik, "Review of *Henry Ford*," 312.

3. While Ford's *My Life and Work,* as will be shown, is unreliable as an account of Ford's life and work, as a polemic, it is quite valuable as a statement of Ford's philosophy and values.

4. Snow, *I Invented the Modern Age,* 17. The Nevins quote was taken directly from *My Life and Work* without attribution.

5. See, for example, Curcio, *Henry Ford,* 7.

6. Ford, *My Life and Work,* 22.

7. Ibid., 29.

8. Snow, *I Invented the Modern Age,* 26.

9. Ford, *My Life and Work,* 26–27.

10. Ibid., 604n.

11. Ibid., 117.

12. Ibid., 33.

13. See, for example, Nevins, *Ford;* Curcio, *Henry Ford;* and Snow, *I Invented the Modern Age.*

14. Simonds, *Henry Ford: His Life, His Work, His Genius,* 47.

15. Curcio, *Henry Ford,* 27.

16. Ford, *My Life and Work,* 30.

17. Quoted in Olson, *Young Henry Ford,* 98.

18. *Detroit Free Press,* March 7, 1896, 4.

19. Quoted in Olson, *Young Henry Ford,* 72.

20. Snow, *I Invented the Modern Age,* 56.

21. "As for the rest of the carriage," Nevins wrote, "Ford undoubtedly learned much from King, for he was present while the latter was developing his test

wagon." "He could see what was being built there," Oliver Barthel noted. King also obtained a chain for Ford to use to drive the quadricycle, to replace the belt that Ford originally planned to install. *Ford,* 153.

22. Simonds, *Henry Ford: His Life, His Work, His Genius,* 18. Although this table-pounding assertion has been widely cited by other biographers, Simonds cites no source. In *My Life and Work,* Ford dates his meeting with Edison to 1887, which isn't possible since Ford didn't begin working for Edison until 1891 (though it is possibly a typo), and places it in Atlantic City; his recollection of Edison's response, while equally enthusiastic, was a good deal more thoughtful and measured. Other accounts have the meeting taking place when Edison visited Detroit in 1898 and sought out his employee to encourage him.

23. Snow, *I Invented the Modern Age,* 68.

CHAPTER 8: SPEED

1. A 1.2-mile "race" was held in 1887 from Paris to Neuilly that featured only two competitors in steam-powered vehicles, Georges Bouton and Albert de Dion, partners in the De Dion–Bouton Company.

2. There is insufficient room in these pages to even begin to detail examples of Bennett's odd behavior. On May 19, 1918, a week after his death, *The New York Times* published "Anecdotes About Gordon Bennett," which recounts just a few examples of the caprices he foisted on his employees.

3. Harmsworth, *Motors and Motor-Driving,* 12. Three years later Chasseloup-Laubat would set the world's first land speed record, just under 40 miles per hour, in an electric car.

4. *HA,* November 1895, 53.

5. King, *Personal Side Lights,* 18.

6. Maxim, *Horseless Carriage Days,* 51–52.

7. King, *Personal Side Lights,* 19.

8. *Chicago Times-Herald,* November 29, 1895, 1.

9. *Rock Island Argus,* November 29, 1895, 1.

10. Ibid.

11. *San Francisco Call,* June 14, 1899, 2. These items did not appear under Bennett's byline, of course, but were all attributed to the *Herald* and almost certainly originated with Bennett himself.

12. Ibid., June 15, 1899, 3.

13. Ibid., June 19, 1899, 4.

14. *Sydney Morning Herald,* September 7, 1899, 5.

15. *Automobile,* February 1900, 455.

16. *New-York Tribune,* June 15, 1900, 4. There was no further report on the dog.

17. *HA,* July 4, 1900, 14.

18. *Automobile,* June 1900, 297.

CHAPTER 9: A ROAD OF ONE'S OWN

1. Ford, *My Life and Work,* 36.

2. Leonard, *Tragedy of Henry Ford,* 19.

3. Ford, *My Life and Work,* 39.

4. *Automobile Club of America* [yearbook], 1900. Also among the members were a number of automobile pioneers, such as Hiram Percy Maxim.

5. Some manufacturers had also exhibited at a bicycle show in February 1900.

6. *NYT,* November 4, 1900, 10.

7. *HA,* January 7, 1900, 61.

8. Some reports have Wills not joining Ford until later, but Charles Sorenson has Wills beginning as a part-time worker about this time. Whenever the date, however, his contributions to Ford's ultimate success are beyond question.

9. Snow, *I Invented the Modern Age,* 82.

10. *Washington Evening Star,* October 11, 1901, 9.

11. *HA,* November 20, 1901, 723.

12. *MW,* December 1901, 121.

13. *HA,* December 4, 1901, 786.

14. As with Wills, there is some question as to exactly when Leland joined the company. Most accounts have him coming on while Ford was still in the shop, which seems most likely; a few after Ford has no longer actively working there. Also as with Wills, it makes little difference to the thrust of the story.

15. Greenleaf, review of Leland and Millbrook, *Master of Precision: Henry M. Leland,* in *Business History Review,* Winter 1966, 517.

16. Ford, *My Life and Work,* 51.

17. Ibid., 50–51.

18. Quoted in Nevins, *Ford,* 218.

19. *MWo,* October 30, 1902, 131.

20. Ibid., 154.

21. *MWo,* September 10, 1903, 925.

22. *Sports Illustrated,* sportsillustrated.cnn.com/vault/article/magazine/MAG10 75655/1/index.htm.

CHAPTER 10: THE ONCE AND FUTURE CAR

1. His father, Mayer, doubtless changed his name upon his arrival in America, but no record survives of the original.

2. A good source for details of Rice's life is Kathy Cunningham, "Prologue: Preparing the Way for the Columbia Cars, and the Formation of the Electric Vehicle Company," kcstudio.com/electrobat.html. Another is his obituary in *The New York Times,* November 3, 1915.

3. *North American Review,* June 1883, 557–67.

4. William Morrison, an engineer from Des Moines, Iowa, was purported to have built an electric car in 1890, but no record exists of his ever putting the machine to any meaningful use.

5. *Harper's Weekly,* December 10, 1898, 1209.

6. *NYT,* March 7, 1897, 10. Rice was not so busy with the electric cabs that he did not take time out to referee an international chess match between the United States and Great Britain, held at the Brooklyn Academy of Music. Whenever he was mentioned in the newspapers for chess activities, he was referred to as "Professor Isaac L. Rice."

7. *Automobile,* October 1899, 79.

8. *Harper's Weekly,* December 10, 1898, 1209.

9. *HA,* March 1897, 5.

10. For a detailed description of Condict's amazing work, see Kirsch, *Electric Vehicle,* 42–43.

11. Lead plates for exide batteries installed in electric cars rose from 7,500 in 1897 to 46,000 one year later.

12. *HA,* March 1897, 15. The magazine engaged in a long and bitter campaign of condemnation for electric vehicles, although, other than a stated prejudice for "hydrocarbons," their reasons remained vague.

13. *NYT,* February 9, 1899, 4.

14. Hendrick, "Great American Fortunes and Their Making," 38. Root was not without political influence himself. He would twice be secretary of war and, under Theodore Roosevelt, secretary of state.

15. Harvey Wish, "*William C. Whitney: Modern Warwick* by Mary D. Hirsch," *Mississippi Valley Historical Review* 36, no. 1 (June 1949): 148–49.

16. Hendrick, "Great American Fortunes and Their Making," 34.

17. Ibid.

18. Rae, "The Electric Vehicle Company," 300.

19. *NYT,* May 6, 1899, 1.

20. Maxim, *Horseless Carriage Days,* 165.

21. *Washington Times,* July 13, 1899, 5.

CHAPTER 11: SELDEN REDUX

1. Hazel's credentials were such that the New York Bar Association declared him highly unqualified for appointment to the federal bench, which dissuaded President McKinley not one bit. For a longer description of Hazel's rather pathetic record, see Goldstone, *Birdmen . . .* a terrific book.

2. Two years later, Judge Coxe, at Thomas Platt's behest, would be appointed to the United States Court of Appeals, where he would eventually cast a vote for the Wright brothers in their infringement suit against Glenn Curtiss.

CHAPTER 12: FORD BEGINS HIS ALPHABET

1. Ford, *My Life and Work,* 51.

2. Barnard, *Independent Man,* 37.

3. Nevins, *Ford,* 230.

4. Kimes, *Pioneers, Engineers, and Scoundrels,* 38.

5. *SciAm,* June 24, 1893, 396.

6. *SciAm,* May 21, 1892, 329.

7. Glasscock, *The Gasoline Age,* 40.

8. The company also later denied that gasoline stored in the building was the cause, although they did not suggest an alternative.

9. Kettering, *American Battle for Abundance,* 51. Kettering was writing for General Motors and as such would certainly be partial to Olds over Ford. Still, the facts as he states them are correct.

10. Glasscock, *The Gasoline Age,* 42.

11. Hyde, "The Dodge Brothers," 53.

12. Quoted in Nevins, *Ford,* 224.

13. Quoted in Kettering, *American Battle for Abundance,* 53.

14. Wells, "The Road to the Model T," 503.

15. Hyde, "The Dodge Brothers," 53.

16. It is unclear whether or not Ford attended this meeting personally. Some Ford biographers imply, but do not state categorically, that he was there, while Couzens's biographer indicates that he was not. In any case, it does not seem as if Ford played a major role in raising money, although his designs certainly did.

17. Here there seems little question that Ford participated little or not at all in the discussions with those who would back the new company.

18. There is some dispute as to why the Dodges were willing to take such an enormous risk and throw in totally with Ford, whether it was because of fervent belief in the Ford product or that there was an uncertain future with Olds.

19. Couzens wanted her listed as an investor in her own right, but Ford refused to have a woman on the rolls, so her shares were subsumed in his.

20. Ford, *My Life and Work,* 54.

21. See, for example, the *Edgefield* (South Carolina) *Advertiser,* July 22, 1903, or *Valentine* (Nebraska) *Democrat,* October 1, 1903.

22. Nevins, *Ford,* 239.

23. Hyde, "The Dodge Brothers," 57.

24. The price must have included shipping, because Ford would set the price on the car and advertise it widely at $750.

25. *Cycle and Automobile Trade Journal,* July 1903, 42.

26. *HA,* September 23, 1903, 332.

27. *Cycle and Automobile Trade Journal,* July 1903, 42.

28. *MA,* April 3, 1903, 10.

29. Quoted in Greenleaf, *Monopoly on Wheels,* 107–8.

30. Greenleaf, *Monopoly on Wheels,* 111.

CHAPTER 13: MAN AND DOG OVER THE ROCKIES

1. The cross-country auto trips of 1903 are detailed in the various trade journals, but also excellently recounted in McConnell, *Coast to Coast by Automobile,* 97.

2. Joy's belief that the Packard's run was his answer to the races in Europe was confirmed by Krarup. The Packard left San Francisco timed to arrive in Salt Lake City when the results of the 370-mile Gordon Bennett Cup would reach America from Europe. "This probable coincidence of dates might lead to a comparison of the relative importance of the two events," Krarup wrote, "one a race at breakneck speed over a smooth course, and the other steady plugging over rough and almost untrodden ground, yet each in its own way intended to demonstrate what this product of modern ingenuity . . . may be trusted to do." Quoted in McConnell, *Coast to Coast by Automobile,* 103.

3. *Lincoln Highway,* 7.

4. *HA,* August 5, 1903, 157.

5. *New-York Tribune,* August 22, 1903, 6.

6. *Around the World in Eighty Days* had been published in 1873, but was still popular three decades later.

7. *MA,* February 25, 1915, 27.
8. Ibid., 37.
9. *HA,* July 29, 1903, 126.

CHAPTER 14: WILLIE K. COMES HOME

1. Although not a single Spanish-made automobile would enter.
2. *Motor Car Journal,* May 2, 1903, 178.
3. *HA,* March 11, 1903, 355.
4. *NYT,* May 24, 1903, 4.
5. *NYT,* May 24, 1903, 8.
6. *Automobile Topics,* May 30, 1903, 432–33.
7. Ibid.
8. Jarrott, *Ten Years of Motors and Motor Racing,* 166.
9. *Automobile Topics,* May 30, 1903, 434.
10. Ibid., 413.
11. *Motor Car Journal,* June 13, 1903, 287.
12. *HA,* June 10, 1903, 670.
13. *Automobile Topics,* May 30, 1903, 414.
14. Ibid., June 6, 1903, 477.
15. *HA,* June 10, 1903, 671.
16. Western Reserve Historical Society, wrhs.org/Properties/Peerless_Manufacturing _Company.
17. *Automobile Topics,* April 18, 1903, 29.
18. Ibid., 17.

CHAPTER 15: COLLISION

1. And might have actually been one, since the author was never identified.
2. *Automobile Topics,* June 6, 1903, 499–501.
3. George Selden received about a tenth of the monies, far from the millions he had hoped for but a great deal more than he could ever make as a patent attorney in Rochester.
4. Greenleaf, *Monopoly on Wheels,* 115.
5. *Hartford Courant,* August 31, 1903, 9.
6. *HA,* October 7, 1903, 378.
7. *Cycle and Automobile Trade Journal,* December 1, 1903, 19.
8. *HA,* October 28, 1903, 445.
9. Sorenson, *My Forty Years with Ford,* 76.
10. Ford, *My Life and Work,* 57.
11. Three years later at Ormond Beach, Glenn Curtiss would travel at more than 130 miles per hour on an 8-cylinder motorcycle.

CHAPTER 16: WILLIE K.'S ROAD

1. Burns, *Thunder at Sunrise,* 19.
2. *NYT,* February 28, 1904, 16.
3. *Cycle and Automobile Trade Journal,* July 1904, 25. The rules were published in every other trade journal, as well as major newspapers such as the *NYT.*
4. The two best sources for information on this and subsequent Vanderbilt Cup

races are Howard Kroplick's *Vanderbilt Cup Races of Long Island* and Burns's *Thunder at Sunrise.*

5. *Cycle and Automobile Trade Journal,* August 1, 1904, 23.
6. *MA,* October 6, 1904, 16.
7. Burns, *Thunder at Sunrise,* 31.
8. *MA,* October 13, 1904, 3.
9. *NYT,* October 9, 1904, 2.
10. Ibid.
11. Ibid.
12. *Brooklyn Daily Eagle,* October 9, 1904, 1.
13. *NYT,* October 9, 1904, 8.

CHAPTER 17: PALACE COUP

1. Nevins, *Ford,* 253–54.
2. Ford, *My Life and Work,* 40. Once again, Ford's ghostwritten autobiography is a reliable account of his philosophy, at least how it had evolved by 1920.
3. Nevins, *Ford,* 269.
4. Ibid., 227.
5. Sorenson, *My Forty Years with Ford,* 74.
6. Nevins, *Ford,* 267.
7. Ibid., 268.
8. Sward, *Legend of Henry Ford,* 43–44. Sward's book was one of the most critical of Ford, dismissed by Ford devotees as character assassination. While many of Sward's more inflammatory judgments regarding Ford's character should be viewed with skepticism, his assessments regarding management issues, and in this case, Couzens's role, seem accurate.
9. Sorenson, *My Forty Years with Ford,* 36.
10. Barnard, *Independent Man,* 60.
11. *MW,* December 28, 1905, 14.
12. Ford and Couzens had tested out this strategy in 1904, when they incorporated Ford of Canada, in which Malcomson was not a stockholder. The open-ended pricing clause was not part of that arrangement, so Malcomson had gone along.
13. Quoted in Barnard, *Independent Man,* 62.
14. Sorenson, *My Forty Years with Ford,* 77–78.

CHAPTER 18: THE FIRST SHOT OF THE REVOLUTION

1. *MWo,* November 1905, 61.
2. This ad appeared in almost every major journal.
3. *Cycle and Automobile Trade Journal,* January 1906, 105.
4. Greenleaf, *Monopoly on Wheels,* 170.
5. *NYT,* January 14, 1906, 10.
6. *Cycle and Automobile Trade Journal,* February 1906, 76.
7. *HA,* January 17, 1906, 103.
8. Ibid., 104. Manufacturers who were paying licensing fees to ALAM were allowed to exhibit in the Garden along with the members.
9. *HA,* January 17, 1906, 104.

10. Ibid., 106.

11. Nevins, *Ford,* 325.

12. Quoted in Nevins, *Ford,* 326.

13. *MW,* August 16, 1906, 16.

14. Ibid., 18.

15. Whether this was coincidence—the earlier production problems were real—or contrivance by Ford and Malcomson can only be guessed at.

16. Sorenson, *My Forty Years with Ford,* 45.

17. Musselman, *Get a Horse!,* 184. Musselman was best known as a Hollywood screenwriter, but his father was an eccentric inventor.

18. Kettering, *American Battle for Abundance,* 60–61. Kettering's most famous inventions are leaded gasoline, an improved electric starter, Freon refrigerant, and the "aerial torpedo."

19. Sorenson, *My Forty Years with Ford,* 45–46.

20. *HA,* July 11, 1906, 47.

CHAPTER 19: MR. SELDEN COMES TO NEW YORK

1. *HA,* February 28, 1906, 341.

2. Maxim, *Horseless Carriage Days,* 172.

3. Greenleaf, *Monopoly on Wheels,* 152.

4. *HA,* July 10, 1907, 45.

5. *MWo,* May 23, 1906, 871.

6. *NYT,* May 19, 1907, 8.

7. Greenleaf, *Monopoly on Wheels,* 149.

8. *Technical World,* September 1906, 2.

9. *New York Sun,* October 28, 1906, 5.

10. *HA,* May 23, 1906, 739.

11. *MW,* May 23, 1906, 871.

12. *HA,* July 10, 1907, 45.

13. Greenleaf, *Monopoly on Wheels,* 154.

14. Ibid., 156.

15. *MWo,* October 11, 1906, 69.

16. *MWo,* December 27, 1906, 767.

17. *HA,* December 12, 1906, 877.

18. *MW,* May 1907, 24.

19. Greenleaf, *Monopoly on Wheels,* 157.

20. *MW,* July 1907, 32.

21. Ibid., 33.

22. Greenleaf, *Monopoly on Wheels,* 159.

23. *MW,* July 1907, 33.

24. Greenleaf, *Monopoly on Wheels,* 159.

25. *HA,* September 11, 1907, 340.

26. *HA,* September 18, 1907, 371.

CHAPTER 20: FORD MOTOR COMES OF AGE

1. *MW,* August 16, 1906, 9. (All *MW* quotations in this section are from this article.)

2. A small portion borders Hamtramck, another island city within the Detroit borders.

3. Greenleaf, *Monopoly on Wheels,* 175.

4. Ibid., 169.

5. Ford, *My Life and Work,* 63.

6. Barnard, *Independent Man,* 57.

7. *Automobile,* December 13, 1906, 847.

8. Apple's performance in the wake of the financial crisis in 2008 is a more modern example of the same phenomenon. Both revenues and net income increased in 2009, and then soared in 2010.

9. Nevins, *Ford,* 342.

10. Dicke, *Franchising in America,* 64.

11. *MW,* December 12, 1912, 20.

12. Quoted in Kroplick and Velocci, *The Long Island Motor Parkway,* 8.

CHAPTER 21: AROUND THE WORLD IN 169 DAYS

1. *MW,* September 1907, 6.

2. *HA,* August 28, 1907, 283.

3. *Spokane Press,* August 20, 1907, 4.

4. *NYT,* August 11, 1907, C3 (Special Cablegram section).

5. *NYT,* November 28, 1907, 1.

6. Ibid.

7. *NYT,* February 11, 1908, 1.

8. *MW,* February 1908, 10.

9. *NYT,* March 28, 1908, 2.

10. *NYT,* April 6, 1908, 1.

11. *NYT,* May 25, 1908, 1.

12. *MA,* July 30, 1908, 1.

13. *NYT,* July 27, 1907, 8.

14. *MA,* August 11, 1908, 10.

15. *NYT,* August 18, 1908, 1.

CHAPTER 22: FORD'S PHENOMENON

1. A practice for which United States automobile manufacturers in the 1960s and 1970s heaped condemnation on Japan, as currently do American technology firms on China.

2. See Sorenson, *My Forty Years with Ford,* 100.

3. Ford, *My Life and Work,* 17.

4. Ibid.

5. Sorenson, *My Forty Years with Ford,* 96.

6. Ibid., 97.

7. *MA,* September 24, 1908, 47.

8. *MWo,* September 24, 1908, 28–29.

9. Ford, *My Life and Work,* 63.

10. Rae, "The Fabulous Billy Durant," 255. Rae's article is, by far, the best and most insightful thumbnail of Durant's life and career.

11. Ibid., 258.

12. Fisher Body was not officially merged with General Motors until 1919, but functioned much as a subsidiary for years before that.
13. Maines, *Men,* 15.
14. Ibid.
15. Rae, "The Fabulous Billy Durant," 261.

CHAPTER 23: FALSE END OF A LONG TRAIL

1. *NYT,* May 6, 1900, 18. The ice pricing scheme ultimately failed amidst revelations of political favors and probably bribery involving New York City's mayor.
2. *NYT,* November 7, 1908, 1.
3. Greenleaf, *Monopoly on Wheels,* 198–99.
4. Ibid., 199.
5. Ibid., 200.
6. Ibid., 202.
7. Quoted in *MWo,* June 10, 1909, 405.
8. The text of the entire opinion was printed in *MW,* September 16, 1909, 1064–6.
9. Bunker, "The New Federal Equity Rules." The notion of pioneer patents, while not specifically addressed in the rules change, soon effectively disappeared from jurisprudence.
10. *MWo,* September 16, 1909, 1053.
11. *HA,* September 22, 1909, 313. It was precisely Hough's *lack* of experience in patent cases, of course, that would make his decision most vulnerable to appeal.
12. *Cycle and Automobile Trade Journal,* September–October 1909, 15.

CHAPTER 24: IT'S NEVER OVER . . .

1. Quoted in Greenleaf, *Monopoly on Wheels,* 211.
2. Ford, *My Life and Work,* 62.
3. Greenleaf, *Monopoly on Wheels,* 215.
4. Barnard, *Independent Man,* 72.
5. Ibid.
6. Ibid., 74.
7. Reports were that Ford was "lying on the floor of his hotel room, suffering from lumbago." Barnard, *Independent Man,* 74.
8. Ibid., 75.
9. Maines, *Men,* 17–18. Maines was a Flint newspaperman and confidant of many in the local elite. His father had made a fortune in real estate. While Durant may have been exaggerating—something that he was known to do—the meeting does seem to have taken place and Stettinius's investment in General Motors is a matter of record.
10. *Automobile Topics,* April 9, 1910, 36.
11. *MWo,* April 21, 1910, 158.
12. See, for example, *MA,* March 1910, 85.
13. Sorenson, *My Forty Years with Ford,* 125.
14. Ibid., 128–29.
15. Greenleaf, *Monopoly on Wheels,* 223.

16. Quoted in Greenleaf, *Monopoly on Wheels*, 225.
17. Greenleaf, *Monopoly on Wheels*, 227.
18. Quoted in *HA*, January 11, 1911, 126.
19. *MWo*, January 12, 1911, 186.
20. *HA*, January 18, 1911, 145.
21. Sorenson, *My Forty Years with Ford*, 121.

EPILOGUE

1. Sorenson, *My Forty Years with Ford*, 135–36.
2. Barnard, *Independent Man*, 86–91.
3. Hyde, "The Dodge Brothers," 49.
4. *Dodge v. Ford Motor Co.*, 170 N.W. 668 (Mich. 1919).
5. Quoted in Barnard, *Independent Man*, 99.
6. A recent biographer has theorized that Ford was having an affair with an assistant named Evangeline Côté, whom Wills also had his eye on—or she on him. But Wills had been gradually squeezed out of the spotlight for a decade and his departure was ensured.
7. Sorenson, *My Forty Years with Ford*, 312.
8. *MWo*, September 16, 1909, 1085. The ad appeared in other trade magazines as well.
9. *NYT*, January 18, 1922, 14.
10. Leonard, *Tragedy of Henry Ford*, 21. Leonard was a prolific science writer, social commentator, and critic. He reviewed Rachel Carson and Carl Sagan and published articles on everything from America's Framers to culinary arts to the atomic tests at White Sands.

BIBLIOGRAPHY

WEBSITES (PARTIAL LIST)

"Albert A. Pope," ConnecticutHistory.org, connecticuthistory.org/albert-augustus-pope-1843–1909
American Oil and Gas Historical Society, aoghs.org
American Society of Mechanical Engineers, asme.org
Automotive Hall of Fame, automotivehalloffame.org
Brooklyn Daily Eagle, bklyn.newspapers.com
California Digital Newspaper Collection, cdnc.ucr.edu
Chess Notes, www.chesshistory.com
Cornell Making of America Collection, moa.library.cornell.edu
Exide Technologies, exide.com
Hathi Trust, babel.hathitrust.org
The Henry Ford Museum, thehenryford.org/exhibits/hf/Did_You_Know.asp
"Henry Selden," New York State Unified Court System, nycourts.gov/history/legal-history
    -new-york/luminaries-court-appeals/selden-henry.html
Internet Archive, archive.org
Library of Congress, loc.gov
NewYork–Paris Auto Race, thegreatrace.com
New York Times, nytimes.com
New York Yacht Club, nyyc.org
Postscripts, notorc.blogspot.com/2006/12/does-mourning-become-electric-1-rise-of.html
Sports Illustrated, si.com
Vienna Review, viennareview.net

PERIODICALS (PARTIAL LIST)

The Automobile. New York: Class Journal Company.
Automobile Club of America [yearbook]. Privately printed. 1900.
Automobile Topics. New York: E. E. Schwarzkopf.
Automotive News. New York: Crain Publications.
Business History Review. Boston: President and Fellows of Harvard College.

Cycle and Automobile Trade Journal. Philadelphia: Chilton Company.
Engineering Magazine. New York: Engineering Magazine Company.
Harper's Weekly. New York: Harper and Brothers.
The Horseless Age. New York: Horseless Age Company, 1895–1918.
McClure's. New York: S. S. McClure Company.
Motor. Garden City, NY: Hearst Corporation, 1924–1934.
Motor Age. Chicago: Class Journal Company.
The Motor Car Journal. London: Cordingley and Company.
The Motor Way. Chicago: L. L. Bligh.
The Motor World. New York: Motor World Publishing Company.
Motor World Wholesale. Philadelphia: Chilton Company.
Official Handbook of Automobiles, 1906. New York: Association of Licensed Automobile Manufacturers; by the National Automobile Board of Trade.
Scientific American. New York: Munn and Company.
The Technical World. Chicago: Technical World Company.

BOOKS AND ARTICLES

Alexander, Amy. "His Drive Paved the Way from Carriages to Cars: Ransom E. Olds' Vision and Stick-to-It Attitude Helped Him Become the Father of the U.S. Auto Industry." *Investor's Business Daily,* March 23, 2006.

Anderson, Russell H. "The First Automobile Race in America." *Journal of the Illinois State Historical Society (1908–1984)* 47, no. 4 (Winter 1954): 343–59.

Bailey, Richard Paul. *Henry Ford and the Press.* Typescript, 1949.

Barnard, Harry. *Independent Man: The Life of Senator James Couzens.* Detroit: Wayne State University Press, 2002.

Batchelor, Ray. *Henry Ford, Mass Production, Modernism, and Design.* Manchester: Manchester University Press, 1994.

Beaumont, William Worby. *Motor Vehicles and Motors: Their Design, Construction and Working by Steam, Oil and Electricity.* 2nd ed. Westminster: A. Constable, 1906.

Bonville, Frank. *What Henry Ford Is Doing.* Seattle: Bureau of Information, 1920.

Bosworth, David. "Idiot Savant: Henry Ford as Proto-Postmodern Man." *Georgia Review* 54, no. 1 (Spring 2000): 11–39.

Brinkley, Douglas. *Wheels for the World: Henry Ford, His Company, and a Century of Progress, 1903–2003.* New York: Viking, 2003.

Bryant, Lynwood. "The Origin of the Four-Stroke Cycle." *Technology and Culture* 8, no. 2 (April 1967): 178–98.

———. "The Silent Otto." *Technology and Culture* 7, no. 2 (Spring 1966): 184–200.

Bunker, Robert E. "The New Federal Equity Rules." *Michigan Law Review* 11, no. 6 (April 1913): 435–45.

Burns, John M. *Thunder at Sunrise: A History of the Vanderbilt Cup, the Grand Prize, and the Indianapolis 500, 1904–1916.* Jefferson, NC: McFarland, 2006.

Bushnell, Sarah T. *The Truth About Henry Ford.* Chicago: Reilly & Lee, 1922.

Cobb, Josephine. "The Duryea Automobile on Pennsylvania Avenue in 1896." *Records of the Columbia Historical Society, Washington, D.C.* 53/56 (1953/1956): 259–64.

Corry, Finbarr F. "Centenary of the Motor Car 1886–1986." *Irish Arts Review (1984–1987)* 3, no. 2 (Summer 1986): 26–35.

Curcio, Vincent. *Henry Ford.* New York: Oxford University Press, 2014.

Daimler, Paul. "The Development of the Petroleum Automobile." *Engineering Magazine* 22, no. 2 (December 1901): 356–66.

de Chasseloup-Laubat, Marquis. "Recent Progress of Automobilism in France." *North American Review* 169, no. 514 (September 1899): 399–414.

Dicke, Thomas S. *Franchising in America: The Development of a Business Method, 1840–1980.* Chapel Hill: University of North Carolina Press, 1992.

Duryea, J. Frank. *America's First Automobile: The First Complete Account by Mr. J. Frank Duryea of How He Developed the First American Automobile, 1892–1893.* Springfield, MA: Donald M. Macaulay, 1942.

Eckermann, Erik. *World History of the Automobile.* Detroit: Society of Automotive Engineers, 2001.

Einstein, Arthur W. *Ask the Man Who Owns One: An Illustrated History of Packard Advertising.* Jefferson, NC: McFarland, 2010.

Flageolet-Lardenois, Michèle. "Une firme pionnière: Panhard et Levassor jusqu'en 1918." *Le Mouvement Social* no. 81, Le Monde de l'Automobile (October–December 1972): 27–49.

Flink, James J. "Innovation in Automotive Technology: After a Long Interval of Stagnation, Automotive Technology May Be Entering a Period of Renewed Creativity." *American Scientist* 73, no. 2 (March–April 1985): 151–61.

Ford, Henry. *My Life and Work.* Garden City, NY: Doubleday, Page, 1922.

Garrett, Romeo B. "Illinois Commentary: The Role of the Duryea Brothers in the Development of the Gasoline Automobile." *Journal of the Illinois State Historical Society (1908–1984)* 68, no. 2 (April 1975): 174–80.

Glasscock, Carl B. *The Gasoline Age: The Story of the Men Who Made It.* Indianapolis: Bobbs-Merrill, 1937.

Goldstone, Lawrence. *Birdmen: The Wright Brothers, Glenn Curtiss, and the Battle to Control the Skies.* New York: Ballantine Books, 2014.

Greenleaf, William. *Monopoly on Wheels: Henry Ford and the Selden Automobile Patent.* Detroit: Wayne State University Press, 1961.

Hargadon, Andrew. *How Breakthroughs Happen: The Surprising Truth About How Companies Innovate.* Cambridge, MA: Harvard Business School Press, 2003.

Harmsworth, Alfred, Viscount Northcliffe. *Motors and Motor-Driving.* London: Longmans, Green, 1902.

Hart-Davis, Adam, ed. *Engineers: From the Great Pyramids to the Pioneers of Space Travel.* New York: DK Publishing, 2012.

Hendrick, Burton J. "Great American Fortunes and Their Making." *McClure's,* November 1907.

Henry, Leslie R. *Henry's Fabulous Model A.* Los Angeles: F. Clymer Publications, 1959.

Hirsch, Mark D. *William C. Whitney: Modern Warwick.* New York: Dodd, Mead, 1948.

Hyde, Charles K. "The Dodge Brothers, the Automobile Industry, and Detroit Society in the Early Twentieth Century." *Michigan Historical Review* 22, no. 2 (Fall 1996): 48–82.

Jarrott, Charles. *Ten Years of Motors and Motor Racing.* New York: Dutton, 1906.

Kettering, Charles Franklin. *American Battle for Abundance: A Story of Mass Production.* Detroit: General Motors, 1947.

Kimes, Beverly Rae. *Pioneers, Engineers, and Scoundrels: The Dawn of the Automobile in America.* Warrendale, PA: SAE International, 2005.

King, Charles Brady. *Personal Side Lights of America's First Automobile Race.* New York: Privately printed by Super-Power Printing Company, 1945.

Kirsch, David A. *The Electric Vehicle and the Burden of History.* New Brunswick, NJ: Rutgers University Press, 2000.

Kroplick, Howard. *Vanderbilt Cup Races of Long Island.* Charleston, SC: Arcadia Publishing, 2008.

Kroplick, Howard, and Al Velocci. *The Long Island Motor Parkway.* Charleston, SC: Arcadia Publishing, 2008.

Lacey, Robert. *Ford: The Men and the Machine.* Boston: Little, Brown, 1986.

Laux, James M. "Some Notes on Entrepreneurship in the Early French Automobile Industry." *French Historical Studies* 3, no. 1 (Spring 1963): 129–34.

———. "Heroic Days in the French Automobile Industry." *French Review* 37, no. 3 (January 1964): 349–55.

Lay, M. G. *Ways of the World: A History of the World's Roads and of the Vehicles That Used Them.* New Brunswick, NJ: Rutgers University Press, 1992.

Leland, Mrs. Wilfred C., and Minnie Dubs Millbrook. *Master of Precision: Henry M. Leland.* Detroit: Wayne State University Press, 1966.

Leonard, Jonathan Norton. *The Tragedy of Henry Ford.* New York: G. P. Putnam's Sons, 1932.

Lewis, David L. *The Public Image of Henry Ford: An American Folk Hero and His Company.* Detroit: Wayne State University Press, 1976.

Lewis, Eugene William. *Motor Memories: A Saga of Whirling Gears.* Detroit: Alven, 1947.

The Lincoln Highway: The Story of a Crusade That Made Transportation History. Written from data supplied out of the day-to-day transactions of the Lincoln Highway Association. New York: Dodd, Mead, 1935.

Maines, George H. *Men . . . a City . . . and Buick . . . , 1903–1953: An Account of How Buick—and Later General Motors—Grew Up in Flint . . . From the Records and Personal Recollections of George Humphrey Maines.* Flint, Mich.: Privately printed in the establishment of Advertisers Press, 1953.

Marquis, Samuel Simpson. *Henry Ford: An Interpretation.* Toronto: T. Allen, 1923.

Maxim, Hiram Percy. *Horseless Carriage Days.* New York: Harper Brothers, 1897.

McConnell, Curt. *Coast to Coast by Automobile: The Pioneering Trips, 1899–1908.* Redwood City: Stanford University Press, 2000.

Musselman, M. M. *Get a Horse!: The Story of the Automobile in America.* Philadelphia: Lippincott, 1950.

Nevins, Allan. *Ford: The Times, the Man, the Company.* New York: Scribner, 1954.

Nixon, St. John C. *The Invention of the Automobile.* London: Country Life, 1936.

Olson, Sidney. *Young Henry Ford.* Detroit: Wayne State University Press, 1963.

Pipp, Edwin Gustav. *The Real Henry Ford.* Detroit: Pipp's Weekly, 1922.

Pound, Arthur. *The Turning Wheel: The Story of General Motors Through Twenty-five Years, 1908–1933.* Garden City, NY: Doubleday, Doran, 1934.

Rae, John B. "The Electric Vehicle Company: A Monopoly That Missed." *Business History Review* 29, no. 4 (December 1955): 298–311.

———. "The Fabulous Billy Durant." *Business History Review* 32, no. 3 (Autumn 1958): 255–71.

———, ed. *Henry Ford.* New York: Prentice Hall, 1969.

Scott, Cord. "The Race of the Century: 1895 Chicago." *Journal of the Illinois State Historical Society* 96, no. 1 (Spring 2003): 37–48.

Simonds, William Adams. *Henry Ford: His Life, His Work, His Genius.* Indianapolis: Bobbs-Merrill, 1943.

———. *Henry Ford, Motor Genius.* Garden City, NY: Doubleday, Doran, 1929.

Snow, Richard. *I Invented the Modern Age: The Rise of Henry Ford.* New York: Scribner, 2013.

Sorenson, Charles E. *My Forty Years with Ford.* New York: Norton, 1956.

Sward, Keith. *The Legend of Henry Ford.* New York: Atheneum, 1948.

Weeks, Lyman Horace. *Automobile Biographies: An Account of the Lives and the Work of Those Who Have Been Identified with the Invention and Development of Self-Propelled Vehicles on the Common Roads.* New York: Monograph Press, 1904.

Wells, Christopher W. "The Road to the Model T: Culture, Road Conditions, and Innovation at the Dawn of the American Motor Age." *Technology and Culture* 48, no. 3 (July 2007): 497–523.

Wik, Reynold M. "Review of *Henry Ford* by John B. Rae." *Technology and Culture* 11, no. 2 (April 1970): 311–13.

Young, Filson. *The Complete Motorist: Being an Account of the Evolution and Construction of the Modern Motor-car; With Notes on the Selection, Use, and Maintenance of the Same; and on the Pleasures of Travel upon the Public Roads.* 4th ed. New York: McClure, Phillips, 1905.

 **INDEX**

ABOUT THE AUTHOR

LAWRENCE GOLDSTONE is the author or co-author of more than a dozen books of fiction and nonfiction, most recently *Birdmen: The Wright Brothers, Glenn Curtiss, and the Battle to Control the Skies.* One of his novels won a New American Writing Award, and another was a *New York Times* notable mystery. His work has been profiled in *The New York Times*, the *Toronto Star, Salon*, and *Slate*, among others. He lives on Long Island with his wife, Nancy.

lawrencegoldstone.com